GREG PERRY

LIVING MIRACLE

If it's meant to be it's up to me!

www.**GregPerry**.com

LIFESTYLES OF SUCCESS, DREAM LIFE, LLC

INTRODUCTION

This is Greg Perry: a successful businessman, entrepreneur, community leader, mentor, family man, and father, who has spent his entire life discovering the steps to successful living. Through Greg's years of joy and pain, success and failure, he has discovered how to play the game of life and win. Greg's life is a true rags to riches story; one that has taken him from poverty to a life of spiritual, business, family, and financial wealth.

Greg Perry wants to share the knowledge he has gained. His dynamic and powerful story will show you how you can achieve true wealth, success, balance, and peace of mind. You too can discover the power within you to change your life.

CONTENTS

Angela, Me, Mom, Michael, London, Adrienne, Gail.

CHAPTER 1

IN THE BEGINNING

I WAS BORN in the South Central part of Los Angeles, California on June 28, 1960. I was the youngest of six children, with four older sisters and an older brother. My mother, Lois Perry, was the best mom in the world. My father was John Perry. My oldest sister, Gail, was 18 years older than me. After Gail came my sister Brenda, my sister Adrienne, my brother Michael, my sister Angela, and then me. I had an incredible childhood in terms of adventure and drama, but on a worldly level, we were pretty poor. My dad was a struggling attorney, and my mom was a clerk at a local department store called Broadway. Our family of eight lived in a two bedroom, one bath unit of a four-plex apartment, on the corner of Kenwood and Jefferson in the South Central part of Los Angeles.

I was running the streets from the time I was four years old. With so many other kids in the family, I guess I got lost in the shuffle because I was the baby. Even as a little kid, I knew I could do just about anything I wanted. What I wanted to do more than anything early in my life was set things on fire. I was a little pyromaniac; I just loved playing with matches and starting fires. First, I set our living room sofa on fire. Another time, I threw some clothes over a lamp in the bedroom and set the wall on fire.

One time when I was five years old, I was at my best friend's house. We were playing up in the attic, and I lit a box full of newspapers on fire. Then my friend and I went outside. A few hours later, when we were playing outside, we heard fire trucks coming through the neighborhood. We ran to see where the fire trucks were going, and when we got to my friend's house, the house was on fire. I remember watching the firemen hitting the house with their axes, trying to put out the fire. It never dawned on me that I had set the house on fire. When we came running back to the house, my friend's parents grabbed him and said, "Oh my gosh, we've been looking all over for you!" They said they didn't know how the house had caught on fire, but they were glad we were okay. Then my friend said, "I know what happened – Greg set the house on fire. He lit the boxes in the attic with some matches."

At that point, it occurred to me what I had done. I immediately turned and ran home as fast as I could, crying every step of the way. I ran straight into my house and told my dad, "Dad, I caught my friend's house on fire!" From the time I was a little kid, my dad had always taught me if I told him the truth, I wouldn't get in trouble. I recall two detectives coming to our house a few days later. My dad stepped outside to talk with them, and that was the last thing I ever heard about that fire. In the end, I didn't even get in trouble, because I had told my dad the truth.

Another reminder of my dad's lesson about always telling the truth came from an incident when I was about five years old, when I went to the store and shoplifted some candy and gum. Later that day, when I saw my dad, he asked me how I was doing, and what I was chewing on. I answered, "Oh, it's just some gum." My dad said, "Some gum, huh? Well, where did you get it?" I said, "From the store." My dad said, "Oh, that's good. How did you get it from the store when you don't have any money?" Before I answered, I thought long and hard, because I remembered my dad's lesson about telling the truth. I thought to myself, "If I lie now, he's gonna know I didn't have any money, and that I stole the gum, and then I'll be in big trouble. If I tell the truth, I won't get in trouble – but then I'll have to face the humiliation of admitting to my dad what I did." So I said, "Dad, I stole the gum." He said, "Okay, go get in my car right now." We went back to the store, where I returned the rest of the gum and candy, and then my father made me apologize to the store manager for stealing it. I was so embarrassed that I never stole from that store again. My father taught me another valuable lesson that day: that the truth will always set you free.

I only got one spanking from my father – for the time I took the girl who lived across the street and ran away from home when I was five years old. My girl and I thought we were just taking a vacation, running away for the day. But I guess my dad didn't see it that way. I remember a guy in a truck pulling up next to us and asking me if my girlfriend and I wanted a ride. My dad had taught me to never accept rides from strangers, so we said no and kept walking. I also remember stopping at the Thrifty store, where we took off our old tennis shoes and put on some brand new shoes so we would be comfortable on our trip. We came around a corner when another car pulled up next to us. This time, it was my father and my sister, Adrienne. My dad grabbed my little girlfriend and I and took us straight home. I'll never forget when we pulled up to our house, there were mobs of people standing around outside. It was only later that I found out that my family, all our friends, and our neighbors were worried to death about us, and that half of South Central was out looking for my girlfriend and I. My dad brought me in the house, closed the door, and whipped my butt good. That was the only spanking I ever got from my dad, but it definitely left a mark, literally and figuratively.

Another great memory I have of my dad is of him taking all the kids in the neighborhood out for ice cream, to the beach, and on family vacations and outings. It seemed like my dad had a different car every month, because he used to leave his keys in his car with the car running, and inevitably the car would get stolen. The police used to get frustrated with my dad, because he would never press charges against the kids who had stolen his car. A few times, the kids got in serious accidents after stealing the cars, but still my dad refused to press charges.

One of the best things about growing up in South Central L.A. was that I always had so much fun. With a big family like ours, there was always a lot going on. I had discovered very early in life that, as the baby of the family, I could get away with some things my siblings couldn't get away with. For example, every summer my friends and I used to have our annual go-cart races. We would steal shopping carts from the nearby market, take off the wheels, then fix up the carts with string, plywood, ironing boards, or anything else we could find to create makeshift go-carts that we could then race in the streets. We also used to get up on the flat roofs of the garages in the back of our houses and go roof jumping from garage to garage. Because the garages were built so close together, we could make it almost all the way down the block. But there was one garage where the gap was almost too big, and all of us kids knew that if we didn't jump far enough and we missed that roof, it was all over – we would probably hit the ground and break a leg, or some other body part. We always got a huge adrenaline rush when we came to that roof, from the sheer excitement and danger of trying to get all the way across.

I always loved to play sports, too. We used to play football in the street, and nothing hurt more than running into the cars that were parked in the street. There was also an abandoned four-plex across the street that had caught on fire. For once, I had nothing to do with that fire. We took all the mattresses out of the house, stacked them up in the backyard, climbed to the top rail of the back stairs, and then did dives and flips onto the mattresses. Another fond memory comes from back when I was about six years old. I had begged my dad to buy me a new bike for Christmas, and on Christmas Day, my dream came true. I immediately took my new bike down the street to show my best friend. We were in his house playing, and when we came back outside, there was some other kid stealing my brand new bike. I chased the thief down the street, crying my eyes out all the way, but with no success. I only had that beautiful brand new green metal-flake bike for less than one hour! Then, just like that, my bike was gone forever. Welcome to life in South Central, L.A.

When I was around seven or eight years old, we used to ride our bikes from our neighborhood over to Santa Monica and Venice Beach. We would catch the bus to the Hollywood Skating Rink on Sunset and Western. I can remember skating all the way home from Hollywood; a distance of about 25 miles. I was also signed up at the USC Sports Club. Our house was about a 15-minute walk from the University of Southern California campus, and the Los Angeles Coliseum. I also remember where I got the courage to jump and dive off ocean cliffs later in my life: from when we were in the USC Sports Club, swimming in the Coliseum's Olympic Pool. My friends and I were in the Olympic Pool, watching the divers jumping off the three-tiered diving boards, into 17 feet of water. In order to get up on the diving platforms, you had to show the lifeguard you could do a one and a half off the high dive. My best friend Dan and I thought we were pretty smart. When the lifeguard was looking the other way, we would get into a tuck position, jump off the board and holler at the lifeguard. When he turned to look at us we'd come out of the tuck and act like we had just done a full one and a half. Sure enough, our plan worked and we were allowed to go on the higher platforms.

The first platform we jumped off was no problem. But we couldn't believe how high the second one was when we got up there. It took us awhile to work up the courage to jump, but we did. Not knowing exactly what to do, we stuck our arms out at our sides to balance ourselves on the way down. But when our arms hit the water, it stung so badly! After that, Dan and I realized that we couldn't jump in the water with our arms out. Then we went up to the third tower, which we had nicknamed Goliath. We're talking about the highest Olympic diving platform. When Dan and I got up there, we saw the lifeguard watching us. We walked to the edge and peered over. It was a long way down to the water. Dan and I looked at each other and said, "No way!"

But when we turned around to go back down the stairs, the lifeguard was standing right there, blocking our escape. He shook his head, pointed to the platform behind us, and said, "Sorry, guys - there's only one way down from here, and it's that way." We had no other choice at that point, so we ran, grabbed our nuts, and jumped as far as we could, screaming out loud all the way down! After we hit the water and realized we were still alive, we knew we had to do it again. Dan and I jumped off that third tower platform so many times that day that there was no more fear, just pure fun. From that point on, we knew we could jump off anything. To this day, I still enjoy jumping off ocean cliffs all over the world: Hawai'i, Bermuda, anywhere there's a challenge and some excitement.

When I was eight years old, I wanted more than anything to

be an NFL player. My hometown team was the Los Angeles Rams, who played nearby at the Coliseum, so I grew up going to the Rams games. I would walk around the parking lot asking people for extra tickets. I got in free to so many games that I lost count. After the game, I would go around to the players' entrance to go into the locker room. I was always pretty clever and slick when it came to getting into places I probably shouldn't have been, and the Rams locker room was no different. I would walk through the security gate with the wives and families of the players, and act like I was just one of their kids. Security would usually let me walk right through. The same security guards also worked the stadium gates, and eventually it got to the point where the guards would recognize me and just wave me on through. They must have figured that I was the son of one of the players. I met Rams stars like Roman Gabriel, Jack Snow, Deacon Jones, Merlin Olsen, Al Clark, and Isiah Robertson. I would carry their bags, wash their cars, and hang around with them after the games. Jack Snow used to give me his wristbands after the game. I truly believed it was only a matter of time before I would grow up and be an NFL player myself. My bedroom at home looked like a shrine to the NFL with all my memorabilia: I had banners, posters, and pictures of all my favorite NFL players and teams.

CHAPTER 2

DAD PASSES

MY LIFE REALLY started to change in a big way when I was eight. One day, I was walking home from the USC Sports Club when one of my friends passed by in the car with his parents. My friend hollered out the window, "Hey Greg, your dad's dead!" I didn't know what he meant, because when we were kids we used to play a game called The Dozens. Part of The Dozens was making insulting jokes about your friend's mom and dad. But when I got home and I walked in the house, I knew right away something was wrong. My mom was lying on the couch, and the house was full of my relatives. I asked my mom, "What's the matter?" She said, "Nothing, honey." I walked into my bedroom, and my brother Michael said to me, "Gregory, Daddy's dead." I didn't know what to think, or even how to feel. It turned out that my mom, my sister Brenda, and my sister Adrienne had gone to my dad's office because he hadn't come home for a couple days and no one had heard from him. When they got there, my dad didn't answer the door, so they had to break into his office. They found my dad sitting at his desk; dead in his chair from a heart attack he had suffered a couple days before. My dad was just 48 years old. Just four months later, my sister Brenda died at 20 years of age from a drug overdose. Losing my dad and then my sister in such a short time absolutely devastated our family. We were a mess after that.

Let me tell you about my older sisters, Gail and Brenda. Gail was the oldest, and she grew up in the Woodstock era of sex, drugs, and rock and roll. Even when I was a little kid, I remember Gail and Brenda were always high on pills, or outside fighting with each other. When I was little, the girls used to get me drunk and spin me around until I would run into the wall. They used to call me "Hickey Head Herbert." The girls thought it was hilarious, but to this day I still have a bump on my head from hitting the wall so many times. All but three of Gail's many friends from that era died of drug-related deaths, including my sister Brenda. Gail was the oldest, but Brenda always wanted to run with the older girls. They used to get high on drugs together and then fight like cats and dogs. My mom told me later that Brenda had always said she didn't believe she would live to see 21, and Brenda was right – she died at 20. Brenda had flown to New York when she was 17 with my aunt Gail Goddard, my mom's baby sister. Gail Goddard used to be a showgirl in New York. After Brenda came back pregnant from that trip, God blessed her with a beautiful daughter, whom she named London. Two years later, God took Brenda and left London with us. London was my niece, but because she lived with us, she was always more like my little sister.

I still remember the day Brenda died. She and her girlfriend Kathy were high on pills and had a fight. Later, they found Brenda lying over the fence. She was rushed to the hospital, where the doctors tried to pump her stomach to save her, but the hospital didn't have the right equipment, and Brenda died that night. At Brenda's funeral, I sat next to Kathy. I remember Kathy crying hysterically and blaming herself for Brenda's death. Later that same day, Kathy rented a room at a local hotel, locked herself in, and took her own life. I think Kathy blamed herself for Brenda's death, because of the fight they had the day Brenda died. In later years, my sister Gail dedicated her life to God and totally changed her life.

I learned at a very young age that pills are deadly. I watched my sister die from overdosing on pills, plus Kathy, and there were several other older friends who were in that same crowd who died from overdosing on pills. I also remember my sister Adrienne, who was the next youngest after Brenda, always hated all the drama and everything else that went on at our house. As soon as Adrienne turned 18, she left home, became a stewardess for Delta, and she never came back. Adrienne told me many years later that she left home because she couldn't stand watching so many people around her dying all the time. Adrienne said that out of all the girls she had known back in the neighborhood, only three or four made it out alive. Over 40 years later, Adrienne is still with Delta, traveling all over the world.

My brother, Michael, joined the Marines at 18. Michael later served in Vietnam, and was one of the few who came back home alive. Michael told me he learned his survival skills from running the streets in South Central. When we were growing up, Michael's favorite TV show was Rat Patrol. It was as if Michael was on a personal mission: he was going to be a Marine and run just like his heroes on Rat Patrol. Unfortunately, Michael had asthma, and he couldn't pass the physical. But Michael had a doctor forge some paperwork for him, just so he could be a Marine. Michael eventually went to Camp Pendleton and became a sharpshooter. When Michael returned home from Vietnam, he would tell me stories about what he did in the war. I would ask Michael, "Did you really kill all those people in Vietnam?" Michael would say, "I didn't kill anybody – the United States Government did." I remember one time Michael and I were out jogging together, and I said, "Michael, wait up." Michael said, "That's what my buddy in 'Nam said – 'wait up' – but he didn't make it out. You can't wait for anybody, Greg."

Michael told me that his team used to go out on suicide missions in Vietnam. Michael's team would get dropped into the enemy camp, blow it up, then run back to their camp – hopefully without getting killed along the way. Sometimes only one or two guys made it back alive. But Michael always made it back. One time, Michael told me about an incident where, five minutes after he got off his watch, the truck he had just been sitting in was blown up and everyone died. It was like Michael always had a guardian angel watching over him. Later on in his life, Michael became a heroin addict. Michael said all the soldiers in Vietnam were addicted to opiates during the war. One time, he caught hepatitis and he was in the hospital with two other Marines when the priest came in and administered the Last Rites. The other two Marines died shortly thereafter, but Michael somehow survived once again. When Michael came home from the war, he changed his life for the better. Michael became a merchant seaman, then a postal worker, and eventually traveled the world. After Michael got off drugs, he became a walking encyclopedia of history.

My older sister Angela was always the bookworm of the family. Angie was a straight-A student her whole life; from grade school, to junior high, to high school, to college scholarships, and then on to USC. Angela has a Master's degree, and was always highly intelligent and at the top of her field, no matter what she was doing. Today, when I look back at that time in my life, it's clear to me that my whole family was just a mess. It started with my dad dying, then continued with my sister dying just four months later. My mom did her best to help all of us kids deal with the loss of two family members, but that was a lot to handle even for someone with her extraordinary faith. As part of the bereavement process, mom took our whole family to see a psychiatrist, which was a complete disaster. I remember the psychiatrist asking my brother, "Michael, did you love your father?" Michael was so angry, I thought he was going to kill that doctor on the spot. That was the first and last time we ever visited that psychiatrist.

Me with David, my second father.

Me with Margy, my second mother.

CHAPTER 3

MEETING MY
JEWISH FAMILY

A FEW MONTHS later, my mom decided to enroll me in a voluntary busing program out in Northridge in the San Fernando Valley. My mom thought the busing program would allow me to attend a better school, get a better education, and even more importantly, hopefully avoid getting into any more trouble in the streets of South Central. I was bused out to Prairie Elementary. The only black kids in the entire school were the few that rode the bus with me every day. I quickly became best friends with a white Jewish boy named Steve. The next thing I knew, Steve asked if I could spend the weekend with him and his family at their house in Northridge.

It wasn't long before I was spending more and more time at Steve's house. In the summer, when the busing program ended, Steve's parents asked my mom if I could stay at their house over the summer and go to summer school out in the Valley with Steve. Before I knew it, Steve's family had pretty much adopted me. Steve's dad, David, was a doctor. Steve's mom, Margy, his older sister Pam, and his little brother, Scott, were like family to me. For the next six years, I spent more time at Steve's than I did at my own house back in South Central. Those years, from age 8 to age 14, were some of the best years of my entire life. To this day, I am grateful for how deeply and strongly those days with Steve's family branded me, in terms of the importance of family. For me, Steve's family was the embodiment of the perfect family, and in later years I modeled my own family life after them.

Steve's family was, and still are, some of the most loving and caring people I have ever met in my life. David has always been like a second father to me, and Margy was like a second mom. David never treated me any differently than he did his own children, despite our social backgrounds, and our racial and cultural differences. At the time, I just assumed everyone had a swimming pool, English horses, and a maid. David also signed up Steve and I for the Little League baseball team he had coached for years. Many years later, when I became a father myself, I realized how coaches could positively impact the lives of their children through the quality time that is spent in sports. I later became a head coach for all three of my sons. I was the only black kid in the entire Little League, and I quickly became a superstar athlete. I batted leadoff, and with my speed, led the league in stolen bases. I played any position where Coach David put me, but I especially loved the outfield, where I could catch all the fly balls and throw out base runners. Eventually, the coaches got the idea that because of my strong arm, I should learn to pitch. That experiment ended quickly when we discovered my accuracy left a little to be desired. I accidentally hit so many batters that the other teams didn't even want to hit against me, so it was back to the outfield for me.

One of my fondest memories of playing Little League baseball concerns one of my teammates, Satcliffe. His parents were very wealthy, and they forced him to play, despite the fact that he had no talent and no desire whatsoever to play. Poor Satcliffe struck out every time he batted, dropped every ball that was hit to him, and was miserable whenever he was on the field. One day we were in the last inning of an important game, which we were winning by only one run. I was playing right field that day, and Satcliffe was in left field. Our coaches deliberately put Satcliffe in left field because they didn't think the ball would ever be hit to him out there. But then one of the best hitters in the league came up for the other team, and he hit a towering fly ball to left field. I knew there was no way Satcliffe was going to catch that ball, so I took off for left field as fast as my legs would carry me. I got there just in time to make a spectacular diving sliding catch. The ball plopped into my mitt, and my teammates erupted with cheers. Everyone said afterward that was the greatest catch they had ever seen a little kid make. I was so proud of myself, and I couldn't stop crying tears of joy. My teammates lifted me up on their shoulders, and carried me off the field. After that, everyone called me "Little Willie Davis" after the Los Angeles Dodgers' great outfielder, Willie Davis.

When we went back home to Steve's house, we would go from house to house to swim in all the pools in the neighborhood. We especially liked swimming at the next-door neighbors' house. Richie and Anna were twins, and they were in the same grade as Steve and I. When we were 8 or 9 years old, we used to joke that Anna was my girlfriend. One day when we were playing outside at their house, Richie and Anna's older brother Eddie came outside and told me, "Greg, my dad said you can't come in our house anymore because something is missing from our house." After all the times we had played together, I couldn't believe their dad would say that about me, but I understood. As the only black kid playing in the entire neighborhood, I knew prejudice when I saw it. David immediately came out of the house and said, "Greg, don't worry about it. I know you didn't take anything from their house. You know what that's all about." We kept right on playing and having fun and I never gave it another thought.

I experienced another example of not-so-subtle racism later that same summer. Our Little League team had made it to the playoffs, and we were getting ready to play a second-round game, when the coach of the other team approached Coach David. The other coach pointed at me and said, "He can't play - he's not from this district." Coach David said, "Yes, he is – he lives at my house with me, so he can play." The other coach said, "No, we already checked him out, and he's not from around here. If you let him play, we're going to play the game under protest, and you'll have to forfeit the game." David turned and looked at me, and I could see the sadness in his eyes. Coach David knew I was the best player on our team, and one of the best players in the entire league. I just wanted to play the game I loved and help my team win. But Coach David knew that if I played it would hurt the team, so he gave in. I sat on the bench and watched my team lose that playoff game, and my insides hurt so bad. After the game, when they handed out the trophies to my teammates, the league officials wouldn't even let me have a trophy. I was a superstar in baseball, but that experience taught me everything I needed to know about politics and prejudice.

Margy used to take us kids grocery shopping. Each of us kids got our own shopping cart and filled it with every kind of soda we could find to put in the refrigerator out by the swimming pool. Fast forward nearly 40 years, and I still keep a fridge stocked with sodas, juices, and Gatorade by my own swimming pool! Margy was a homemaker who catered to our every need. She was always positive, and as sweet as can be. Margy was very creative and talented with arts and crafts, and she was always making belts, bags, purses, tie-dyed shirts, and other homemade creations. Steve's family had a live-in Mexican maid, Maria, whom they treated like family. Steve's sister Pam had English horses, and Steve's family had private tennis courts. I basically grew up in a Jewish household, with Passover, Bar Mitzvahs, and all the other Jewish cultural rites. Steve's family hosted a lot of large social gatherings, and I always felt perfectly at home in those settings. But my comfort level changed in certain social settings. Sometimes when David would take us all out to dinner at a nice restaurant, when we walked in together I could see the staff looking at Steve's family, and then looking at me, as if to say, "What is that nigger doing in here?" Nevertheless, I always felt thoroughly loved and protected by Steve's family, and I never doubted my place in their family.

When I was at Steve's house, Steve and I and the rest of our friends used to love playing pranks on the rest of the neighborhood. One of our favorite games was to go down to the Magic Shop, and buy packets of fake vampire blood. We couldn't wait to get back home to pull our favorite prank. We'd go down to the end of our street, and then cut through to the next block over. Then we'd take the vampire blood and pour it all over my face. I'd lay down in the street, and the rest of the guys would stand around me yelling and acting like they were kicking me and beating me up. People driving by would see a group of white kids seemingly beating a helpless black kid, and they'd stop to help me. As soon as a car stopped, my friends would scatter in every direction, while I lay on the ground, writhing and moaning in pain. The people would come running over to help me, but when they got close, I'd jump up and yell "Mickey Mouse!" and then run away as fast as I could. That was just good clean fun for us kids out in the Valley, in Northridge.

Me at age 13, with my Afro.

CHAPTER 4

RUNNING WITH THE CROWD

DURING THOSE SIX years with Steve's family, I went back home to South Central only sparingly on the weekends. As soon as I was back on my home turf, I fell right back into my routine: hanging out at the Hollywood Skating Rink, Venice Beach, the Santa Monica Pier, and running the streets like there was no tomorrow. One time when I was about 12, I came home for the weekend and I was introduced to marijuana. My friends Mark and David had stolen their father Duke's stash, and that was the first time I ever tried to get high. Duke was a counterfeiter who was always in and out of jail. I don't know if I was doing something wrong, or if we just had some bad weed, but that first time didn't affect me at all. The next time we tried it, though, I got very high and I remember exactly how it felt. We were at a James Brown concert at the L.A. Sports Arena, and I could feel that funky music pulsing through my whole body, and I thought that was pretty cool.

Growing up in the South Central neighborhood, there was a girl named Debbie, who was a real tomboy. Debbie always liked me, and if anyone else liked me or ever threatened me, Debbie would go after them. Debbie had a big family with five or six brothers. We always used to say you didn't want to mess with Debbie or her family, because you'd have to go through all those brothers. I was always the baby of the group, and all my friends were older. I was totally influenced by the older guys I hung out with. One time we were at the Hollywood Skating Rink, and a riot broke out. We were hanging around outside, when suddenly we saw all these guys running around in the streets with tire irons and crowbars. They were chasing people, banging on cars, and just scaring the hell out of everyone.

I'll never forget one scene from that episode: there was a white guy who got stuck at a red light in traffic right in the middle of the riot. To make matters worse, he was driving a convertible. All of a sudden, one of the fellas, one of the boys in the 'hood, came up to his car and busted out the windshield with a crowbar. The smartest thing that man ever did was act as if absolutely nothing had happened. He didn't breathe, he didn't move a muscle, and he didn't even turn his head to look at the crowd around him. He never even flinched; he just sat there frozen like a statue. He kept his hands on the wheel and stared straight ahead until the light turned green and traffic started to move along. After that, the police sirens started getting closer, and by the time the cops came, we were long gone. That was just another Saturday night in Hollywood with the fellas. By the following Monday, I was back out in the Valley with Steve's family, living the good life again.

CHAPTER 5

CRIPS AND BRIMS

AT THAT POINT in my life, I started to hang out with a different crowd at school in the Valley. Even though I still lived with Steve, and I loved him like a brother, he wanted no part of the people who were doing drugs and getting in trouble. I felt the powerful lure of being in the party crowd. Before long, I was getting high and hanging out with the "cool" kids in the Valley. My school grades started to decline, and when I came home to South Central for the weekend it was time to really get crazy. I remember one time in 1972 when we went to a big concert at the L.A. Coliseum. It was billed as the WattsStax Show, with Isaac Hayes, Rufus Thomas, and other R&B/Soul stars. Every black gang in the city turned out for the event. There were The Crips, The Cripplettes (the female version of the Crips,) The Brims, The Family, and many more gangs. I remember watching as the inevitable fights and riots broke out, and feeling like I was right in the middle of the action.

I was only 12, but all my friends were 16, 18, 20, and older. I loved being part of that crowd, and once again, because I was the baby of the group, I knew I could get away with anything. Nobody messed with me because I had the protection of my older gang brothers. I may have looked like a little smurf, but I was always talking trash, keeping the crew energized, and instigating trouble. It was like I was living a double life. Out in the Valley with Steve and his family, it was like the Brady Bunch - everything was nice, clean, and happy. But in South Central, it was more like Boyz In The Hood - crazy, violent, and out of control. I bounced back and forth between my two lives, and I somehow felt equally at home in both worlds. Nobody out in the Valley had any idea of my lifestyle in South Central, and nobody in South Central knew what a good life I had out in the Valley.

My crazy life in South Central finally caught up with me when I was 13, when I got shot. I was home from Steve's for the weekend and hanging out with my friends Short Arm Sammy and Cissy. On Sundays, all the gangs went to downtown Los Angeles to go to the movie theaters. All of us Crips went to the L.A. Theater and the State Theater. Our rival gang, the Brims, went across the street to the Palace Theater. The latest kung fu movie, Black Belt Jones, was playing at the L.A. Theater, where all of us Crips went. There were about 50 of us hanging out that day, but the line was so long at the L.A. Theater, we decided to go down the street to the State Theater instead. As usual, I was out front and instigating the move, with the rest of the crew behind me. It was 3 or 4 in the afternoon, broad daylight, in busy downtown Los Angeles. As we approached the State, a group of Brims came running out from the Palace and cut straight across the street in front of us. As soon as they got to the sidewalk in front of us, the Brims whipped out their guns and started shooting.

The rest of my gang turned and ran, but because I had been in front of the pack, when everyone turned I suddenly found myself in the back of the line trying to escape. An old lady had walked across the street and stepped right in my way when the shooting started. I paused to avoid her and I felt a bullet hit me in the hip. It felt like I had a bad charley-horse but with a fire burning inside me. I didn't know exactly what happened, but when I got hit I dropped to the ground and tried to crawl away. It was total chaos; bullets were flying, people were screaming and running everywhere. Some cops who were outside the L.A. Theater grabbed me, dragged me into the Theater, and told me I'd been shot. Later on, after the police got the situation under control, an ambulance came to take me to the hospital. When the ambulance attendants tried to cut off my pants so they could see the wound, I told them they couldn't cut off my brand-new Levis because I didn't want them to ruin my pants.

Like a lot of the guys in my crew, I had been carrying a "cake cutter" comb in my back pocket that day. A cake cutter is a big steel hair pick on a steel bar, with a rosin handle. It was perfect for grooming the big Michael Jackson-style Afro I had back then. They also made great weapons if you needed something handy in your back pocket. In my case, the guardian angel that had always watched over me growing up made sure that cake cutter saved my hip. The doctors told me later the bullet had hit the steel part of the comb and split it in two before lodging in my hip. The doctors said if that comb had not been there, and that .38 slug had gone straight into my hip, I might never have walked again, because the bullet would've blown my hip apart, as the shot came from such close range. I was rushed into surgery at Kaiser Hospital that night and had the bullet removed. When the doctor came to visit me the next day, he brought along a souvenir: the .38 slug he had pulled out of me.

I knew after the surgery that I wouldn't be able to make it back out to Steve's house in time to go to school the next day. I decided to call David and let him know what happened. I was reluctant to talk with David, because I knew he knew nothing of the reality of my South Central L.A. lifestyle. But I felt compelled to tell him the truth because I loved him, and I knew he loved me like I was his own son. I will never forget that conversation. "Hi David, it's Greg." "Greg, what's going on?" I hesitated, and then took a deep breath. "I'm in the hospital." I could hear the shock in David's response, "Are you okay?!" I responded with a very nonchalant, "Yes…I'm fine." David then asked, "What happened?" I said, "I got shot." David shouted, "Oh my gosh, Greg! Are you okay?! Where are you?!" I told him I was at Kaiser Hospital, and it seemed like only about 15 minutes passed before David was standing next to me in my room. I will never forget the look on David's face when he saw me. He was dumbfounded that his little man was lying in a hospital bed when just 72 hours earlier I had been sitting in his house having dinner with their family.

When I got out of the hospital, I was on crutches for a while and had to learn to walk again. Once I returned to school in the Valley, I was the most popular kid in school for having survived being shot. Someone told me later that the L.A. Times had run a front-page story on the shooting, with the headline, "Innocent bystander wounded in downtown shooting." Little did they realize, I was no innocent bystander. Back in the 'hood, I became like Superman – not even a bullet could stop me! Even at 13, I already had a reputation of being the Little King in the gang, and the bragging rights that came with surviving a gunshot elevated me to a local legend. I was right out in front of the trouble, just like always. Unfortunately, my ego grew just as quickly, and my escalating drug use only made it worse. My mom had recently remarried, and she and her new husband, James had bought a house in Gardena, between El Segundo and Crenshaw. Gardena was a nicer middle class black area. Our family left South Central at that point, and my mom took the chance to put me on notice about my rapidly declining grades. My mom said that if my grades did not improve immediately, my party out in the Valley with Steve's family would end.

When I reflect on that time in my life, I'm struck by my mom's unconditional love and compassion for me. She had let me go to live with Steve's family for those five critical years of my childhood because she knew it was best for me and that it was what I wanted. I now have seven kids of my own, and to this day, I don't think I could do what my mom did for me. I love my kids so much, and I am so protective of my children. I couldn't let my kids go like that, even if it was in their best interests for me to do so. My mom did what she had to do out of her capacity to love me unconditionally, and by doing that, she set an example that would stick with me for the rest of my life.

My mom had let me go be with Steve's family out of love, but as soon as she saw that my circle of friends in the Valley had changed, and that my lifestyle was taking me down the wrong road, she pulled the plug and brought me back home. Mom thought that with the move to the new area, plus the presence of a new father figure in her new husband, the time was right for me to come back home. Life as I had known it with Steve's family was over. I never could have imagined it then, but it would be seven years before I had any contact again with Steve's family. I came back home to live with my mom in the middle of my second semester of 9th grade, after transferring from Holmes Junior High to Henry Clay Junior High in Los Angeles.

For all her great intentions, my mom had no idea we were simply moving from the old 'hood into the new 'hood, which was run by a gang called the OG Shotgun Crips - and those niggas was crazy. The Original Gangster Shotgun Crips controlled the entire territory, which we called the set, bordered by Crenshaw and

Western on the east and west, and El Segundo and Rosecrans on the north and south. Back in those days, if you came into the 'hood and didn't belong there, you were as good as dead. My new life in the new area signified another turning point, which began at my new school. Henry Clay Junior High was located in the Harbor Gangster set. I met one of my best friends in life at that time. Keith and I connected right away, and we remain close today. After school, we'd hang out at the record shop.

I remember one day I was standing outside the record shop in my new gangster attire - a double-breasted waistline black leather coat, cul-de-sac shoes (which were considered Crips shoes), and one-cuff Levis – when three guys approached me and surrounded me. One of them spoke up and said, "Hey brother, that's a nice leather coat – let me try it on." I said, "Sorry man, this is my brother's coat. I can't let you try it on." He said, "Hey man, let me just try it on – I'll give it right back." I repeated, "It's my brother's coat, and I can't let you try it on." I knew these guys were getting ready to jack me and take my coat. The group closed in tight around me and the guy said, "Hey homeboy, you better take off that coat." I knew if I took off that coat, I'd never see it again. So I said, "I can't do that." Just then the leader said, "Hey, aren't you that new homeboy who just moved in over on Cashmere, in the set?" I said "Yeah, that's me." Then he said, "You're one of us!" I said, "Yeah, that's right, I'm one of you!" I was not going to be a victim. At that point, I was down with the program – whatever that entailed. It had nothing to do with right or wrong – you were either all the way in, or all the way out - and I was in from that point forward. As soon as I stepped out of my front door, I was in the 'hood – because I lived right in the middle of it. I became one of the boys.

CHAPTER 6

DEEDEE AND FRED

I WAS 14 years old by then, and even though my family had moved, I still loved to go to some of my favorite old hangouts, such as the Hollywood Skating Rink. That's where I met my new girlfriend, DeeDee. DeeDee's stepfather, Fred, was one of the top guys in the local organized crime scene in Inglewood. DeeDee lived with her older sister Mimi, her mom, and Fred. Mimi was a beautiful light-skinned black girl who was also a groupie; she only dated star athletes and a Who's Who of famous men. I remember meeting a certain world-famous Olympic gold medalist boxing champion at DeeDee's house. When I met him, I asked him if the boxing game was fixed and if he knew who was going to win or lose before the match. His response was, "Greg, there are no losers in boxing." He left it open to my interpretation, but I knew exactly what he meant.

DeeDee and I were boyfriend and girlfriend from the time I was 14 until I was about 20, and it was assumed that DeeDee and I would eventually get married. Her stepfather, Fred, loved me like a son, and he took me under his wing and taught me the ropes. Fred's best friend Joe was a hit man, who used to dress up like a mailman when he went out to do a hit. If Joe came to your house dressed like the mailman, you weren't getting any mail - your time was up. When I went to Inglewood to see DeeDee, I'd see Fred and Joe too, and they treated me like their new little protégé. Fred knew DeeDee loved me and since we were going to be together in the future, it made sense for him to groom me as his future son-in-law.

I remember one time when Fred's gun accidentally went off and wounded him in the leg. I asked DeeDee why Fred hadn't gone to the hospital. DeeDee told me Fred had been AWOL from the penitentiary for many years, and that he couldn't risk getting caught in the hospital. Fred taught me several valuable lessons and schooled me up on the rules of the game in the streets. One of Fred's rules was, don't ever pull out a gun unless you're going use it – because if you pull it out and don't use it, the person you pull it on will come back and kill you first. Another lesson Fred taught me was, don't put cash in the bank – put it in a safe deposit box or in a safe. Fred also used to tell me to always wear a mask and don't let people know who you really are.

I was 14 or 15 when the light came on in my head regarding finances. I realized I had lived the good life all those years out at Steve's house, with their swimming pool, horses, tennis courts, maid, etc. Now the meaning and value of money really started to sink in. When I was just a kid having fun at Steve's house, I never thought about where that good life came from, or who paid for it. But as I got a little older, and was away from that kind of wealth for a while, I started to understand that not everyone lived like that. When I saw guys in the 'hood driving fancy low rider cars, I asked someone, "Man, how do you get a car like that?" They said, "You gotta wheel and deal, Homeboy!" So I said, "Hook me up!" I was determined to live that same lifestyle I'd had at Steve's house, since that was what I was accustomed to. I didn't care what it took; I just knew I had to do whatever it took to get there.

I knew I needed some money to get started, so I stole $100 from my brother Michael and I set it up to make it look like Michael's friend Daryl had stolen the money. I bought a half-pound of marijuana and after that, I was off and running. That was my first step toward making money for myself. I was wheeling and dealing to the fellas in the 'hood, guys in the gangs, people at school, friends at Hollywood Skating Rink, and anyone else who needed to get hooked up. By the time I was 17, I had the low rider car, tailor-made clothes, jewelry, girls, and all the accoutrements of success. My buddies and I were the kings of the neighborhood. I had my gang life, my wheeling and dealing life, and my organized crime life.

Looking back on those times, I realize that my life was on the line on a daily basis. It seems like God's guardian angels were always watching over me and protecting me when everyone around me was either getting shot, getting killed, or going to jail. It was crazy rolling through the streets of L.A. in the '70s. We stole cars, broke into houses to get guns; you name it - we did it. It was never about right or wrong - it was about handling our business and doing whatever we had to do to survive in the 'hood. I never felt like I had a choice; I lived in the 'hood, and that meant I had to be down with the program, because I was not going to be a victim or a statistic like so many of the people I knew. It was life or death, and I chose to live - by whatever means necessary.

WE LOVE YOU MOM!

CHAPTER 7

MOM'S PRAYER OF PROTECTION

MY MOM USED to wait up for us to come home at night. Mom didn't know everything we did, but she knew just enough about life on the streets of L.A. to be worried about us. My mom used to leave inspirational and spiritual sayings taped to the mirror in the bathroom where I washed up before I went to bed. Even in the darkest times of my young life, when I was up to my neck in trouble, my mom always found a way to remind me that God loved me, and that all things were possible through God. I always knew there were a greater meaning and a higher purpose to my life. I was hooked on my gangster lifestyle, addicted to the power and the material possessions that came with having money – but I always believed in God. I hated the trouble that came along with the lifestyle, but it seemed like I couldn't have one without the other.

To this day, I still remember my favorite of all the notes and spiritual sayings my mom left taped to my bathroom mirror. It's called the Prayer of Protection:

The light of God surrounds me

The love of God enfolds me

The power of God protects me

The presence of God watches over me

The mind of God guides me

The life of God flows through me

The law of God directs me

The peace of God abides with me

The joy of God uplifts me

The strength of God renews me

The beauty of God inspires me

Wherever I am, God is

My mom always played some kind of spiritual message on the radio early in the morning, and she turned it up real loud, whether I liked it or not. She never said a word, but the message was crystal clear. Thank God mothers know best, because I sure didn't have a clue back then.

CHAPTER 8

GOING TO JAIL

MY TROUBLES STARTED to escalate as I got into my mid-late teens. It seemed like everyone I knew was getting killed or going to jail. One day, I was out of mind on a rowdy high. My friend Leon (L.C.) from the Shotgun Crips and I had smoked some weed, drank several beers, and taken Valium. We broke into a house down the street in the neighborhood. As we ransacked the house looking for guns, Leon looked out the window and said, "They're home!" As the owners walked in the front door, we flew out the back door. Leon jumped over the fence in the backyard, but I slipped as I tried to jump the fence and the man caught me by the collar. He dragged me back into the house and grabbed a vase to threaten me with until the police could come.

I thought that guy was going to crown me with that glass vase, and his wife was so upset that we had turned her house upside down, she was ready to kill me herself if he didn't. His two little kids were tugging on my arms and singing, "We caught you, we caught you!!" The wife called the police, and when they got there, I looked outside and saw Poncho from the 'hood standing out there. He happened to be there when the police came into the house, and so he came over to see what was going on. Poncho just shook his head when he saw me, because he knew I was going to jail that night. My mom came downtown and bailed me out just as quickly as the police had checked me in. I had to go to court after that, and I got a year of probation.

The very next week after I got probation, I found myself in jail again. I couldn't believe it. I had been at my buddy O.J.'s house. There was O.J., Frog, who stood about 6-5; and me at about 5-7. We were bored, and decided we all needed some quick money, so we hatched a plan for Frog to snatch a purse. O.J. had a white low rider, so he drove us all down to the bank, dropped off Frog and I, and then parked down the street in the alley. The plan called for Frog and I to hide where we could watch for ladies coming out of the bank, then Frog would jump out, grab a lady's purse and we would take off back to the getaway car. Unfortunately, the plan didn't go quite as expected. Every time a lady came out of the bank, I'd say, "Go get that one!" But after three ladies came out, Frog kept getting scared and chickening out, so finally I just said, "I'll do it myself."

The next time a lady came out of the bank, I waited until she was unlocking her car door and then I ran up fast and snatched her purse. Frog and I took off back to the car where O.J. was waiting. We headed for O.J.'s house in Gardena, and I remember passing a Gardena police car on the way. We were at O.J.'s house only for about 15 minutes when we heard the Gardena police pounding on the door and telling us to open the door. We were hiding in O.J.'s bedroom, and I told him not to answer the door. But O.J. was worried about the police knocking down the door to his mom's house, so he left Frog and I in his bedroom and let the police in the front door. Next thing I knew, all three of us were facedown on the carpet, with the cops' revolvers pointed at our heads.

When we got to jail, the police played the Prisoner's Dilemma game with the three of us by telling each of us that the other two had already ratted out the other one. Once again, my mom came downtown and bailed me out and I was back at home that night. It wasn't until we got to our hearing that we realized that the purse-snatching victim was also a probation officer! She stunned everyone by saying Frog had snatched the purse. It also came out in the police report that Frog had fingered me as the thief. My guardian angels must have been working overtime that day, because there is no way that anyone in their right mind could mistake Frog at 6-5 for me at 5-7. The lady insisted Frog was the one who grabbed her purse, so he went to jail and I got off with more probation and weekends at Juvenile Hall correction facility.

When I got back on the streets, the word was going around that Frog was coming to get me as soon as he got out of jail. I told all the fellas that I was glad that Frog went to jail because he had snitched on me. The code on the street was simple: you never, ever snitched on anyone. Nothing is worse than a snitch. When Frog got out of jail, I didn't bother waiting for him to come to my house. I went straight over to his house and confronted him at his front door. I said, "Frog, the word is you're coming to get me. Well, here I am – what's it gonna be?" Frog didn't know what to think, or whether I was packing a gun, or a knife, or whether I was there to kill him. I said, "I'm glad you went to jail, because you snitched on me. You got a problem with that?" Frog said, "No, I don't have a problem." We shook hands, and that was the end of it. It was all part of what I had learned growing up in the streets: you handle your business on the streets before it handles you. All you have on the street is your reputation, and you never, ever let anybody punk you. After that, the word on the street was that I had confronted Frog straight up, and everything was back to normal.

CHAPTER 9

O.J. AND MOODY

WHEN I WAS on probation and had to spend my weekends at Juvenile Hall, I had to go in on Friday night and I didn't get out until Sunday night. I'd stop by my friend O.J.'s house on Friday to drop off my cash and my stash so he could hold it for me until I got out of Juvenile. One time, when I came back to pick up my money from O.J.'s, he told me that my money was gone. O.J. figured somebody had broken into his house and stolen it. I trusted O.J., so I sat him down and we tried to backtrack and figure out who could have stolen our money. It turned out that O.J.'s buddy, Moody, had stopped by that weekend, and when they were getting ready to leave, O.J. couldn't find his house keys. When O.J. got home that night, his keys were on the kitchen table, but all the money was gone. I knew immediately that Moody had taken the money. I also knew that on Sunday nights, Moody used to hang out at Washington Skating Rink on Rosecrans and Western. I told O.J. we were going to round up some fellas from the 'hood and head up to Washington to find Moody and get my money back.

Now, O.J. was a player, not a fighter – he had all the girls, but he wasn't a gangster. When we got to Washington Skating Rink, I saw Moody in there with his buddies, spending my money and having a good time. His good time ended as soon as he saw us. I could see in Moody's eyes that he knew something was up. We got there right before closing, so Moody knew we'd be waiting for him when the rink emptied out. I had to keep pressuring O.J., telling him that when Moody came out, to take the first swing at him and then the rest of us would jump Moody and get the money back. As soon as the rink closed and people started coming out, we surrounded Moody. I told O.J., "Hit him, and we'll get him." I could see in O.J.'s eyes that he was scared, but finally he took a big swing and hit Moody square in the jaw. O.J.'s timing was perfect, because he swung at Moody just as Moody was reaching for a gun in the back of his pants. Moody dropped the gun as he hit the ground. We grabbed the gun and Moody's wallet, and the fight was on.

The security guards from the rink came out and started grabbing guys who were fighting. Moody got up, ran to his low rider and took off, and we got out of there as fast as we could. On the way back home to O.J.s house, I told O.J. that I could see he didn't really have it in him to confront Moody for the money, because he was scared of Moody. I told O.J. I didn't care if he was too scared to fight - I just wanted my money back, period. O.J. nodded and said he'd pay me back my money himself in the next week or so. Days went by, and O.J. still hadn't paid me back my money. I kept asking him for it, and O.J. kept telling me he'd pay me. Everyone in the 'hood knew that Moody had taken my money from O.J.'s house while I was in Juvenile detention.

Pretty soon, word got around that O.J. still hadn't paid me back my money. Just as I kept grilling O.J. for my money, the fellas in my crew kept grilling me, asking me if O.J. had paid me back yet. I kept telling the guys, "Yeah, it's under control – O.J.'s gonna pay me himself." I felt like I was trapped in the middle, with my friend O.J. on one side and the respect of my crew on the other side. I couldn't win. One day, my crew confronted me and asked, "Bono, did you get your money from O.J.?!" Bono was my gang nickname, which I took from the Bruce Lee movie, The Chinese Connection. I said, "No, I'll handle it." The next day, when they asked again, and I said no again, the crew started telling people that I was going to take O.J. out. I never said I was going to take O.J. out – I just said I'd handle my business. But that's how it works in the streets: the gangs exert tremendous peer pressure on their members to do things the way they're supposed to be done. Now, with the gang saying I was going to take O.J. out, I felt I had no choice but to do it. If I didn't take out O.J. soon, it wouldn't be long before the gang would be taking me out instead. The worst thing that could happen to me would be for the other gang members to think that I'd gotten soft and lost my edge. It was simply a matter of principle and respect.

The very next day, I called O.J. and told him I was coming over to get my money. O.J. told me to come by the house later that evening. I had already made up my mind that if O.J. didn't have my money that night, I was going to have to do something hard and heavy. I couldn't take the fellas grilling me again. I got to O.J.'s and it was the same old song: "Greg, I'm gonna pay you, man." But he still didn't have my money. I took O.J. out in the front yard, and I knew right then and there that I was going to have to take O.J. out just on principle. I couldn't have the gang questioning my toughness. O.J. started making excuses for not having my money, and while he was talking, I was counting to 10 in my mind. When I got to 10, I swung at O.J. and knocked him down. For the next several minutes, I beat O.J. until he was knocked out cold. When O.J. stopped responding to me, I hauled him into his house and laid him on his bed. Then I got in my car, and drove to my house.

When I got home, I called O.J., but when he answered the phone, he was in a senseless daze. "Greg, Greg, what happened?! I woke up in my bed, and I'm all bloody – what happened?!" I said, "O.J., you know what happened!" O.J. said, "Greg, I'm looking in the mirror and I'm all bloody – what happened?" I told O.J., "I knocked you out, and you're lucky I didn't take you out for good!" He said, "Oh, it's like that?" The very next day, O.J. gave me all of my money. Even after I got my money back, I felt terrible because O.J. was my good buddy. But I did what I had to do, even though it broke my heart to do it. That was life in the 'hood, and I was not going to be a victim. Either you handle the streets or the streets handle you. In the end, everything was back to normal. O.J. was still my friend, and in my crew's eyes, my reputation had been restored.

CHAPTER 10

ON TOP OF OL' SMOKEY

ONE TIME WHEN I was living in my mom's house in Gardena, I came home from school and discovered someone had broken into our house and stolen my stash, which had been hidden under a floorboard in our crawl space. My immediate reaction was that I felt so violated by the robbery that I never wanted to break into another house again. I also knew it had to be my friend Smokey who had ripped me off, because he was the only person who knew where I kept my stash. Smokey lived across the street from me on the corner. Smokey was so black he was purple, and he was real big and buff like a gorilla. Truth be told, I was scared of Smokey, but he was just one of the boys in the 'hood.

When I got home the day we were robbed, my mom also told me her diamond jewelry was gone. I didn't care so much about Smokey taking my stash, but I was enraged that he had taken my mom's diamonds. That was crossing the line – the code in the 'hood was, you never, ever messed with anyone's mom. I took off and went over to L.C.'s house, which is where we all used to hang out. I was screaming and yelling that someone had broken into my house and they were going to die when I figured out who it was. The fellas in the crew immediately piped up and said, "It was that stupid-ass nigga Smokey! We told that fool we wanted no part of that. We're just tellin' you straight, because we don't want no trouble with you, Bono."

I left L.C.'s and drove my low rider straight to Smokey's house. He wasn't there, so I waited for him. I was sitting on his fence when Smokey came walking up. The anger within me was like a raging volcano, but I had to maintain the appearance of cool and calm. So I said, "Hey, Smoke – what's going on?" Smokey said, "Oh, I've been over at my girlfriend's house all day." I knew he was lying, because Smokey didn't even have a girlfriend. Smokey was so big and so ugly, all the girls were afraid of him. I told him I had some weed, and I offered him a joint. When Smokey went to light it, I reached back and swung my fist at him with every ounce of strength I had in my body. Smokey fell to the ground, and I immediately jumped on him and started beating on him with all my might. I weighed about 140 pounds soaking wet, and Smokey was built like a professional bodybuilder. But I caught Smokey off guard, and I was so full of rage, he didn't stand a chance. I was screaming, crying, and cussing all at the same time as I beat Smokey and accused him of stealing my mom's diamonds. Smokey kept screaming and crying, saying the fellas were lying and that he didn't steal my mom's diamonds. Once again, my heart was heavy because Smokey kept swearing he didn't do it. Finally, I stopped beating Smokey and let him up. But I told him, "If I find out you're lying, and you took my mom's diamonds, I'm coming back here to kill you."

I left Smokey, went back over to L.C.'s house, and confronted the fellas who were still there. The guys insisted Smokey had stolen the diamonds, saying he had brought the diamonds to L.C.'s house to try to sell them. After that, Smokey disappeared for about a week.

One day when we were at Rowley Park, where all the Shotgun Crips used to hang out, someone said, "Hey, look! There goes Smokey on his bike!" I ran up behind Smokey and socked him in the side of the head, and knocked him to the ground. Then I grabbed Smokey's bike and started pounding him with it. I told Smokey to go get my mom's diamonds or I was going to take him out right then and there. Smokey got on his bike, and we followed him in the car. When we got to Smokey's house, he went inside and came back out with his two older brothers, Billy and Wildman. As soon as I saw Billy and Wildman come out, I ran at Smokey and punched him again. Then Billy hit me in the temple and knocked me off Smokey and into the bushes. Pretty soon, the fight was on – my brother, my cousin, and the rest of the guys from the park jumped in until the Gardena police came and broke everything up.

The next day, my mom got her diamonds back. It turns out that while I was trying to kill Smokey with my bare hands, my mom was busy killing him with kindness. It seems my mom had written a note to Smokey, asking him to please return the diamonds he had stolen. Smokey obliged and returned everything intact. As soon as my mom told me she had gotten her diamonds back, I knew it wouldn't be long before things would be back to the usual level of insanity in the 'hood. My mom always had such a gentle, loving, and compassionate spirit, and her wisdom has always been a guiding light in my life. Unfortunately, my business with Smokey wasn't finished just yet.

A week or so later, a friend of mine who I knew from Saturday Continuation school stopped by my house to visit. When he went to leave, his car wouldn't start, so he left it parked at my house overnight. When he came back for the car the next day, his 8-track tape deck was missing from his car. He asked me if I had taken it, but of course I knew right away who the thief was – the neighborhood kleptomaniac. We went over to Smokey's house, and my friend told Smokey, "Go get my tape deck right now, and bring it down to Greg's house." Smokey didn't even try to hide the fact that he had taken it. He just said, "Okay." I thought Smokey should have lied, like he always did, because my friend was not someone you wanted to mess with, and now he was angry. When Smokey showed up with the tape deck, my friend said, "We should just kick his ass and teach him a lesson." I agreed, and the next thing I knew, my friend had knocked Smokey down, jumped on his chest, and was just beating the life out of poor Smokey. I started to feel bad for Smokey, and I tried to stall my friend out and make him stop hitting Smokey, but he was just too big and strong, and I couldn't stop him. That guy beat Smokey to a pulp. I saw Smokey's eyes start to roll up in his head, and I finally managed to pull my friend off Smokey.

After a few minutes, Smokey staggered to his feet and tried to walk away. Some neighbors had come out of their houses to see what was going on, but as soon as they saw it was Smokey getting beat up, they just went back to their business. Smokey had broken into almost every house on the street at one time or another, and had developed a reputation for being quite a kleptomaniac. I'm sure the neighbors felt justice was finally being served for all the times Smokey had gotten away with stealing. I heard later from the fellas that Smokey wound up in the hospital as a result of the beating he took that day. He was in pretty bad shape, but I didn't even care, because Smokey had it coming, and he messed with the wrong guy. Little did I know that it wouldn't be long before I'd be joining Smokey in the hospital.

The very next day, I was walking down the alley on my way to Rowley Park. A car pulled up beside me, and Smokey's older brothers Billy and Wildman got out. Wildman grabbed me and pulled my arms behind my back like I was handcuffed. I barely remember Billy swinging at me, and then everything went black. When I came to, my buddy Curtis was helping me up off the ground. I didn't know what happened, but I knew I was hurt bad. Curtis said, "Oh man, Bono, that's messed up. That ain't right what they did to you." Billy and Wildman had knocked me unconscious, and as I was walking back home I didn't feel right. When I got home, my sister Angela freaked out and started screaming when she saw my face. It was a crazy scene at my house that night. My brother was there, with my cousin, and some of the fellas. Everyone in the crew was saying we should go shoot up Billy and Wildman's house in retaliation, or throw some Molotov cocktails at their house and burn it down.

Even in my battered condition, and in the middle of all the chaos at my house that night, I had a rare moment of clarity. I knew if this situation escalated any further, people were going to die. All I could think of was my mom being endangered if the violence blew up out of control. I knew that if my friends and I went back for revenge on Smokey's brothers, his sister and her kids and other innocent family members would die too. I also knew that it wouldn't stop there, and that my mom and my family would soon get caught up in it as well. Through all of the screaming and yelling in the house, my mom was saying she needed to take me to the hospital. I told all the fellas to calm down and that we'd deal with this situation when I got back from the hospital. My mom took me to Kaiser, where I was diagnosed with a concussion and internal bleeding. My face was virtually unrecognizable from the beating I took, and Angela told me several years later that my eyes were so swollen they looked like they were about to come out of my head.

While I was in the hospital, someone suggested I should press assault charges against Billy and Wildman, because they were both adults and I was a minor. I went ahead and pressed charges, and

Smokey's brothers went to jail for 90 days plus probation. The same day Billy and Wildman got out of jail, it just so happened I was planning to have my car painted. I parked my low rider outside, and when I came out to go to school the next day there were about five gallons of house paint poured all over my car. My car was white, but it was covered in red, blue, yellow, green, and orange paint. Fortunately, it had been a cool evening, and the paint hadn't completely dried. I spent the entire day cleaning that paint off my car, but what Billy and Wildman didn't know was that I was going to paint that car anyway.

When I saw Smokey coming down the street, I stood right in front of his car until he stopped, then I snatched him out of his car. Smokey started singing like a bird. "I didn't do it, Bono - I swear! It was Billy and Wildman. They just got out of jail last night!" The recent episode of violence between Smokey and I had spun out of control, but it finally ran its course that day. Billy and Wildman were on probation and couldn't touch me. Smokey was still terrified of me from all the beatings he'd received. Once I recovered from my injuries, it was time for me to get back to running my business and being the king of the streets with my buddy Keith.

CHAPTER 11

THE RAYMOND CRIPS AND R.B.

ONE NIGHT, I went over to my best friend Keith's neighborhood, where the Harvard Gangsters hung out. They were like wannabe Crips. We decided to head down to the dance at Raymond Park, in the Raymond Crips' neighborhood. The Raymond Crips had a reputation: shoot first, and ask questions later. There were about 15 of us hanging out together that night, so we thought we'd be safe. We got to the party, and right away I could tell something wasn't right. We didn't have any guns on us that night, but we all acted like we were packing heat. I knew there was something wrong about the way the Raymond Crips were sizing us up. I just had a bad feeling about the way they were looking at us. We all huddled together, and then Gary from the Harvard Gangsters piped up and said he had told his friend from the Raymond gang that we didn't really have any guns, and that we were just acting tough. I thought to myself, "We're dead." I told the fellas, "Let's get out of here before they light us up."

We started moving toward the door, with our hands in our coats like we had guns. We finally got to the door and broke for it, just as the bullets started flying all around us. Those Raymond Crips lit us up like it was the Fourth of July. We ran as fast as we could for about eight blocks. Yet again, despite the constant danger, and my life flashing before my eyes for a few minutes, none of us got shot that night. We made it home safe and sound and lived to run the streets another day. As usual, when I got home that night I found my mom had stuck some more of her little spiritual sayings to the mirror in the bathroom where I cleaned up before going to bed.

I remember going to bed that night and thanking God that I didn't get killed, because even by my standards, that episode with the Raymond Crips was a little too close for comfort. I realized that in the gang life, everyone plays tough – but deep inside, everyone is scared to death, and nobody wants to die. It was a terrible, dirty feeling to live in that constant state of fear and hopelessness. I would come home and take a shower before bedtime, but it was like I could never get clean. Everyone wore a mask of fake courage and fake toughness, but on the inside we were all just scared little kids living in an inner-city gangster nightmare. The only problem was, for us the nightmare was real – it was our daily life. It seemed like every day our lives were on the line, but over time we became immune to it. Living and dying was just part of the game; but the bottom line was, don't ever get caught with your guard down. The fear of dying was actually an asset, because that fear kept us sharp and on top of our game.

My sense of fear saved my life one Saturday night at a party in the 'hood. Everyone knew that you never go to a party in another gang's set. On that night, a trio of members from another set crossed neighborhood lines and came looking for April and Yvette, two girls from the 'hood, at a party in our set. All the fellas from our neighborhood were there, including Ralph, Buddha, Bear, Bacon, Poncho, L.C., Frog, Curtis, Kent, and me. The party was at the home of Smooch, one of the regulars in our group. Ralph, aka R.B., had a reputation for being crazy. R.B. was a career criminal who had become thoroughly institutionalized. R.B. was always getting busted for one thing or another, and as a result spent most of his life bouncing back and forth between the jail and the streets. On the night of this particular party, R.B. had just been released from jail yet again. R.B. knew all the fellas in the 'hood, so as soon as he saw the rival gangsters with April and Yvette, he was ready for a fight. R.B. immediately turned on the lights, drew his gun, put the three guys on the ground, stuck his gun in their faces, and told them they were about to die. For the next several minutes, R.B. belittled and humiliated those guys, and threatened to kill them on the spot. I knew these three guys were tough guys, but R.B. had them in a bad position so they wisely kept their mouths shut and took his abuse. Smooch told R.B. not to shoot the guys in his house, while April and Yvette screamed and pleaded with R.B. to let the guys go.

R.B. finally relented and let the guys get up. Then he told them, "If you ever come in our neighborhood again, you're dead." As I watched this scene unfold, I recalled the lesson I had learned from Fred: "Don't ever pull a gun on someone unless you're going to use it. Because if you pull it and don't use it, the guys you pull it on are going to come back and get you." For the next few hours, I couldn't stop thinking about Fred's words, and how R.B. had let those guys go after humiliating them in front of the girls and everyone else at the party. After those three guys got up off the floor and left, R.B. went right back to having fun - but I just couldn't relax.

Several hours later, I was outside with a bunch of the fellas, sitting on the trunk of a car parked in front of the house and talking with my buddy, Victor. I kept thinking, I should keep a look out for those three guys. I turned my head for a second and my worst fears came true: there they were - the same three tough guys R.B. had sent home earlier. They were in a car, cruising by the house real slow, with the windows rolled down. I knew instantly why they were there. Just like James Brown used to sing, it was time for the Big Payback.

In the blink of an eye, I saw one of the guys in the backseat of the car pull up a gun and point it at us. Instinctively, I jumped off the trunk of the car and ran straight toward the house as fast as I could. As I ran through the yard and dove into the bushes, I could hear bullets whistling past my ears. Those guys sprayed the house with gunfire, and Victor, the guy I'd been standing right next to just moments earlier, was shot four times. The craziest part of that situation was that, when I went home that night, I didn't even give the shooting a second thought. I had become so numb to the insanity of my life in the street. Shootings were the norm in the 'hood in the '70s, and the fact that I had so narrowly avoided such grave danger didn't even register in my mind. It wasn't until many years later that I realized how divinely protected I was. My mom was always praying for my safe return home, and her prayers were always answered – my guardian angels were there watching out for me. Every so often, the spiritual side of me got the best of the dark side of me, and I'd see an opportunity to help another brother survive the insanity when it appeared his time was about to run out.

Chapter 12

Slim and The Centerviews

I HAD A friend from the skating rink, Slim, who was a Brim. The Brims were the same gang that had shot me when I was 13. We used to see Slim and the rest of the Brims at the skating rink all the time. The rule was, the gangs left each other alone at the skating rink, because we all went there just to listen to the music, have a good time and be with the girls. One day, a bunch of the Shotgun Crips decided they were going to take out Slim, for no good reason. The plan was to go up to the Hollywood Skating Rink, where Slim liked to hang out, find him and kill him. I liked Slim and didn't want to see him get taken out, so I told the fellas, "When we get there, I'll go in, find Slim and set it all up. When he comes out, you guys shoot him."

I went inside, found Slim, and told him, "Slim, listen to me – the fellas are outside, and they're here to take you out, right now. If you walk out the front door, you're dead. I'll tell them I got you all set up, but you gotta find a way out of here if you want to live."

Slim said, "Ok, Greg - I got it. Thanks for saving me, man." I went back outside and told the fellas in my crew it was all set up, and that Slim would be coming out any minute. The fellas were ready and waiting, but after several minutes, Slim still hadn't come out. I told my guys, "Man, I don't know what happened – I had it all set up to get him!" If the fellas had known what I had really done, it would have been me that got taken out that night. Fortunately, the fellas believed me, and Slim and I both lived to see another day.

I had a friend, Michael, whose dad lived in our set. Michael's parents were divorced, and his mom lived in another set, called Centerview. I used to go over to Michael's mom's house in Centerview, and all the guys over there were cool with me. I had a lot of friends in Centerview, but those same guys could never ever come over to our set – even though Michael was cool and lived in our set. The Centerview guys were considered a rival gang. One day, some of the guys from the Centerview gang pulled up to my house. I came outside and said, "Hey, what are you guys doin' over here? You can't come into the 'hood!" Just then I looked down the street and saw Paul, L. C.'s brother, drive by in his car. Paul had a reputation as a shooter. I told the Centerview guys they needed to get out of there fast before Paul and the rest of the fellas came back and tried to shoot them. I finally convinced them to go, and just in time too.

As soon as the Centerview guys were out of sight, Paul and several of his friends came rolling up fast. They were packing guns and grilling me about the Centerview guys, but I just passed them off as Michael's friends. Those guys from Centerview had no idea how lucky they were to avoid Paul, because he was always ready to shoot first and worry about the consequences later. It was chaos at the highest level, on a daily basis. There was always something crazy going on, always some random violence waiting for those unlucky enough to get in its way.

That reminds me of one semester when I went to Dorsey High School in Los Angeles because I'd been kicked out of Gardena High. Dorsey High was right across the street from the Jungle. The Jungle is the neighborhood that was featured in the Denzel Washington movie, Training Day. The rule of the Jungle was simple: you either had a pass going in or you didn't come out alive. I heard from one of my homeboys, saying the Centerviews were coming up to Gardena High to jack some of the fellas in my crew. Gardena High was home to several rival sets that barely managed to coexist, and as always, tensions were running high. The Centerviews were bringing in some reinforcements to even the odds. I left school early that day and caught the City Transit bus over to Washington High School on the other side of town to pick up one of my homeboys, who was known as a shooter, from another Crips gang. I wanted this particular brother with me because I knew he would be packing his gun even at school. When we got to Gardena, we could tell something big was about to go down. When classes got out for the day, I rounded up my boys and told them we were packing and that we were ready for whatever the Centerviews had in mind.

The school buses were lined up out in front of the school as always, ready to take everyone home. Even the school's security guards could tell something was up. We always had armed security guards at the high schools in our area because the tension between all the rival gangs was always on the verge of exploding in violence. My boys and I got on the school bus that would be going back to Gardena to our set, but before we even left the school, everything started going down. When we got on the bus, I saw a group of the Centerviews start heading toward us, and even more of their reinforcements were pulling up in their low riders. Fred had always schooled me to case out every situation and be ready to take action.

He also taught me to take out the other guy before they could take me out. My sense of fear was very finely tuned and it had always served me well. I knew the time to act was right now.

When I saw one of the Centerviews coming right up to our bus just as we started to pull out, I told my shooter homeboy, "There's one of them – pop him!" My homeboy pulled out his .38, reached out the window of the bus and fired off two quick shots. Boom! Boom! The crowd of students standing around the buses reacted just as we had always been taught to whenever we heard gunshots: some dropped to the ground, screaming and covering their heads, while the rest scattered in every direction. Even the security guards hit the deck, not knowing where the shots came from or what would happen next. We were still on our bus home to Gardena about 15 minutes later when we heard a helicopter overhead, and looked up to see an L.A. Police helicopter tracking our bus. I knew then that the guards must have figured out that the shots came from our bus and the cops were following us home. As soon as the bus came to the next stop, my boys and I bailed out and we all took off in separate directions.

CHAPTER 13

LIFE WEEDS YOU OUT

EVEN THOUGH EVERYONE involved somehow escaped without any bloodshed on that particular day, it wouldn't be long before the gang lifestyle caught up to us and started weeding out a lot of the guys in our crew. The truth of the matter is, the gang lifestyle is a kind of collective insanity. We were all slowly going crazy every single day, we just couldn't see it at the time because we were right in the middle of it. Everyone was always so hyped up on fear, anger, drugs, and the thrill of the danger that constantly surrounded us. By the time I was 15-16 years old, it seemed like things only got worse. I watched as the fellas I ran with started dropping, one by one. We were just like kids, acting out and trying to make it through to another day, every day. Maybe if we had known how things would turn out for us, we would've stopped - but we just couldn't see that far ahead.

Leon had no idea that when he was 18, they were going to shoot him in the head and kill him. Poncho had no idea that when he was 25 they were going to kill him and throw his body on the freeway. Mark and David had no idea they were going to be shot and killed.

Dan had no idea they were going to shoot him in the chest. Melvin had no idea he was going to get shot. Gregory and Jeff had no idea they were going to flip over a Volkswagen and die in a car accident. That's just a few of the guys who I knew that ended up dead, and there were so many others. Gang life weeds everyone out. I always knew that there was no escaping or moving on from our lifestyle. We all had a one-way ticket to hell, and we were riding in First Class, Row 1.

As if all the violence wasn't bad enough, by the mid-late '70s drugs started claiming their share of victims as well. It was dangerous enough when we were all just drinking and smoking weed. But as soon as harder drugs like cocaine and angel dust started showing up, things changed for the worse, especially for the people who got caught up in that. My buddy L.C. had always been pretty reliable, but when he started smoking angel dust, he started getting sloppy in his business. He paid the ultimate price for it. L.C. had been flashing too much of his money and carrying too much drugs around. One day L.C. left for Vegas with a carful of the fellas, and lots of money and drugs. Next thing you know, the other guys came back from Vegas…with the car, the cash, and the drugs – but no L.C. Nobody ever said anything, but it didn't take a genius to figure out what happened. That's just the way things worked in the hood. Gangster life has a way of weeding everyone out. For a lot of guys, the only way out was in a body bag.

One night I was walking home from Keith's house, which was in the Harbor Gangster set. The Harbor Gangster set was a group of wannabe Crips, who were on the border with the Raymond Crips. One of the rules of the street was that you never walked anywhere alone late at night, no matter which area you were in. Because it was late and I was alone, I took a shortcut through an industrial area. I was headed down an alley when I saw a carload of Raymond Crips drive by. They must have seen me too, because they immediately hit the brakes and turned down the alley behind me. I took off running as fast as I could, with the Raymonds in pursuit. I quickly realized that I was boxed in, with no way out but the same way I had come in. My life started flashing before my eyes, because those Raymond Crips had me dead to rights. I thought about my mom, and how she had always told me that God was with me everywhere I go. I started praying with all my heart, "Dear God, please help me!"

I got to the end of the alley and there was nowhere else to turn. I saw a bush off to the side of the street, so I jumped behind it, worked my way into it as far as I could and curled up in a ball. A few moments later the Raymonds pulled up right next to me. Their car was idling only a few feet from where I was hiding. I thought to myself, "So this is how it's gonna end…with me getting killed right here." My heart was beating so fast I thought the Raymonds would hear it and find me. I just kept praying, over and over, for God to help me. I heard one of the Raymonds say, "Where'd that nigga go?!" They sat there waiting for a few minutes before they turned around and drove away.

That night when I finally made it home, I once again came face-to-face with my mom's favorite spiritual verse, The Prayer of Protection, still taped to my bathroom mirror. The difference was, on that particular night, I saw that verse in a different light, and I realized how much it meant to me. I knew that my mom had brainwashed me, but in the best possible way. I had read that verse every day for I don't know how long, and it finally started to sink in. To this day, The Prayer of Protection remains my favorite prayer, and I repeat it to myself every single day of my life. Here it is again, in case you missed it the first time:

The light of God surrounds me

The love of God enfolds me

The power of God protects me

The presence of God watches over me

The mind of God guides me

The life of God flows through me

The law of God directs me

The peace of God abides with me

The joy of God uplifts me

The strength of God renews me

The beauty of God inspires me

Wherever I am, God is

Through all of the madness of my gangbanging lifestyle, my mom continued to be a reckoning force for me. She was my spiritual advisor and truly the rock in my life. Even in my darkest hours, my Mom had a way of programming my mind, my heart, and my soul with her positive spiritual messages. Although my mom never said anything about my lifestyle, I'm sure she knew I was involved in some pretty dark stuff. But Mom never gave up on me, and she never stopped building me up with her wisdom. From the spiritual shows Mom played on the radio every morning, to the spiritual verses and sayings she taped to my bathroom mirror every night, I was constantly absorbing all of her messages of faith, hope and salvation. I didn't think about it at the time, but my mom's unconditional love and compassion supported me wherever I went and in whatever I did. My faith in God was growing despite the nature of my business and my life. I owe all of that to my Mom.

I didn't realize it when I was younger, but my mom was so smart – because every time I said that prayer, I was actually putting a prayer of protection around myself. I honestly believe that's why, when everyone around me got killed, I didn't get killed. When other guys were going to prison, I was coming home every night. Mom used to tell me things like, "Time waits for no man." I had no idea what she was talking about back then, but now I know exactly what it means: that when the sun goes up and comes down, you paid your life for that day. All the money and power in the world is not going to buy you one more hour, minute, moment, or second. Because of my mom's influence and programming, I now say to myself every day, "Oh, what a beautiful morning. Oh, what a beautiful day. I've got a beautiful feeling, everything is going my way." That reminds me to live every single day like it's my last day. My mom would say things like, "Gregory, you need to get some rest." I would say, "Mom, I'll catch up on my sleep later." She would say, "Gregory, you can't catch up on your sleep, you can only get some rest." My mom was always my anchor. There were so many times when I would be in danger, and somehow some way, I would come out of it without a scratch.

CHAPTER 14

PULL THE TRIGGER

JUST TO SHOW you how absolutely insane things got sometimes: I'll never forget one time when I was 17 or 18 and I was out in front of my mom's house washing my white low rider. By that time, a lot of the real bad guys in the 'hood had been weeded out in one way or another. The guys like me who were still around were big-time dealers in the high end of organized crime. Al and a couple of the boys from the set pulled up as I was washing my car. Al said, "Hey Bono, what's up, man? We just copped a whole lotta blow, and we know you're the man, so we want you to come over and test it for us real quick." I said, "Okay, hold on man, let me go get my Roscoe." My Roscoe was my gun. Fred had always told me, "Never go anywhere without your gun. You always take your gun." Al said, "C'mon Bono, you don't need your gun, man. Just jump in the car and let's go to the house and check it out real quick." I wanted to run in the house and grab my gun, but I said, "Okay, let's go." I jumped in the car with the boys and we rolled over to Al's house. When we got to Al's house, we went in the garage and Al closed the garage door behind us. Al said, "Wait here, man. Let me go get my brother and the stash and we'll check it out."

Al came back out to the garage with his brother, who walked straight up to me, socked me in the jaw, put me in a headlock, put a .38 to my temple, and said, "Nigga, you're dead. We got you. Here's the deal." Al said, "Hey, Homeboy. I told you I wanted my mom's diamonds back." Al had bought some blow from me and given me some diamonds as collateral because he didn't have the cash yet. My life flashed in front of me, once again, because I realized those guys had set me up. I thought, "The one time I let down my guard and don't have my gun with me, I'm getting jacked by guys from my own set." I knew I had to think fast and come up with something, or those guys were going to kill me right then and there.

Immediately, I decided to turn the tables and go off on those guys. I said, "Nigga, go ahead and pull the trigger. You think you're gonna come and jack me from my house, bring me over here and fire on me like this?! Pull the trigger. My mom saw me leave the house with you. The boys are gonna come over here and blow up this house. Who the f--- do you think you are, doing me like this?! I ain't no punk!" Then I could see they got scared. All of a sudden Al's brother let me loose and put the gun down. Al said, "Look, Bono – all I wanted was my mom's diamonds." I started screaming, "Listen, nigga – you gotta give me my money before you get those diamonds back. You think I'm a punk?!" Al and his brother started apologizing, saying, "Okay, calm down, Bono. We'll work it out. We're sorry man, we didn't mean anything by it." The next thing I knew, we were back in the car together, heading back over to my house like nothing had ever happened. That's how crazy that lifestyle was. Every single one of us was absolutely insane.

I loved the lifestyle that came from being big-time dealers and the power that we had over people, but I hated the trouble that came with it. Unfortunately, as I learned the hard way, I couldn't have one without the other. I was in a constant state of inner turmoil, caught in a tug-of-war between me, myself, and I. The ugly truth of the matter is that, in the gang way of life, there's really only three things that can happen: you either go to prison, or you end up dead, or you mess up your life so badly that you wish to God you were dead. Because we were all sick and insane, it wasn't a matter of "if" - it was only a matter of "when" our number would come up. That's how things work in the street. The sick and the insane becomes normal when you live it every single day. You get immune to it, and you just learn to adapt. It's all part of the environment you live in.

There are rules to the game on the street, and when you break the rules, you die – plain and simple. Somehow, some way, I always seemed to have guardian angels watching over me. I was fortunate to have been schooled up by the best in a lot of different aspects of my life. I had my gang life with the boys, my rich life with Steve's family, and my organized crime life with Fred. All of that schooling prepared me for anything. My street sense was so well developed and so finely tuned that it allowed me to avoid most of the pitfalls that took down so many of my gang brothers. At the same time, I also had all that spiritual wisdom that my mom had infused in me, plus my faith in God and my guardian angels protecting me.

One of the things I started noticing as we rose higher and higher in the ranks of organized crime was that the game changed. At Fred's level of organized crime, they didn't have my problems, but they had their own kinds of problems. The biggest thing to watch out for was getting set up, because all the deals were done in cash, and the deals were so big. You'd go to do a deal, but it was all a setup. The guys on the other side of the deal would ask to see the buy money, and then they'd pull their guns, kill you, and take all your money. There were no rules and no recourse; it was just a dead end, literally. That was a whole new level of insanity that we always had to be on guard against. After my previous episode with Al and his brother, I never again forgot what Fred taught me, and I never went anywhere without my Roscoe.

CHAPTER 15

GET A JOB

ABOUT HALFWAY THROUGH my junior year of high school, I realized I'd had enough of Gardena High. I was thinking about transferring to Crenshaw, or maybe dropping out altogether if that transfer didn't come through. I met with the Principal of Gardena to discuss my options, and he suggested that I consider going to a Technical School instead. He said I could learn a craft or a skill, get a certificate, and put myself in a better position to get a good job when my high school class graduated. I thought that sounded pretty good, so I left Gardena, enrolled in Harbor Point Occupational School, and learned to be an Electronics Technician. I took my technical classes and took care of my requirements for high school at the same time.

When my high school class graduated, I graduated as an Electronics Technician, and I got my technical certification. One of the instructors at Harbor Point Occupational School was also an executive with Pace Communications; a company out in San Pedro. He really liked me, so as soon as I turned 18, I got hired to work at Pace. It was the perfect cover, because I could work my straight gig at Pace during the day, and still run my dealing life at night.

My new job at Pace, which was the first straight job I ever had, also had a major impact on my mom's marriage to her new husband. James had always hated me. He resented me because he thought I was a spoiled brat who had all the trappings of success that he could never afford to have. James and my mom had gotten married when I was 14, which was right before I hit my stride as a dealer. James had already told my mom, "If Greg doesn't have a job by the time he's 18, I want him out of this house." James thought he could control me like he was my dad, but nobody was going to be my dad. Even Steve's dad David, who always loved me like a father, never tried to get tough with me as if he was my dad. James sure wasn't going to be the one to do it.

When I started my job at Pace on my 18th birthday, James was furious because he had no more excuse to try to kick me out of the house. So, he told my mom, "It's either me or Greg – one of us has to go." My mom, who had always loved me unconditionally, said, "I'll see you later. I'm not kicking Greg out of my house at 18. Period." Many years later, James and I made amends, and James admitted that he had been jealous and envious of me, and that he hated me because I had all of the things as a teenager that he never had when he was a young man.

CHAPTER 16

LESSONS FROM FRED

ANOTHER LESSON FROM Fred came right around the time I was turning 18. Keith and I had really been rolling for a few years; making lots of money, wearing fancy clothes, driving our low riders, and just generally looking and acting like we were Hollywood. I even had long permed hair down to my shoulders like Superfly. One day, we told Fred that, since we were wheeling and dealing big-time, we were each going to buy a new Cadillac Seville. Those cars were so clean and tight they looked like a little top hat. Keith and I thought the new Seville was like a baby Rolls Royce. We were so proud of ourselves, but when Fred heard that idea, he told Keith and I to sit down, shut up, and listen.

Fred said, "You little punks...let me tell you something right now. First of all, you guys are only 18 years old. If you buy brand new Sevilles, you're gonna be in jail in 5 minutes. Your neighbors are gonna call the police on you. They're not gonna let some little 18 year-old punk drive around in a brand new Cadillac when they can't even afford a brand new car. And they have real jobs. So here's what you're gonna do – you're gonna wear a mask. Cut all your hair off. I want you guys to be GQ, like you're on college scholarship at USC or UCLA. You need to sell your low riders. I want you guys to buy sports cars. I want you to get a new fashion style, and buy clothes that make you look like you're going to college at Oxford."

After that speech from Fred, Keith and I sold our low riders, cut off our hair, and bought brand new 280Z sports cars. We bought new clothes, and we started wearing our masks. In reality, we were becoming high rollers, but we were under the radar. We looked like straight-up, legit guys; we could go anywhere and fit right in. We had the money, the style, the look, the sports cars, and the kinds of jobs that created a great front. As far as anyone knew, we could've been college kids who came from wealthy families. We were clean-cut, presentable, everyone loved us, and no one had the slightest idea who we really were or what we were up to. Keith and I were dialed in after that, and ready to take our business to a higher level.

When cocaine hit the drug scene like a neutron bomb in the late '70s and early '80s, we were ready for it. It was the rich man's high, it was the cool drug, it was supposedly non-addictive, and being a coke dealer was considered cool. We weren't some low-life drug dealers running in the streets. We catered to the high-end clientele. In reality, there was a cocaine epidemic going through America back then, and Keith and I had the product that was on the scene and in high demand. Unfortunately, even with our new image, there were still occasions when things got a little crazy just like they used to back in the old days when we were running with the gang. One night we cruised out to Hollywood to score our supply of blow. When we left, the guy we bought the coke from told me to make sure we didn't show our stash to anyone. I said, "Of course, we're not fools – we already know that." It was pretty late when we got back, so I just left the stuff at Keith's house and went home.

I called Keith the next morning to tell him I was coming over to cut it up and get it ready to sell. Keith said, "Greg – I ain't got it. It's gone." I started laughing, figuring Keith was messing with me. I said, "Yeah, right. C'mon man, don't mess with me like that." Keith said, "Greg, I'm serious, man…the stuff is gone." I didn't believe him, but I hung up the phone and went straight over to Keith's house. I looked Keith straight in the eye and I asked him again, "Where's our stash?" Keith said, "G, I don't know where it is – it's gone." I couldn't believe it, so I sat down with him and we brainstormed together. We retraced all our steps to try to figure out what happened to our blow. I told Keith to think real hard about everything that happened before I got there that morning.

It turned out that Keith had a friend from the 280Z club over to his house earlier that morning before I'd gotten there. They were going out for awhile, but when they got in their cars to leave, the friend said he needed to use Keith's bathroom, so he went back in the house alone for a few minutes. I said, "Okay, so he came over… but you didn't show him our stash, did you? Tell me you didn't show him our stash. You know what Fred always taught us – you never show your stash to anyone!" Keith said, "Bono, I showed it to him." I said, "Keith, homeboy stole our stash when he came back in the house! We gotta go find him right now. Where does he live?" Keith said he didn't know where he lived, but homeboy's best friend always played tennis up at Rowley Park, right in our own 'hood.

I went to the 'hood, rounded up Curtis, who was crazy, and another fella too. I told Curtis to bring the 12-gauge, and we headed over to Rowley Park. Sure enough, there was homeboy's best friend, playing tennis. We walked up to him, Curtis stuck the 12-gauge shotgun right in his face, and I said, "Nigga, get in the car." We threw him in the car and took him back to Keith's house, and I asked him, "Where's our stash? We want it back, right now." He said he didn't know what we were talking about, so I told Curtis,

"Shoot this nigga right now." Keith said, "G, don't cap that nigga here in my mom's house." Homeboy's friend started singing like a bird, saying his buddy had stolen our stash. He was screaming and crying and probably crapping in his pants, he was so scared.

He told us everything we needed to know, including where to find the thief. We threw him back in the car, took him back to Rowley Park, and kicked him out. We were going over to get homeboy and retrieve our stash, but later that morning we heard that he had crashed his 280Z into a telephone pole, totaled his car, and practically killed himself in the process. He was probably so high from our stash that he couldn't even drive straight. The bottom line was, Keith and I ended up with no stash, no money, no homeboy, no nothing. That's about the time it started occurring to me that the whole world was corrupt. We were selling blow to people whose job description during the daytime was, "To Serve and To Protect." We were selling blow to star athletes from sports leagues with three capital-letter names. We were selling blow to celebrities, executives, doctors - you name it. It seemed like everyone was part of that cocaine scene, even world-famous gold medal Olympians. People who you would never suspect of doing coke were becoming some of our best customers. I was 18, and I started recognizing it was all corrupt – the whole world. Fred had told me years before, "It's not about right or wrong, it's about handling your business." Now I knew what he meant. I couldn't make sense of the insanity I was a part of, because there was no sense. It was all crazy, and we were all crazy.

Throughout this time, Fred's daughter DeeDee was still my girlfriend. In her own way, DeeDee was crazy too. Not from the usual drugs or gangs, but because she was so jealous and possessive of me. DeeDee always said she loved me, and I knew she did. Fred always loved me like a son, and he treated me like one too. It was always assumed DeeDee and I would be together forever. But her jealousy was just too much to take sometimes. There were times when I couldn't take it because I felt like I couldn't make a move or even breathe without DeeDee checking my every move. But that was just the kind of relationship we had. It seemed to fit right in with the rest of my life. Insanity was the rule of the day. It was all just part of the crazy game of life, and me, Keith, DeeDee, and Fred, were all playing it the best we knew how. And we were good at it. We were all living a lie, but we were good at it. The fellas always had girls on the side back then. If DeeDee had known then that I had girls on the side, she probably would've killed me herself. I wouldn't have doubted that for a second. But she never knew anything about it until I told her myself, which wouldn't be until it was too late to do anything about it.

CHAPTER 17

WHEELING AND DEALING

AFTER WORKING AT Pace Communications for a little while, I heard that Todd Shipyards was hiring ET's (Electronic Technicians) in San Pedro. I applied for the job, got hired, and at 19, I started working at Todd as a Weapons Control Technician. Todd had a contract with the Navy to build FFG frigates, and my job was installing hi-tech wiring for the Navy's weapons systems. I was already making so much money from my drug dealing business that I didn't need a paycheck, let alone a job, but it was all part of Fred's plan of wearing a mask to hide what I really did. My job at Todd was just a front. When I came home from work at night, I led a different life altogether. Keith and I were rolling down the street late at night, doing drugs, and living the high life. But as I said before, life always weeds you out. When I look back on it now, I see that life had already started to weed me out...I just didn't know it yet. All the years of spiritual programming by my mom had stayed with me, and in some ways my conscience always haunted me. On one hand, I couldn't stand it – but on the other hand, I couldn't get enough of it.

Keith and I used to say, the way we were going, we would be millionaires by the time we were 21. We'd come home from collecting from our customers, and we'd stack up all our cash on the bed in huge piles of 1's, 5's, 10's, 20's, 50's and 100's, like we were running a bank. We ran our drug dealing business just like a regular business. Over time, though, I gradually became my own best customer. I became hooked on my own stash. The rules in our game were, you never used your stash and you never spent your buy money; meaning, you don't use for your personal use the stash you're going to sell, and you don't blow the money that you're going to need to buy your next stash. If you broke the rules, it wouldn't be long before you'd be out of business completely. I was definitely using more and more over time, but I just couldn't see it. I stayed high constantly from age 15 until I was 25. Being high all the time was a state of mind – my insane state of mind.

To my way of thinking back then, I never had a drug problem because I never ran out of drugs. There was no problem, there was just me doing whatever I wanted, using and abusing whatever I wanted, whenever I wanted. If anything, my only drug problem was that I had so many drugs. It was just too easy. Once everyone started smoking coke, it was over. You'd take one hit off that freebase pipe, and you were hooked like a fish. I was using drugs, but the truth of the matter is, the drugs were using me - and I didn't even have a say in it anymore. I may have looked like a good guy from college, but on the inside I was really sick and I didn't have the slightest clue. I thought I knew everything and no one could tell me anything. It was life in the fast lane, going 1,000 miles an hour. But my world was nothing but a fast track to hell. It was only a matter of time before my world would come crashing down on me. Until it did, I thought I was the King of the Streets.

When my sister Angela graduated from USC, her husband

Patrick got hired by ARCO, the oil company. They moved up to Bellingham, Washington, which is about two hours north of Seattle. When I looked at the map, Bellingham was just a little black dot. I thought to myself, "Where is Patrick taking my sister? I better check this out." I was the man of the house, and my head was as hard as penitentiary steel. If I said, "Jump," you'd better say, "How high?" When I went to see Angie in Bellingham, I got up there and it was just this tiny little college town. It was like The Land That Time Forgot - there was nothing to do up there. Angie suggested I go up to Canada and check out Vancouver, B.C., which is just a short drive across the border from Bellingham.

I got up to Vancouver in 1979, and it was like I'd landed in paradise. The city was clean, the clubs were jumping, the people were GQ, everyone was doing coke, and it was a non-stop party. I was so insane back then that, when I went to Canada, I crossed the border with my weed and my blow in the car. It's a miracle they didn't bust me at the border and throw me in prison right then and there. When I got back home from Bellingham, Fred told me to invest my money and buy property out of state. Angie and Patrick had just bought a house right around the corner from Lake Whatcom, where there was a new condo development going in. So, at 19, I bought my first house; a condo on the lake. I had Angie rent it out for me, and I was in business as a homeowner. I told Fred all about it, and he said that was a smart move.

Meanwhile, my drug use was spiraling out of control. I was constantly high, hitting the pipe, smoking coke, and it was never enough. It got to the point where I'd give DeeDee my stash and tell her to hang on to it for me. I'd say, "Do not, under any circumstances, give it back to me, no matter how hard I beg." Sure enough, as soon as I started getting high, I'd ask DeeDee for my stash so I could do even more. She'd say no, and then I'd really get mad. Eventually, after I'd threatened her enough, she'd give it back to me. She probably thought I was going to kill her if she didn't give it up, and knowing my state of mind back then, I might have. I was so sick, so crazy, and so out of control. The coke had taken over my mind, my soul, everything. I would do anything for it. It got to the point where, if I was going to get high, I'd have to just lock myself up somewhere and do it alone because I knew I'd go berserk once I was high and I didn't want anyone around to see me. That was part of wearing the mask: keeping the appearances up, like everything was cool, when in reality I was gone off the deep end.

In my daily life, nobody knew the truth about me. But behind the scenes, I was making a wreck out of my life, and it was all self-inflicted. I was physically, mentally, emotionally and spiritually bankrupt. I was smiling on the outside, and crying on the inside. But nobody ever knew, because I was wearing my mask. Once I started using drugs, there were only three ways I was going to stop: I was either going to run out of drugs, run out of money, or run out of life. I never ran out of drugs or money, but my life was slipping away. Through it all, I would still go home every night and pray as hard as I could. My mom had brainwashed me with all those spiritual messages, and I found myself returning to them over and over again. Throughout my time in the gang life, my heart was always pulling on me. I was begging God every day and night for a way out of the insane world I was living in.

CHAPTER 18

I DON'T WANNA DIE
LIKE THIS

PROBABLY THE BIGGEST turning point of my early life came one day when I went over to Fred and DeeDee's house in Inglewood. I knocked on the door, which had metal bars for security, just like a prison. A familiar voice asked, "Who is it?" I said, "It's me, Bono." They opened the bars and the front door, and I walked in. That's when it hit me. I looked around the same room I had been in a thousand times, and for once I could see everything clearly. I saw the Dobermans that were there for extra protection. I saw the guns everywhere, the huge piles of money and drugs all over the place; everything was there just like always. But this time it struck me differently. My heart condemned me, and made me see my future, then and there, and I knew I had reached my limit. I said to myself, "God, I don't wanna die like this."

I saw in my mind exactly how this game that we were playing was going to end. Fred was already AWOL from the penitentiary, and he wasn't going back. Joe was a hit man; he definitely wasn't going down without a fight. It was all going to end right here. Someday, when we least expected it, a SWAT team was going to come in here, clean house, and everyone here was going to die. I thought to myself, "I might as well order my casket right now, because they'll be carrying me out of here in a body bag." I walked out of that house that day, and I knew beyond any shadow of a doubt that it was over – I was done with that life, and done with those people. I was 20 years old. I had been working with this same crew since I was 15. I didn't know how to get out, but I knew I was getting out. I didn't want to die in that house, living that life.

I already had a date with DeeDee lined up for that night. We went out for dinner at my favorite restaurant in Marina Del Rey, and I never said a word to DeeDee about the change of heart I had experienced earlier that day, or what I was planning. The next night, I had another date, this time with Rae, who was my longtime girl on the side. We went out to the same restaurant, and I asked Rae to marry me. She was elated and said yes, and I knew then that there was no going back. The most ironic part of the entire situation was that, all of the various aspects of my life that had been part of my mask, and my front, were now lining up perfectly in terms of helping me plan my new life.

It's so clear to me now that God and my guardian angels were working the highest good for me in everything I was doing. It was yet another miracle at work in my life. I had my job at Todd Shipyards in San Pedro, and Todd also happened to have a shipyard up in Seattle, which would help me make the transition up north. I had my condo on Lake Whatcom in Bellingham, which would also help me make the transition out of L.A. Suddenly, every part of my life was lining up perfectly to facilitate the positive life changes I was so determined to make.

I brought Rae back to my mom's house that night after we had dinner out in Marina Del Rey. The next morning, my phone rang, and Rae picked it up. It was DeeDee, looking for me. DeeDee said, "Who is this?!" Rae said, "This is Rae." DeeDee said, "Put Greg on the phone. Right now." I took the phone, and DeeDee said, "Who is that b---- that answered the phone?" I said, "It's Rae. Baby, we're getting married." DeeDee said, "Oh baby, we're getting married!" I said, "No - I'm marrying Rae." Click. DeeDee hung up the phone, and that was it. DeeDee and I were done, and Rae and I were on. As soon as I hung up that phone, I thought to myself, "I'm a dead man - Fred is gonna kill me." But I didn't care. Because I was not going to die in that house, living that life. I'd rather die from Fred killing me because I broke up with DeeDee than die from living that old life that I was trying so hard to escape. I knew Fred was going to kill me, and it wasn't a matter of if, it was only a matter of when before someone walked up and shot me in the head. I didn't care. In my mind, in my heart, and especially in my soul, I was done with every part of that life. I was 20, and I just didn't want to do it anymore. I was more than willing to risk the consequences of trying to quit organized crime. My heart was always tugging on me, and I was finally ready to listen. I told myself I was not going to be a victim like so many others I had known. I was going to do whatever it took to escape.

Rae and I started planning our wedding, but the whole time we were preparing, I was looking over my shoulder, waiting for someone to run up on me and kill me. Rae worked at a bank, and after we were engaged, she told me she had $30,000 in her account from her grandfather selling his gas station. Our plan was to live off my money for a month or so before we left L.A., and then use the $30,000 that Rae had from her grandfather to get everything set up in Washington. Meanwhile, I still hadn't seen or heard from DeeDee, which only confirmed to me that I was a dead man walking.

At the wedding, my best man Keith and I were fighting backstage. We had been best friends for what seemed like forever, but on my wedding day, Keith kept grabbing me and shaking me, and telling me I couldn't marry Rae. Keith probably had the same concerns I had about Fred coming after me, and didn't want me to risk my life, but I didn't care. I'm sure there was a part of Keith that felt like I was divorcing him and marrying Rae. Keith had always been my #1 homeboy, and we had been through so much together. I finally had to push Keith away, and tell him to let me go. The wedding music was playing, Rae was waiting for me, and it was time for me to step forward into my new life.

Rae and I got married as planned, and I quit my job at Todd in San Pedro because Rae and I were getting ready to move up to Bellingham. Once we were there, I would be working at Todd up in Seattle. Rae and I basically had a month-long honeymoon of wining and dining. Shortly after we were married, and after we had blown through all my money, Rae tearfully confessed that she had lied about having the $30,000 in the bank. When I told Keith that story, he once again tried to convince me to get rid of Rae, but I wasn't about to do that. Another friend of mine, George, was also upset with me for letting Rae play me like a fool, and he suggested I drop her to the bottom of the ocean. Although I was upset that Rae had lied about the money, I knew she had done so because she was trying to impress me. Keith begged me to stick around L.A. to make some money and get back on my feet, but I refused to dump Rae or stay in L.A. After I borrowed some money from my mom in order to make my next buy, Rae and I packed up and moved up to Bellingham.

CHAPTER 19

BELLINGHAM AND SEATTLE

AFTER WE GOT to Bellingham and got settled in, Rae told me I didn't need to keep dealing, since we both had good jobs and were making good money together. But wheeling and dealing was my specialty, and I was such a smooth operator from all those years of dealing in L.A. that the dealers in Seattle didn't stand a chance. I commuted two hours a day each way to Todd for a couple months, and then Rae and I got a waterfront condo on Alki Beach in Seattle. Three months after I left L.A., I was back on my feet, wheeling and dealing and living life in the fast lane all over again. I had a great job as an Electronics Technician on the Navy weapons systems, I was making good money, with excellent benefits, driving a BMW, and living like there was no tomorrow. I'd gotten married to Rae when I was 20 years old, then we had my daughter, Raquel, when I was 22, and my second daughter, Royale, when I was 24. I was a family man, with a straight job, and the perfect mask. You never would have known from looking at me on the outside how messed up I was on the inside.

Once Rae and I left L.A. and moved to Seattle, I stopped worrying about Fred coming after me. But it didn't matter anyway, because my drug addiction was becoming a more immediate threat to my life. I had left Fred, DeeDee, and L.A. because I didn't want to die in the life that I had there. Shortly after I was settled in Seattle, I actually tried to quit drugs for the first time since I started using when I was a teenager. I had always thought drug addicts were junkies with needles hanging out of their arms. I had always thought alcoholics were the winos we used to mess with in the streets of L.A. I had no awareness that when I looked in the mirror, I was looking at a full-blown drug addict and alcoholic. I quickly grasped the truth of the matter, however, when I tried to quit dealing and using and then found myself buying drugs from other dealers in Seattle. I had been dealing and abusing drugs from the time I was 15 until I was 25, and over all those years, I had learned how to function at a high level while living in complete chaos. I was high as a kite, 24/7, 365 days a year. I was what you'd call a high-functioning addict. I was doing very complex and technical work while I was stoned out of my mind. That was just normal for me. From time to time, I would fly back to L.A. to buy coke, and then end up using most of it myself.

Free-basing came on the scene in Seattle in the early '80s, and I was already a seasoned veteran. Fred had taught me all the tricks of the trade of making, testing and smoking coke years earlier in L.A., and by the time it hit Seattle, I was an expert. My tolerance for coke was so high a normal person would overdose trying to keep up with me. I could out-smoke anyone. One time when Rae was out of town, I flew to L.A. and bought an ounce of cocaine, thinking I would sell 22 grams and keep the rest for myself. Instead, I started binging. I stood in my kitchen for two days and smoked 22 grams by myself. My heart was beating so fast, I thought it was going to explode out of my chest. I'd smoke coke to get high, then I'd drink alcohol to bring me back down and balance it out, then I'd smoke some weed to stimulate my appetite and smooth everything out. Then I'd pump myself full of vitamins and amino acids to get my system going again. It was the most vicious cycle of drug abuse you could imagine.

I'd always said that the only way I was going to stop using drugs was if I ran out of drugs, ran out of money, or ran out of life. Thank God I ran out of drugs that night, or I probably would have killed myself right then and there. I was standing in my kitchen, breaking out in a cold sweat and shaking like I was having a seizure. After I came down from that two-day binge, I had a moment of clarity - and I saw that something was terribly, horribly wrong with me and my life.

When I first started using drugs as a teenager, it was all fun and cool. By the time I was 25, the drugs were using me and I no longer had any say in the matter. At that point, the drugs were in complete control of my life. When I reflect back on it now, I realize that I loved my drugs more than I loved God, my wife, and even my children. Unfortunately, I was still so concerned with wearing my mask, I couldn't allow anyone to see the real Greg. Over my years of dealing and abusing, I had become a master of disguise. I could have won an Oscar for my acting ability. I was so sick and miserable in my mind, body, and spirit during the final stages of my addiction that, even though I knew it was destroying my marriage, my finances, and every other aspect of my life, I still couldn't get enough of it. My life was crumbling all around me, but just like in my gang years in L.A., I had become immune to the fear of death, because death was so commonplace to me.

CHAPTER 20

GOING TO REHAB

MY GREATEST FEAR in facing up to my addiction was that I would mess up my life so badly from the drugs that I would wish to God I was dead, but God would make me live. Then everyone would see how messed up I really was. Rae knew I was using, but she didn't know the full extent of it, because I hid it so well. That changed when Rae and I were planning a vacation to L.A. to visit our families, and she told me, "If you go back home and start getting high and smoking coke, I'm going to tell your family and your friends that you're a drug addict and an alcoholic." When Rae said that, I panicked because I was scared she was going to tear off my mask. I was always camouflaged. I was GP, I was The Man, and I had it all together. I had everything: the wife, the kids, the job, the clothes, the car, and all the trappings. The stone cold truth is, Skid Road is just a state of mind, and I was no different than the winos sleeping under the bridge. I was 100% gone from my drug addiction. Rae had seen through all of that, and she was going to blow my cover if I slipped up.

We got to L.A., and sure enough – my demons got the best

of me. I had a bunch of money, so I went and got some coke and started smoking. I ran out of money, and I knew I couldn't ask Rae for any more because she'd know what I was doing. So I stole $40 that my brother Michael had hidden, got some more coke, hooked up with Keith, and started smoking again. It was 4:30 in the morning when I came to another major turning point in my life. I broke down and started crying. Keith just looked at me and said, "G, what's up? What's the matter with you?" In an instant, my life changed forever because I said the most sincere prayer a man could ever say. I said, "God, please help me – I'm a drug addict." When I heard myself say that out loud, there was a part of me that couldn't believe those words had just come out of my own mouth. In that very moment, my life changed, because I felt God's grace and mercy came upon me. The truth and humility of my prayer opened the door for God's power to change my life.

I got up the next morning and confessed to Michael that I had stolen his money and that there was something wrong with me. I told my mom I was a drug addict, and then Rae called Steve's father, David, to tell him what was going on with me. David and his wife, Margy, had been back in my life for several years, and were the godparents to my oldest daughter, Raquel. David said, "Greg, what's the matter?" I said, "I don't know, but something is wrong with me." David said, "Are you asking for help?" I said, "Yes, I am." David called another doctor he knew in the Seattle area, Dr. Paul, who was the Director of the Care Unit in Kirkland. Dr. Paul told me that, if I put myself in rehab for 28 days straight, and made a sincere commitment to my recovery, I would learn more about myself and about addiction than I ever believed possible. I was 25 years old when I voluntarily entered rehab for the first time. I was as open and receptive to the process as I could possibly be, and I wanted to change my life for the better.

My biggest problem had always been that I couldn't deal with life on life's terms. I had always worn a mask, which helped me cover up my true feelings and hide my true self. Once I got into recovery, I realized that I wasn't the only person who had created a mask to hide their addictions and obscure the truth of who they really were. There were so many people in rehab who had the same kinds of problems I had. I remember one young guy named Gordy, who would come to my room at night with some of the other patients and ask me to tell him stories about my crazy gang life back in the 'hood. Recovery was one of the most humbling experiences I ever faced, because I didn't know the rules of the game. Out on the streets, I had been the grand master, cheating and manipulating situations to get whatever I wanted. I was accustomed to hustling and scheming my way through life.

But in recovery, none of my schemes worked, because I had to confront life on its own terms. I was always the guy who would come in the back door and end up in the front row. I never met a situation I couldn't control one way or another. After the initial shock wore off, I found myself learning to love the process and the system. I met people I could identify with, and I learned so much about the nature of addiction. When I started in rehab, it seemed like reality was the worst high I had ever experienced. All of a sudden, I could feel everything. I had been so high for the past 10+ years that, once I was sober, I mistook feeling good for feeling normal. Before rehab, I had been numbed out and immune to everything. After rehab, I discovered that when you eat regularly, and you get enough rest, and you don't use drugs, you feel pretty good! That was how life was supposed to be, but it had never been my life.

I made it to about four months of clean living during my first shot at sobriety before I relapsed. I'd be going along, doing well, and then when I couldn't get my way like I always had on the street, I'd say "Forget this, I'm out of here" and go back to my old ways. I was in and out of rehab for a few years to the point where it felt like I was stuck in a revolving door and couldn't escape. The truth is, I couldn't escape myself. But I kept on trying to come to grips with my life, and my sobriety. The Center would sometimes bring in recovering addicts and alcoholics from the outside who were in Alcoholics Anonymous, Cocaine Anonymous, Narcotics Anonymous, and various other 12-Step programs.

One of the people who came in to talk to us, that I especially liked to see, was named Harold. Harold was a recovering addict who had long-term sobriety, and who had gone on to be very successful and do some great things with his life. Harold was my hero, my knight in shining armor, because his background story was very similar to mine, with all the wheeling and dealing. It seemed like every time I saw Harold, he looked bigger, stronger, and healthier. I'd see Harold and I'd think to myself, "Man, whatever he has, I want it." One of the core values of the program is giving back to others, and Harold always came back to give back.

One time, Harold called on me to talk, but when I opened my mouth to speak, no words would come out. Instead, I just started bawling my eyes out. It was like I had been transported back in time to when I was a little kid, crying at my father's funeral all over again. I couldn't say a word. After that incident, it took me two weeks to figure out why I had started crying like that. I came to realize that my addiction was the greatest hurdle I would ever face in my entire life. My gang life was completely insane, and that was bad enough. But my addiction was even worse than that. It was bigger than me, bigger than anything I had ever known. It was as if I was under some kind of remote control, like a robot, and I was powerless to do anything about it. Sometimes I would ask myself questions like, "What is this thing inside me? Why am I like this?" Most importantly, I asked myself, "How am I going to stop this?" My revolving door in and out of rehab eventually slowed down enough to where I was able to make significant progress. It took me four years to get one year of continuous sobriety, but my faith in God sustained me through even my darkest hours, and I never stopped believing.

CHAPTER 21

MIRACLES AND SOBRIETY

WHEN I THINK back on all the things I went through in my life, sobriety was the greatest turning point, because getting clean and sober connected me back to God. I got a second chance to start my life over when I was still just 25 years old. It was like being born again, before I had started using drugs at age 13. Now, I sit here today with 26 years of sobriety, but in reality, I've had 26 years of overtime. I should have been dead years ago! There are so many people I knew who are dead, or in prison, who did so much less than I did. That's miraculous in itself. I realize it's not because I'm so hip, slick, and cool, or because I know so much. In fact, it's the opposite. For all these years, no matter where I was or what I was doing, my guardian angels were watching over me. God was always working the highest good in my life, even if I wasn't consciously aware of it. I couldn't deny God if I tried! I sit here now and my eyes still see, my heart still beats, and my legs still walk - after I've put enough drugs in my system to kill everyone in South Central and Seattle combined. I'm still here, and I've lived to tell this miraculous story.

There has to be a God. I'm healthy in mind, body, spirit and soul. But it's not me that got me this far. I can't sugarcoat it, or act like I'm The Man, or like I had anything to do with it – it's none of that. Because the truth is, I'm the guy who can tear down Rome in a single day. If you leave it up to me, without God, I'll ruin everything. I've proven that, over and over again. Now, I love God more than anything. I realize it's the foundation that came from my mom. It's the unconditional love she always showed me, even through the darkest, most desperate times in my life. My mom was always there, setting the ultimate example of compassion and forgiveness. You could do just about anything to me and I'd forgive you, because unconditional love is in my heart. I remember someone said living is all about giving and forgiving, and I agree wholeheartedly with that. The only thing I couldn't forgive is if someone hurt my kids, because I love my kids so much. I'm just protective of children in general.

One of the reasons I'm so blessed is because my success is really God's success. It's all because of Him. I'm a living miracle, and it's because I have so much faith in Him. I have a boldness for life, and it's because I'm not afraid to die. I'm not afraid of death, so that allows me to live every day like it's my last. I live like there's no tomorrow. I've learned that when the sun comes up and goes down, I paid my life for that day – so I'm going to live it for all it's worth. I'm going to live every hour, minute, moment, and second like it's my last. The truth is, the last time I checked, no one gets out of here alive. So, knowing that, I'm bold for God. Nothing is going to stop me, ever. When you tell me I can't do something, I don't even hear you. God has worked so many miracles through my life and through my sobriety. For me to now have what you would call a normal life - even though my wife says there's nothing normal about me – and to live my life without drugs and alcohol, are you kidding me? In this modern-day society? That is an absolute living miracle right there. Remember, no one was a better customer than me when it came to doing drugs - I was my own number one customer, and my own worst enemy.

I loved drugs and alcohol, but what I realized in recovery was that drugs and alcohol weren't my problem – Greg was my problem. I had a living problem, not a drug problem. I couldn't live life on its own terms. So, I had to get to know myself. It's like the old saying, "Know Thyself." That is the ultimate truth, and the key to everything. Greg was my biggest problem, and everywhere I went, Greg followed. I realize now that I used drugs and alcohol because I couldn't deal with my reality. I put all those mind-altering substances in my body in order to change the way I felt, to numb myself out, because I didn't feel good on the inside. In order to conquer that, I had to get to know myself, to go through and take inventory of my thoughts and feelings. I had to sit down and figure out why I did the things I did. It was a matter of holding myself accountable. After I got sober and grew spiritually, mentally, and emotionally, I realized that I had been bankrupt in all those aspects of my life. Most importantly, I understood that every blessing in my life was a result of the grace of God, not the grace of Greg.

At 25, God gave me a free pass out of hell, and I got to start my life over. When I came out of rehab, I realized that I didn't know how to meet life straight up, on life's terms. I only knew how to cheat and play the game that way. I couldn't handle the reality of life, only the reality I created in my own mind. Once I got sober, it wasn't that it was so hard; it's that it was just so different. I didn't know the rules to the game, because I had never followed the rules anyway. Suddenly I could feel everything, just the way it's supposed to be. I could no longer manipulate and scheme to get whatever I wanted. In sobriety, I couldn't get what I wanted. I knew if I was going to change my life, and do things the right way, I had to stop cheating. Through it all, some of the most important things I had to learn about myself were the various character defects that always held me back. Going through the steps, living the program, helping others, and working with my sponsors, I was able to identify my defects. Then, in my daily prayers and meditation, I used affirmations to overcome my limitations.

CHAPTER 22

RAE GOES AWAY

AFTER I EMERGED from my first round of rehab at the Treatment Center, I came back home to Rae, Raquel, and Royale. Rae had been with me throughout my drug-addicted years, getting high and partying right alongside me. I was working hard to stay sober, but Rae didn't share my desire to clean up and get sober. I was busy going to my meetings and trying to do the right thing, but then I'd turn around and Rae would ask me to go buy her some weed so she could get high. I did it a few times, but then I told Rae, "I'm trying to stay on the straight and narrow path over here, and you always want me to go backwards. It's like you're trying to sabotage me." Rae just shrugged it off and said, "No, I just want to smoke some weed, that's all. If you don't want to, that's your choice, but I wanna get high."

Rae and I occasionally struggled with that issue, but I kept working the program and doing my best to be strong and push forward to sobriety. Something had changed inside me, and even though sobriety was a constant challenge, I knew I was on the right track. As my daughters got a little older, Rae and I eventually outgrew our beautiful but small waterfront condo, and we bought my cousin Stephanie's house near Seward Park in Seattle. Despite my occasional battles with Rae over her desire to get high, we were doing well. We both had good jobs and my efforts at sobriety had us moving in the right direction.

One day, Rae decided she wanted to take Raquel and Royale on a trip back east to visit my sister Adrienne, who lived in New Jersey with her husband and their 2 daughters. I was going to stay home, because I had to work. Rae had always been a fashion whore – she loved shopping at Nordstrom, and she had a lot of nice jewelry, shoes, furs, you name it. Rae was GQ all the way, and that was one thing we definitely had in common – our love of nice clothes. Rae was packing for the trip to New Jersey and had left her open suitcase sitting on our bed. I walked by, glanced at her suitcase, and noticed Rae had packed 5 pairs of her most expensive lingerie. I picked up a handful of lingerie and jokingly said, "Hey, what's all this lingerie for? Who you going to wear this for? You got someone to see in Jersey?"

I had said it as a joke, but as soon as those words came out of my mouth, I saw the guilt on Rae's face. I had struck a nerve. She was busted, and she knew it. Rae froze like a statue, with an "Oh s---" look on her face. I said, "Oh my God, I don't believe this. You little ho - you're going to see someone, aren't you? Well, I'll show you what you can do with that lingerie!" I grabbed the suitcase, threw the lingerie back in it, went downstairs, threw Rae's stuff in my car, and took off. I went to the store, bought a big garbage bag, and put all Rae's clothes inside. When I came back home a little while later, Rae was freaking out and asking me what I had done with her clothes. I told her, "Guess what – your clothes are swimming in Lake Washington." Rae immediately went crazy, and started throwing literally everything but the kitchen sink at me. I was dodging flying dishes, pots, pans, silverware, and whatever else she could get her hands on in our kitchen.

I retreated to the other end of the house, locked myself in a room and called my sister Adrienne in New Jersey to tell her what was happening. I told Adrienne, "Rae is coming to see you, and I just found out she's cheating on me. She's coming back there to see someone, and I just busted her." Adrienne told me, "Whatever you do, don't get violent or hit Rae, because the police will come and throw you in jail for domestic violence." Less than an hour after I hung up the phone with my sister, I called the police myself. Every time I came out of the room, Rae was after me, screaming and throwing stuff at me. Raquel and Royale were asleep in their beds upstairs, and Rae was still going nuts. The cops finally showed up just before midnight. One officer took me downstairs, while the other officer took Rae upstairs. The officers questioned us separately and then brought us back together. One cop pointed at a family picture hanging on the wall and said, "Listen – you guys have a beautiful family. We don't want to take anyone in for this. You need to stop all this and work everything out without any more violence. If we have to come back out here, someone is going to jail. Understand?" The cops told me to sleep downstairs, and told Rae to stay upstairs and cool off until the morning. Rae and I apologized and agreed to work it out. The officers left, I went downstairs, and Rae went upstairs.

The cops hadn't been gone 5 minutes before Rae busted in my room downstairs and came at me with the big cake knife from our wedding. Rae was a skinny little bird, so I just pushed her away. Then she went after my suits and leather jackets that were in the closet. Rae was shredding some of my favorite clothes like she had a machete in her hands. I ran back upstairs and called the cops again. When Rae heard the police sirens outside, she dropped the knife, ran upstairs, and locked herself in our bedroom. A moment later, the same two officers came back in our house. I pointed at the knife and my sliced up clothes and said, "Look – she came at me with that knife and then she went after my stuff." The officers arrested and handcuffed Rae, and took her to jail on domestic violence charges. After they all left, I just stood there alone for a few moments; stunned by what had transpired in the past few hours. From the moment I first saw the lingerie in the suitcase, to the time the cops took Rae away, my whole life as a family man had come completely unraveled.

Rae had been arrested for domestic violence, and according to State law, she wasn't allowed to return to the family house for two weeks. Rae got out of jail, and immediately flew home to visit her family, who lived in L.A., just down the street from my mom. Rae went to see my mom and told her, "I'm gonna divorce Greg and take everything – the house, the cars, the money, all of it." My mom called me and said, "Rae's down here talking up a storm - I think she's lost her mind." A few days later, Raquel and Royale both came down with the chicken pox. I was alone with the girls in the house, so I asked my mom if I'd ever had chicken pox as a kid. She told me I had, and not to worry. My mom must have confused me for one of her other five kids, because just a few days later, I got the chicken pox too. I was trying to take care of both girls and myself, but I couldn't even function. I've never been so sick in my life. Rae's best friend, Nyla, came over to check on all of us, and she volunteered to clean up the house, and take care of the girls for a few days until I felt better. Nyla used to babysit the girls for us sometimes when Rae and I went out, and the girls were very comfortable with her, so I gratefully accepted her offer.

When Rae heard that Nyla had come over to help me out and take care of our daughters, Rae threw a fit. She called Nyla's workplace and talked to Nyla's boss. Rae said, "You tell that no-good whore to stop f------ my husband and to stay the hell away from my kids and my house." Nyla called me that same day and said, "Greg, I am so sorry. But you deserve better than that little whore of a wife you got, because the truth is, I cannot live with myself any longer. Rae's been having an affair with your brother-in-law, your sister's husband, whenever he comes to town for business. I know because I babysit your girls for Rae when he's here. I'm so sorry for hurting you." I said, "Okay Nyla, it's alright. I believe you."

My sister Adrienne's husband was a distributor for a large and very popular sportswear company. He made a lot of money and traveled all over the world for business. Apparently, he came to Seattle often enough to maintain an affair with my wife. Since Rae had tried to get Nyla fired from her job earlier that day, Nyla figured it was time to come clean. Nyla dropped a dime on Rae, but the next move was up to me. I called up several of Rae's girlfriends, and I said, "Look – don't even try to hide it. I already know the truth. I'm only going to ask you once: is Rae having an affair with my sister's husband?" The response from all five of Rae's girlfriends rang in my ears: "Yes, Yes, Yes, Yes, Yes."

Then I got on the phone and called my sister, Adrienne, in New Jersey to tell her the truth about what was happening. Adrienne started crying and said, "Gregory, why would you say those things and hurt me like that?" I answered, "Because it's true, and your no-good sonofabitch husband and Rae, they're gonna pay for this." I got off the phone and was so enraged I was practically numb. I couldn't think or feel anything. If I'd stepped off the curb and gotten hit by a Mack truck, I wouldn't have known if I was dead. My first thought was, "He is dead. This episode is gonna send ripples through our family, and they're gonna kill that sonofabitch." I instructed my family, "Don't anybody go after him – he's all mine. When he comes to L.A., I'm gonna set him up. I'm gonna cut off his d--- and stick it in his mouth."

As for Rae, her and I were finished from the moment Nyla told me what was going on behind my back. First, I got a good attorney and filed for divorce. I was still plotting my revenge on Rae and Adrienne's husband when God's grace and mercy came upon me. God made me see that I wasn't perfect, that I had slipped up many times in my life. God made me examine my own heart and my motives, and He showed me that everyone deserves compassion and forgiveness because we're all just human beings. I realized how blessed I had been through the power of forgiveness, and I knew that I had to forgive Rae and Adrienne's husband before I could move forward with my life. I couldn't live with myself for having so much anger and so little mercy, when I was no saint myself.

I also decided my sobriety was more important than revenge, and I didn't want to open up the Pandora's Box of my old life of violence. I knew that, unless I allowed my heart to forgive, I'd end up paying a greater price than Rae and Adrienne's husband. I prayed about it for a long time, and God told me, "If I can forgive you, then you can forgive Rae and Adrienne's husband." I said, "Okay, Lord. I understand. I'll let it go." So I did just that. In reality, Rae and Adrienne's husband couldn't shake a stick at some of the stuff I'd done in my life. I let it be, and then I was at peace again. I divorced Rae, Adrienne divorced her husband, and we all moved on with our lives. I got full custody of Raquel and Royale, and Rae moved into her own place.

CHAPTER 23

DEEDEE AND THE BMW

THROUGHOUT MY MARRIAGE to Rae, DeeDee would still call me on occasion. Usually it was on my birthday, or maybe for Christmas or New Year's. DeeDee would call and say, "Greg, I still love you, baby." Of course, Rae threw a fit every time DeeDee called, and she'd start screaming at me, "I don't want that b---- calling here no more!" I never said anything to encourage DeeDee, but it still went on for about 5 years, and each time, Rae would go off on me. Once Rae was out of the house, and I had filed for divorce, I called DeeDee in California and said, "Hey baby, I'm sorry about the way everything turned out. Why don't you come up here and be with me." I flew DeeDee up to Seattle, and when she got to the house, I showed her the closet full of Rae's fancy clothes. I told DeeDee, "First of all, I want you to go through here and take whatever you want. Those furs and diamonds should have been yours anyway." DeeDee cleared out Rae's closet, and we started making our plans to be together. I put my baby, my black-on-black BMW with Recaro seats, in DeeDee's name and set everything up for her to take the car and Rae's stuff back to California and wait for me there.

DeeDee took the car full of Rae's stuff back to L.A., and I called her every few days to check in. One day, I called DeeDee at work, but they said she wasn't there. When I tried to call her again a few days later, they told me, "DeeDee doesn't work here anymore." I thought, "What? DeeDee quit her job?" Then they told me, "DeeDee hasn't worked here in 2 weeks." I thought to myself, "What the heck is going on here?" I started to get a funny feeling that it was a setup, and that I was getting screwed. So I called DeeDee's house - and Fred answered the phone. Now, I hadn't talked to Fred or heard from him in about 7 years. When I'd left town, I assumed Fred was going to find me and put a bullet in my head. The exchange that ensued with Fred was one of the most illuminating and entertaining conversations I've ever experienced:

Fred: Hello?
Me: Fred?

Fred: Who's this?
Me: It's Greg.

Fred: Greg who?
Me: Greg Perry.

Fred: Greg Perry?! Greg Perry?! Man, how you doin'?!
Me: I'm good, Fred! How you doin'?

Fred: Man, I'm good.
Me: It's good to hear your voice, Fred!

Fred: It's good to hear your voice too, Greg!
Me: Fred, I gotta be honest with you…I've been trying to get ahold of DeeDee, but I kinda got this funny feeling like I'm getting screwed.

Fred: Yeah! You are getting screwed!
Me: I am?

Fred: Yeah, you are.
Me: Oh, it's like that?

Fred: Yeah, it's like that, Greg.
Me: Hmmm...okay.

Fred: So what you gonna do?
Me: Well, I know what I would do, what you taught me to do – I would handle my business. But I can't really handle my business in this case because my business is DeeDee.

Fred: Handle your business.
Me: How am I gonna do that when I don't even know where DeeDee is?

Fred: I'll tell you exactly where she is - she's at my house in Louisiana.
Me: What? I didn't even know you had a house in Louisiana. I've never even been to Louisiana, and I don't know where your house is.

Fred: Well, here's my address...
Me: Okay, I got it.

Fred: By the way, there's a gate in front, with a Jag in the driveway, and a boat.
Me: Okay. I know I'm getting screwed, but I want my damn car. I want my BMW back.

Fred: Then go get it. Handle your business.
Me: Okay, Fred. I'll handle my business.

Fred: Good! By the way, Greg – we never had this conversation. Is that clear?
Me: That's crystal clear, Fred. I'll talk to you later.

Fred: Goodbye, Greg.
Me: Goodbye, Fred.

I hung up the phone, and it struck me how much Fred had always loved me. I was the son Fred never had. That's why he didn't kill me after I'd broken up with DeeDee and left town all those years earlier – because he couldn't kill his own son! Fred had groomed me from the time I was 14 until I was 20 – and he taught me everything. Come to find out later, DeeDee and Mimi and their mom had been stealing money from Fred for years. Fred knew about it, but he didn't sweat it. But when I called, he probably figured DeeDee had a little something coming to her. I jumped on a plane and flew down to Baton Rouge, Louisiana to get my car. I had a taxi take me to a spot just down the road from Fred's address. I found the house, with the Jag and the boat in the driveway - but no BMW. I went back to my hotel, waited a few hours, and then about 11:30 that night, I called the house. DeeDee answered, but I hung up without saying a word. I got another cab and went back out to the house. I walked by the gate, and sitting there in the driveway was my BMW. The adrenaline started pumping through me. When DeeDee left my house in Seattle a month earlier, she left a pair of her nice designer jeans behind. I brought those jeans with me to Louisiana; that was my little calling card for DeeDee.

I sneaked into the back yard, and set the jeans on the porch, right where DeeDee would be sure to find them. I started to quietly push my car out of the driveway, but then I thought, "What the hell am I doing? This is my car!" I jumped in, fired up the engine, and burned rubber all the way out of the driveway and down the road. I flew out of town and hit the freeway at full blast. I was driving for hours, and I'll never forget how the sun came up and went down that night, and I was still in Texas. That was the longest stretch of highway I'd ever seen! I finally pulled over in El Paso to call DeeDee and see how she was doing in light of the most recent developments.

When DeeDee answered the phone, I laughed and said, "Yeah, DeeDee – so what's up now?" DeeDee said, "Oh, I'm great, Greg. By the way, the police are looking for you, because I told them you stole my car, since it's in my name now. There's also a gun under the seat, so when they find you, you're going to jail. Bye." She hung up just as I screamed, "You f------ bitch!" I almost broke my hand slamming down that phone. That sudden rush of adrenaline gave me all the energy I needed to jump back in the car and hit the road.

I made it all the way from Baton Rouge to Los Angeles in 28 hours, with only a few breaks in between. When I got to L.A., my brother Mike was there. I knew from when we used to steal cars in the old days that it would take about 72 hours for the BMW to hit the police hot sheet for stolen cars. I told Michael I needed to get some sleep, and to wake me up in a few hours. Mike woke me up a few hours later and told me I better get going. I made it as far as Grants Pass, Oregon, when I started seeing double. I stopped and got a hotel room for the night, and made it home to Seattle the next day. After it was all said and done, DeeDee's mom made me give her $6,000 to have DeeDee sign off on the title of the BMW. I had my car back, but that was the last I ever heard from DeeDee, and the last time I ever talked to Fred.

My beloved wife, Sheri.

CHAPTER 24

SHERI

IN THE SPACE of three months, I had gone from being happily married (or so I thought) to Rae, to Rae cheating on me with my sister's husband, to Rae and I getting divorced, to DeeDee being back in my life, to DeeDee stealing my car and disappearing, to going to Louisiana to retrieve my car, to driving cross-country to L.A., to being back in Seattle, to being alone with Raquel and Royale. I was used to living a life of chaos, but that had to be some kind of record, even by my standards. When all that drama finally died down, I started looking ahead to my new life alone with Raquel and Royale, and without Rae or DeeDee. I was ready to just be a dad to my little girls without the distractions that came from my crazy romantic relationships. I was still in the treatment program, working on my sobriety, and taking one day at a time. I had a great job as an Electronic Weapons Technician at Todd, where I was responsible for wiring the Navy's classified weapons systems. Who could've guessed that Todd Shipyards would also be the place where I would meet Sheri, the love of my life, who later became my wife? Sheri has been the best wife, and the best mother to my children that I ever could have imagined, and then some.

Sheri worked in the Accounting department at Todd. Friday was payday for me and my crew, so we used to go down to a little booth where Sheri would come and hand out our paychecks. I had seen Sheri before, but I never really paid attention to her. The truth of the matter is, on payday, I only had one thing on my mind: getting my paycheck and seeing how much money I had earned. One particular Friday, Sheri handed me my check as always, and when I looked up, this beautiful blonde girl was looking at me with bedroom eyes. It caught me off guard, and I thought, "Oh my gosh, what is that all about?" I'd never really interacted with Sheri before, but she was making it clear she was interested in me. Sheri admitted later that she had been checking me out for almost a year before I noticed. I asked Sheri for her phone number, but she gave me the number for her office phone upstairs, so I didn't even bother calling her after that. I wasn't about to call Sheri at work to discuss our personal business.

The next time I came to the booth to pick up my paycheck, I told Sheri, "You gave me your office number – I want your home number." Sheri gave me her personal number, and we started dating almost immediately. Sheri would come over to my house, and she was great about helping me with Raquel and Royale. Every once in a while, Rae would come to see the girls, and if Sheri was there, all hell would break loose. Sheri was so restrained in those situations, and always kept her cool. But Rae had a mean streak, and a nasty mouth that wouldn't stop. Rae would be yelling and cursing at Sheri, and calling her names. A few times, Rae ripped the antenna off Sheri's car. That was probably quite a shock for a classy girl like Sheri, but it was just another day in the life for my ex. Rae was always going ballistic about something and instigating one drama or another. It especially bothered me that Rae would go nuts in front of my daughters, calling Sheri a "white b----" and every other name in the book.

Rae always was a little crazy anyway, and as our divorce proceedings got closer to completion, she summoned a little extra crazy for Sheri and I. In reality, Rae was a late-stage alcoholic and drug addict who refused to seek help or even admit she had a problem. She never once went to rehab or tried to go clean. Sheri and I just blessed Rae, and wished her well. We did our best to keep things civil in front of Raquel and Royale, but Rae always went the other way – she wanted to use the girls to hurt me as much as possible. Rae's personality was edgy enough when she was sober; but when she was high, she was impossible. One time, my beautiful niece London came to visit us from the east coast. Rae started shooting off her mouth about something, and London just hauled off and decked Rae and knocked her out cold right on my bed. I had to pick London up in my arms and carry her out of the room, or she might have killed Rae. Through all the drama with Rae, my love for Sheri grew every day, because I saw how Sheri carried herself with such class.

Sheri and I fell in love, and before long we started talking about getting a house together. Sheri had a nice home in Ballard, which had been in her family. When Raquel and Royale wanted to spend more time with Rae, I set the three of them up in a nice apartment and I moved out of the house I had shared with Rae. I was spending more and more time at Sheri's, while we looked for a house. Eventually we found a nice new development in the Harbour Pointe neighborhood out in Mukilteo. We picked out the lot we wanted and worked with the builder on the custom plans. We made arrangements to move as soon as the home was completed. As part of the financing process, I had Sheri put my name on her bank account for my asset verification. Sheri had about $35,000 in the bank, and we thought we were good to go. Everything was going our way. I was doing service work in the program, going to my meetings, and teaching Sunday school at Unity Church. Sheri and I weren't married, but we were definitely committed to one another.

Pretty soon, the new house was completed. I signed all the papers, and I got the keys to the house. Sheri and I were so excited to start this new chapter in our lives together. I went out to the house alone right after I picked up the keys because Sheri had to return to work. I had just pulled up to the house when our agent called me and said something had gone wrong at the last minute with my loan, and that the purchase was off. He said, "Sorry Greg, but I need the keys back. It's not your house, after all." In an instant, I imploded and lost my mind. Everything had been going along so perfectly for Sheri and I, and now this house deal was going to ruin everything for us. I was mad at God, because I felt like He had let me down after all the hard work I had done to try to get clean and sober. I had been doing my best, trying to give back to the program and still deal with my own sobriety challenges. I was trying to raise the girls the right way, but now it seemed like all my good work was for nothing. My soul was crushed, and that old monkey of addiction jumped on my back once again.

I went straight to the bank and took some money out of Sheri's account. Then I bought some coke, and started smoking my brains out yet again. It was just after Christmas when I rented a hotel room, locked myself up, and hit the pipe hard for a few days. After the whole debacle with buying the house, my only thought was, "I'll show you, God." Sheri was worried sick about me, and she didn't know what to do. She finally called Emmitt, who had been my first sponsor in the program years earlier. Emmitt came and got me out of the hotel, and helped me pull myself together just enough to go see Sheri. Emmitt took me to Sheri's house, where I apologized to

Sheri for everything and talked with her for a while. When we were done talking, Emmitt said, "You can't stay here, Greg. You have to go. This is going to take some time for Sheri."

Back when I was in the hotel room, God came upon me and said, "Oh ye of little faith. The first time something goes wrong, you bail out and go back to your old using ways." I knew I was my own worst enemy. While Sheri took a break from me, I kept trying to work everything out with our lender so we could still buy the house. I kept writing letters and calling the bank to appeal the process, and the bank just kept turning me down. Finally, after my third letter to the bank, they approved us for the loan and we got the house; again. This time it was really happening and we could move right in. But when we were packing up Sheri's house and getting ready to move, I could see Sheri was struggling with the whole idea of taking this huge step together. She didn't say much, but she didn't have to. I had let Sheri down before, as well as myself, and I had hurt her too. Sheri already had her life together long before she ever met me. She had a great job, a house of her own, money in the bank, and stability. Living in a state of chaos had always been my specialty, but Sheri didn't know any of that in her life. The last thing Sheri needed was me messing up her life with my drama.

Even when we were first dating, I dragged Sheri through the mud with me. Sometimes I would ask her, "Why are you hanging with me? You deserve better than this." Sheri would say, "I'm still hanging with you because you said you were going to do all these great things and make a great life with me. And I believed you." One time, I said, "But you don't understand - I'm a drug addict! You need to get the f--- away from me!" Sheri was so resilient and strong, though. She said, "No, Greg. I'm not leaving. I'm gonna stay here with you and help you, and you're gonna get it together – period." With the house deal finally done, and our future hanging in the balance, all those times I had stressed Sheri created doubt in her mind. It was weighing hard on her. We were all packed and ready to go, when I said, "Okay, Sheri – this is it. The truck is ready. Either you're with me, or you're not with me. Which is it?" I thank God that Sheri still believed in me, despite myself, and we walked out of her house that day and into our new life together.

CHAPTER 25

YOU CAN'T GIVE AWAY SOMETHING YOU DON'T HAVE

SHERI AND I got set up at our new house in Harbour Pointe, and things slowly got better again. I was secretary of the meetings at the Care Unit, and was doing my best to get sober. But one day, just as I was getting off work, my old familiar nemesis jumped up and bit me again. It was as if I couldn't handle all the goodness in my new life and I had to sabotage myself. Just a few days before, I'd been leading the meeting at the Treatment Center, and now I had that monkey on my back again. I got off work, drove straight to the dope house, and bought some blow. Then I went home, locked myself in the bathroom, and started smoking my brains out all over again. When Sheri came home and discovered I was locked in the bathroom, she knew something was up. She asked me if I was okay, but I just played it off like everything was cool. Boom! The next thing I knew, that bathroom door came flying off its hinges and Sheri blew in there like Wonder Woman. Sheri confronted me once and for all, and said, "I love you, Greg, but this has to stop. You've got two choices: either I'm calling the police, or I'm taking you back to treatment. Which is it?" I was high as a kite, so I said, "Don't call 911. Just take me to treatment."

Sheri drove me straight to the Treatment Center, and I went in. I was just in the Center three days earlier, leading the meeting. When the staff saw me come in, they started talking to me just like always. It only took them a few moments, however, to realize that something was different and I was not in my right mind. I made it through a week of residence treatment before I had a meeting with my counselor, Millie. I told her I finally recognized that I was at a crossroads in my life, and this time it was do or die. I had already fallen off the wagon twice before after a full 28-day cycle of treatment, so I told Millie the typical program wasn't going to work this time. I knew I needed to make a serious decision about my sobriety, or I wouldn't live long enough to take another shot at treatment. The Center agreed to release me early so I could make a more rigorous commitment to getting clean. I already knew where I was going to start, and the very next day I called Harold to see if he would sponsor me. Harold was the one person who I thought could actually help me.

My drug rehabilitation took a major leap forward the day I asked Harold to sponsor me. Harold just looked at me and said, "Absolutely not. You're full of s---, Greg, and you don't know s--- about being sober." I was stunned by his response. Harold said, "You know a lot of things, and yet you don't know anything. And your problem is, you don't listen to anybody. The answer is 'no' – I'm not doing it." I always looked up to Harold, so I begged and pleaded with him to help me. I said, "Please, it's not like that anymore - I'm serious this time." Harold shook his head and said, "You already asked me once before, and you were lyin' your ass off even then. Your wife called me and said you told her you were over at my house – and you don't even know where I live! You were probably out getting high and smokin' somewhere."

I told Harold I wanted what he had, and that I didn't know how else to get it. Harold took a deep breath and said, "I will sponsor you…but only on one condition: if you do absolutely, positively, everything I tell you to do. If you don't, I'm done." I told Harold, "I'll do it, I promise – just tell me what you want me to do." He said, "Alright, it's simple - you only have to change one thing. Do you think you can do that?" I said, "Yes, what is it?" Harold said, "Everything. You have to change everything. You have to change the things you do, the places you go, the people you see, all of it. The bottom line is, you gotta do it all, one day at a time. You can't get there in a hurry." The whole time I was listening to Harold, I was thinking, "Oh my God - he's setting me up."

Then Harold sat me down and started laying out his expectations for me, point by point. He said, "I want you to go to 90 meetings in 90 days. The only way you can miss a meeting is if you're at a funeral, and if you miss a meeting, it better be your own funeral. I want you to call me every single day for the first 30 days to check in with me. I want you to come over to my house once a week – we're gonna have a men's group for all the guys I sponsor. I want you to do service work in the program, starting with Step One. If anyone in the Program asks you for anything, you need to help them. Do not turn down a single request. I want you to go to the meetings, take the cotton out of your ears, and stick it in your mouth. Shut your f------ mouth and listen. Do not talk - because you can't give away something you don't have. If anyone calls on you, tell them that your sponsor said you don't know s--- about sobriety, and that you can't give away something you don't have. Is that clear?"

I said, "Yes, that's clear – I'll do it." After that reality check from

Harold, I realized that he was the first man I had listened to since my dad had passed away. I was used to being The Man and calling all the shots – I answered to no one. Steve's father David had always treated me like a son and given me lots of love, but he never tried to be my father. Fred had been my mentor in organized crime, but he never tried to be my dad. Harold gave me some tough love, like a father, but most importantly, he held me accountable. Because I had always liked Harold, and I respected him so much, I listened intently and allowed him to hold me accountable. I did exactly what Harold had told me to do. Right away, I knew something was different this time. I could feel myself making serious progress. I was Secretary of the 12-Step meetings we had at the Treatment Center every Sunday night, and I made it to six straight months of sobriety.

Before Harold sponsored me, I'd make it one week, then two months, then six weeks, whatever – but I never made it as far as six months of continuous sobriety. Six months was a real milestone, a turning point in my sobriety. One day a kid came up to me at the Center and said, "Hey Greg, I want what you have. Will you be my sponsor?" I thought to myself, "Now what was it Harold told me?" I eyeballed the kid and said, "Absolutely not. You don't know s--- about sobriety." I then proceeded to give that kid the same speech that I'd gotten from Harold, word for word, right down to the list of my conditions. The kid listened intently, and when I was finished talking, he agreed to my conditions for sponsoring him. I had my first sponsoree and I was on my way.

The next time I went to Harold's house for our weekly men's group meeting, I walked in like I had a big "S" on my chest. I was so proud of myself because I had picked up my first sponsoree. When I told the guys in my group why I was so happy, they just rolled their eyes and laughed at me. They said, "Great – talk about the blind leading the blind. That's never going to work. How are you going to sponsor someone else when you can't stay sober yourself for more than five minutes?!" Those guys in my group roasted me good. I was steaming on the inside, but I didn't say a word. I left Harold's house that night more determined than ever to make it. I was the baby of the group that met at Harold's house, in terms of my length of sobriety. But I knew I was on the right track, and I was going to show those guys what I was all about.

I had always been the kind of person who, if you told me I couldn't do something, I'd find a way to walk on water to prove you wrong. I was committed to helping that kid work his way through the steps, and I knew the best way to accomplish that goal was to keep working the steps myself with Harold. Sure enough, next thing I knew, my one sponsoree had turned into 22 sponsorees. I hosted my own meetings at my house every Tuesday night for 12 years in a row. When I looked up, my whole life had transformed. I had been focused on doing the right thing, giving back, and not worrying about keeping score. Before I consciously realized what happened, I was at my best in every single area of my life: physically, emotionally, mentally, spiritually, in my business, in my family – all of it had changed radically for the better. I went from being happy just to have six months of sobriety to having 14 years of sobriety, and it seemed like it all happened in the wink of an eye. My recipe for success had been simple: put God first, help others, and clean house within myself. When I did, all that goodness came flowing back to me many, many times over.

To top it all off, all 22 of the people I sponsored went on to have happy, healthy, and productive lives. Some of them started businesses and became millionaires, but all of them were successful in their own way, and on their own terms. It was a beautiful thing to behold, and I couldn't take credit for any of it. We had simply followed the steps in the system, stayed diligent in our effort, and supported and loved each other through every challenge we faced. It was a miraculous time, to say the least. After 12 straight years of meetings at my house, the group drifted apart as many of us faced new challenges that came with our growing success. Everyone was having families, buying houses and cars, traveling, making money, and enjoying the fruits of their sobriety.

We also got a little complacent, and satisfied with the success that was borne out of those years of meetings. Nevertheless, Harold remains one of my closest, most trusted friends to this day. In hindsight, those 22 guys I sponsored will never know it, but they helped me more than I ever helped them. That day in the bathroom with Sheri turned out to be the last time in my life I used drugs of any kind. My 26-year streak of sobriety started the very next day when I called Harold and asked him to sponsor me, and it continues unbroken to this day. That day was the ultimate turning point in my life, because I've discovered it is only in sobriety that I am alive anyway.

Harold already had his life together when I met him. I believe the Law of Attraction brought us together because Harold had what I needed: a model of sobriety, a path to follow, and the tough love to get there. The whole key to my sobriety was that I learned I had to surrender in order to win. Surrender was simply not in my vocabulary. Back on the streets of South Central, surrender meant only one thing: you're dead. The only way I was ever going to surrender to anything was if I was wearing a toe tag. I had grown up in the streets thinking and believing that in order for me to win, I had to cheat, manipulate, and control my environment. Surrender just wasn't in my DNA. Surrender was for losers. I had always said, I was not going to lose, and I was not going to be a victim, no matter what I had to do. But in my quest for sobriety, the opposite strategy was actually the best strategy.

In battling my addiction, I realized I couldn't fight it, or cheat it, or manipulate it, or even control it, because my addiction knew me better than I knew myself. Once I saw that my addiction was bigger, stronger, and smarter than I was, I realized that I couldn't win without changing my strategy. As soon as I learned to surrender, I became worldly weak, but spiritually strong. I let go of it all, and stopped trying to cheat the process. When I did that, God's higher power kicked in, and that gave me the willingness to start my life over. I learned the power of taking it one day at a time. I learned to grow as a person, as a father, and as a husband to Sheri.

I had never followed directions in my life before Harold laid down the law with me and held me accountable when he agreed to sponsor me. I always cheated, and I always won. Work was a four-letter word to me. I was a master of cheating and winning. But I wanted what Harold had, and I was willing to do whatever I had to do to get it. I remember one time when I confided to Harold, "You could've told me to jump off the Golden Gate Bridge and I would've done it. No questions asked." That's how badly I wanted my sobriety. Just as Harold had served me and guided me when he was my sponsor, that's how I served and guided the 22 guys who I sponsored. Those 22 guys helped me grow so much. Just by making myself available, helping them out of love, with no expectancy of return, I realized how life really works. Whatever you dish out, you get back in return. That's one of the Laws of the Universe. I was giving love unconditionally, and no one knew about it. I did it anonymously, and I didn't get any credit or glory for what I was doing. Because of that, God blessed my life from A-Z, top to bottom, inside and out, backward and forward - across the board.

When I looked up several years later, my entire life had been transformed. I had given back wherever I could, from speaking to the fellas in the penitentiary to talking to the kids in Juvenile Hall. I had mentored everyone who I thought could use my help, from the young kids in the schools to billionaires and world leaders. What I really did, more than anything, was I just got out of my own way. It was like my sobriety took care of itself, because I was so busy living the right way. I got to 14 years of sobriety by doing the right thing, trusting God, helping others, and giving back; all the things the Program taught us to do. Harold had always told me, "There is an easier, softer way to clean house" and he was right. Everything came together for me once I got long-term sobriety.

CHAPTER 26

THE NFL

WHEN I FINALLY came out of the fog after working my way through sobriety, it felt like someone had hit the rewind button on my life and I was back at age 12, when all I wanted to do was play professional football. That was my dream as a kid before I got derailed by the gang life and all the wheeling and dealing that came with it. I had been a superstar athlete as a kid, but once I started getting high at age 12, I really stopped growing mentally, emotionally, and spiritually. Physically, I was a full-grown man – but a man who had no ability to navigate life's peaks and valleys without numbing myself out with drugs. Many of my childhood friends who had stayed in sports in their younger years later went on to play in the NFL. Nesby was a safety for the Colts. George was a receiver for the Rams. Ray was a safety for the Bengals. Doug was a defensive lineman for the Vikings. Toussaint was a running back for the Saints. Tony was a linebacker for the Raiders. Willie was a defensive lineman for the Redskins. Several other friends of mine had also been in and out of pro football, and all of them were supportive of me in my quest to make it to the NFL.

Sobriety had saved my life, and it was a fantastic first step. But I knew if I were going to have any chance whatsoever of fulfilling my NFL dream, I'd have to get in the best shape of my life. I hit the gym with several of my NFL friends, and mastered the same workouts they did to prepare themselves for an NFL season. It wasn't easy, but before long, I was hard as a rock physically, and as strong and fast as I could possibly be. I had done everything I could to prepare for this. I was 28 years old, and I was ready to climb the final mountain toward one of my major life goals. I wrote a passionate letter about myself that described my commitment to my NFL dream. I gave the letter to my friend Tony, who passed it on to his teammate Greg, and Greg in turn gave it to the General Manager of my hometown team, the L.A. Raiders.

In 1988, I got my first shot at my dream when I received an invitation to the Raiders' training camp. Unfortunately, reality soon hit me like a blow from a middle linebacker. Although I was primed and ready physically, my mental state wasn't where it needed to be. I was so excited to finally have a chance at my dream that on the first day of camp, I froze up. I couldn't run, and I could barely breathe because I was so amped up. Just being in the Raiders training complex and seeing their Super Bowl trophies, Championship rings, and that notorious silver and black logo everywhere was completely overwhelming for me. I had watched the Raiders play since I was a little kid, and I couldn't even believe I was actually there in that environment. Despite my pleas to the Raiders' Director of Player Personnel to give me one more chance, I was cut after the first day of camp. The next thing I knew, I was on my way back to Seattle to ponder my next move.

I had never played a down of organized ball at any level throughout my junior high, high school, and college-aged years. Sitting at home in Seattle, I started to question myself and I wondered if it was even realistic to think that a 28-year old man with no football experience could make it all the way to the NFL. After reflecting on my situation for a short time, I came to the conclusion that I needed some sort of standard to measure myself by. I needed to find out if I was even good enough to play football at any level, so I decided to join a semi-pro team in the Seattle area.

It only took me six games of semi-pro ball to realize that, at the very least, my skills were far beyond that level. I was a starting safety and a kick returner, and I ran circles around those semi-pro players. I may not have been ready for the NFL just yet, but I was also not ready to give up on my dream just yet. Apparently, the NFL wasn't quite ready to give up on me either, because just a short time later, I received a letter inviting me to a free agent tryout in Irvine, California. I had no idea who the letter came from, or how they knew where to find me, but I figured the Raiders must have seen something in me and passed my name along to someone in a position to help me. The bottom line was, if someone thought I was worthy of a second chance, I wasn't going to ask too many questions.

Apparently the NFL, the Canadian Football League, and the World Football League sometimes held combined camp tryouts to scour the market for undiscovered talent. I had continued to work out just in case, and was ready to give it another shot. A few weeks later, I flew down to Irvine and found myself on the field with 400 other athletes who shared my dream of playing pro ball. I had pulled my groin while working out a few weeks earlier, and it was still sore, but a friend who was already in the NFL said, "Greg, this is it - you gotta go." I was on the field, going through all the drills with the other players when a man named Tim approached me and introduced himself as a scout for the San Diego Chargers. Tim told me he had been watching me all day and that he was so impressed with my performance that he wanted to extend me an invitation to the Chargers' training camp. I was one of only 10 players out of the 400 who were good enough that day to get signed by an NFL team.

By the time I got to the Chargers' training camp, passed the team physical, and hit the field, I was dialed in mentally. When Tim the scout came over to me during one of the drills and asked me how I was doing, I said, "Tim, I can't talk right now – I'm dialed in." My focus was paying off too, because the next time the action paused and I looked up, I noticed that half of the players who had started the day were already gone. I made it all the way down to the final six defensive backs before the Chargers cut me. Once again, I came back to Seattle to reassess my situation. I decided enough was enough and that it was time to let go of my football dream. I hammered a nail into the wall and literally hung up my cleats. I was done with football.

But football still wasn't done with me. A week later, I got a call from the Edmonton Eskimos of the CFL, saying they wanted to send a scout to Seattle to check me out. I immediately said yes, and the workout went well. The Edmonton scout said I definitely had talent and could play, and that the team would be in touch with me. I waited as long as I could, but eventually reality took over. I had already sacrificed my previous job to pursue my football dreams, and it was time for me to move on. I took a job on a fishing boat out of San Francisco and was out at sea when the Eskimos finally called to invite me to their training camp. I missed the call, and the tryout, and my dream of playing pro football came to an end.

CHAPTER 27

AN ORDAINED MINISTER?

BEING AT SEA on that fishing boat for an entire month gave me a lot of time to think about my life. Sheri met me at the dock when the boat came in, and she no doubt sensed something was up. I loved Sheri, and she was the best woman I had ever been with. Sheri was true blue, as loyal as they get, and had stuck with me through hell and high water. But I knew I had to make a decision about Sheri, because even though I loved her and she was my girl, I sensed I could love her even more deeply and strongly than I did. Shortly after Sheri and I got back to Mukilteo, the phone rang at our house. I picked it up and a man's voice said, "Hi, Greg - do you know who this is?" I said, "Yeah, I know who it is." The voice said, "Well, who is it?" I said, "It's Short Arm Sammy." The caller let out a loud scream, and said, "Awww, man - how did you know it was me?!"

It was my old friend David, who used to be known as Short Arm Sammy back in the 'hood. I'd known David since we were 4 years old, living in South Central. The last time I had talked with David, I was 18, and he was about to be sentenced for armed robbery and assault. Everyone in Gardena figured Short Arm Sammy was going to prison for the rest of his life. More than 15 years later, David called me up out of the blue. I said, "Man, what happened to you? I thought you went to prison?" David said, "Nah man, they let me off. They nailed the other guys and I got off because the jury didn't believe I was in it with those guys."

I asked David where he was living and what he was doing with his life. David said he was living in Texas and that he had become an ordained minister. I started laughing out loud. I said, "What? Get the f--- outta here, man! You're an ordained minister? How can you be an ordained minister when you're a dope-dealing, lying, cheating, hustling, shoot-em-up gangster?!" David said, "Nah man, that old stuff is all in the past. Listen to this, Greg…one night I was just sitting there when the spirit of God came over me, and it changed my whole life right at that moment. I'm straight now." I couldn't believe what I was hearing from David, but I had already experienced so many miracles in my own life that I had to give David the benefit of the doubt. I told David, "Man, you gotta come up and see me." David agreed, and within a few weeks, he was at my front door.

David came into my house, and back into my life, filled with the spirit of God. It was a beautiful thing to see. I was in a real good place myself by then, with my first few years of sobriety under my belt. I had Raquel and Royale with me, Sheri and I were doing well, and I was still teaching Sunday school. David and I were talking and he told me, "Greg, God told me to reach out to you. I see a vision for you, brother. You're gonna do great things, make a lot of money in real estate, and have a great quality of life." I nodded and soaked it all in, then David added, "But here's the deal, Greg – God is telling me right now that this situation you got here with this girl you love, it isn't right. God isn't gonna honor that. You need to marry Sheri and make it right, or you need to let her go. So what are you gonna do?" I stepped back and said, "Aww, come on, David. Why are you coming in here and trying to bust my balls like this?"

The conversation continued, and David persisted. He not only refused to back down, he actually elevated his point to where he and I were huddled together and praying hard on it and talking it all out. It occurred to me that God was using David to speak to my heart, and eventually David got through to me. We had a meeting of the minds and of the spirits, and I knew exactly what I had to do. I called Sheri at work and told her, "I'm coming to get you right now – we're getting married." Sheri said, "What? What's going on, Greg?" I went and picked up Sheri, while David went to K-Mart and bought a $40 wedding ring. We made arrangements to meet at the home of a minster we knew, and that's where Sheri and I were married later that same day. David served as my best man, which was appropriate after the role he'd played in helping me see my relationship with Sheri from a more Godly spiritual perspective. David returned to Texas a short time later, while Sheri and I started our new life as husband and wife.

CHAPTER 28

KEITH TURNS IT AROUND

IT TOOK ME four years to get one year of nonstop sobriety, but once I made it to my first anniversary, I had some serious momentum in my recovery. I had been through so many ups and downs in my own sobriety that I could understand what others were going through, and I was always eager to help a fellow addict. Unfortunately, no one needed my help more than my main man, Keith. I'd go back to L.A. every so often to visit my mom, and when I did, I'd always stop by to see Keith. A couple times when I went to see him, Keith was still smoking up a storm. He'd be higher than a kite, and I'd be straight. I'd tell Keith, "C'mon man, you gotta knock it off before that stuff kills you." Keith would always say, "I know, G – I'll get right. I promise."

I'd go back to Seattle and continue on with my good habits of clean living, helping others, and giving back. Then I'd come back to L.A. and Keith would still be smoked out. I tried to talk to him brother-to-brother, because we'd always been so close. I wanted to show Keith the other side of life, the sober side, and hopefully inspire him to make the same kinds of positive changes that I had made. But Keith was in too deep, and he couldn't see it. I figured it was only a matter of time before he'd hit the wall and either smoke himself to death or clean up. I prayed it would be the latter. One time, I went to L.A. on short notice, and Keith didn't even know I was coming. I stopped at my mom's first, then I rolled over to Keith's house, just like always. When I walked in, Keith was sitting there like a zombie. He was all smoked out, and completely fried out of his mind. I looked at Keith in that sorry state, and all I could see was myself just a few years earlier.

My heart condemned me in that moment, and it told me, "Greg, you can't do this anymore. Your sobriety is too important." I knew right then that, as much as I loved Keith, I couldn't be around that destructive behavior. So I said to Keith, "Hey man, I love you. You're like a brother to me, and you always have been. But my heart is broken right now, seeing you like this. I'm watching you slowly kill yourself, and I know you're better than that. I can't see you like this. I can't see you no more. Our friendship is over right now, buddy. I can't come here anymore, and I can't be around you until you're ready to get right. I love you, and I'll always wish you the best, but I'm done. I'll be praying for you, but we're done, man. I'll see you later." Then I got up and walked out the door.

Keith told me later that moment was the biggest turning point in his entire life, because it broke his heart so bad. Keith and I had always been like Butch Cassidy and The Sundance Kid - if you go, I go. We went through it all together, for so many years. We used to say that someone would have to kill us both at the same time, because we'd done everything together from the time we were kids. But just as Keith couldn't have helped me overcome my addiction, I couldn't help him with his either. We were in the same boat, in that sense. I sat in that room with Keith, and I looked at him with nothing but love, but my heart was broken. It felt like a divorce, because I had to walk away from the guy I loved so much. Keith and I had been through thick and thin together, but my sobriety was more important, because without my sobriety, I had nothing. I saw Keith standing at the same crossroads where I had stood a few years before, when I needed to get straightened out.

That moment in his living room turned out to be so important for Keith, because it prompted him to do an about-face. Keith told me later that, after I told him I couldn't be his friend anymore, he told himself, "No more." He made a life and death decision right after that, got himself into the Program, and got cleaned up for good. Fast forward 20+ years, and Keith is a self-made millionaire in his own right. He owns millions of dollars of real estate, including apartment buildings and other properties. Keith is still one of my best friends, and the two of us are among the very few who made it out of the 'hood alive.

Keith is now a very successful businessman, as well as the Chairman and Financial Manager of his church. He is also the Team Chaplain for a pro sports team. When teams come to town for games, Keith leads the players in their chapel meetings before and after the games. This is the same guy who I used to run the streets with, wheeling and dealing, and now look at him! I'm so proud of my friend. It's an amazing and miraculous story in itself, to see how Keith has turned his life around. He's committed to sobriety, he's giving back to the Program, he's helping others – and it all started that day we sat in his living room. I gave Keith some tough love that day, just like Sheri and Harold had done for me years earlier. It was hard, and it hurt both of us to go through that. But out of that heartache came the beautiful life that Keith has enjoyed since he found lasting sobriety.

CHAPTER 29

CASH FLOW SYSTEM

ALMOST IMMEDIATELY AFTER Sheri and I got married, the vision that David had seen for me began to take shape. God had given me a glimpse of it through David's eyes, but the reality was even greater. At the time, I was working as a Lead Electrician for an electrical contractor near Lake Union in Seattle. Late at night, after Sheri and the girls had gone to sleep, I'd stay up late and watch TV. I had always said sleep was overrated and a waste of time. My favorite late night show was Dave Del Dotto's real estate infomercial called Cash Flow System. I watched that show every time it came on, and pretty soon I started dreaming of big houses, nice cars, lots of money, and the rest of the lifestyle that came from being successful in real estate.

Dave Del Dotto was simply selling a lifestyle that I already identified with from my years spent living at Steve's house. It dawned on me that there was a way I could finance the lifestyle I had always figured should be mine anyway. One night, after seeing Cash Flow System for about the hundredth time, I said to myself, "That's it - I'm done. I'm not gonna be an electrician anymore.

I'm gonna be a superstar real estate agent." All of a sudden it was obvious. There was no way my big dreams were ever going to come true if I remained an electrician for the rest of my life.

Any normal person would have looked at my life back then and said I already had it all: a union job with full benefits, 2 healthy kids, a beautiful wife, a nice house, dependable income, leading my own crew, the whole thing. By any rational standard, most people would have been perfectly content with my quality of life. But I'm not most people, and I wanted to do more, and be more, and make more. So I did what I had always done when I wanted to change my life: I took bold, decisive action. The next day at work, I took my lunch break and walked to a nearby park. I sat in the sun by Lake Union and prayed, "God, I want to be a superstar real estate agent. I know I can do it." God spoke in my heart and said, "Go ahead – do it." I went back to work, but I knew deep inside I was done with my old business and my old life.

I found my boss, the owner of the company, and told him, "I need you to double my salary right now." That was a ridiculous demand for me to make, and of course I knew it. But I had a plan. The owner looked at me like I was crazy. "Greg, what are you talking about? I can't double your pay – you're already my top-paid guy." I said, "I know, I'm sorry. I was hoping you'd get mad and fire me." My boss said, "Why in the world would I fire you? You're running my crew." I said, "Well, the truth of the matter is, I've made a decision anyway. I'm gonna do something else." The owner eyeballed me with a mix of skepticism and surprise. Then he said, "What is it that you're going to do?" I said, "I don't want to say, because I've learned that if you tell people your dreams before you make them happen, it takes the wind out of your sails. But I'm starting today." The boss narrowed his eyes at me and said, "So let me get this straight…you go to lunch and you're running my business. You come back from lunch, and all of a sudden you're leaving? Today?" I said, "Yep, that's it. I gotta get started right away." My boss just stared at me for a moment, then he said, "Okay, Greg – if that's what you want, I wish you well. But can you do me a favor? Can you please leave out the back door so I don't have to explain to everyone what just happened to you?" I shook the boss's hand, walked out the back door, and I never looked back.

The sun was shining on me all the way home, and it seemed like a positive symbol for my new direction. I was so excited by the time I got home I could hardly contain myself. Sheri got home, saw me bubbling over, and said, "You're sure happy today, what's going on?" I said, "Honey, check this out – I'm gonna be a superstar real estate agent and take care of you and our family. I just quit my job!" Sheri sighed, and said, "Oh God, are you back on drugs?" I said, "Sheri, I'm serious." Sheri said, "Have you lost your mind?! We're doing great, there is nothing wrong with our life. You quit your job? What is wrong with you?" I said, "Listen to me, Honey…I'm gonna be a superstar real estate agent, make lots of money, and really take care of you and the kids. My old job was never gonna get me there, not where I want to go." Sheri closed her eyes and said, "Oh my God, you're crazy. You've officially gone off the deep end." I quickly added, "Not only that, but I want you to quit your job and stay home and take care of the kids full time." Sheri shook her head and said, "You've lost your mind. What is wrong with you? I've worked hard for ten years to make it to corporate. There's no way I'm quitting my job. What is all this? Why are you trying to ruin our lives when there is absolutely nothing wrong?"

I wasn't getting anywhere with Sheri, so I called my mom to tell her the great news about the big decision I had made. Her first words to me were, "Gregory, have you lost your mind? You can't quit your job – you have to take care of your family." I told my mom all about my big plans to be a superstar in real estate. My mom listened very politely, and when I finished she said, "Okay, Gregory. I'm gonna pray for you." I hung up the phone, went back to Sheri and told her that, in order for my plan to work, she needed to quit her job. Sheri said, "Listen to me, Greg...I'm not going to quit my job, not in this lifetime. You've lost it. You can just forget about all of this." I tried again and again to convince Sheri that my plan was our ticket to a better life. I said, "You don't need to work anymore. You take care of the kids, and I'll take care of the rest. A man's got to take care of his family, and this will let me do that in the best possible way." I rode Sheri like a bull for several days, and finally she agreed to quit her job. Sheri really didn't want to quit her job, but she got tired of me constantly bugging her, and she knew quitting her job was the only way I would stop.

It took me three tries to pass the real estate exam, but I finally got my license and went to work. Nine months later, I still had not made a single copper penny. I was working hard, but I had nothing to show for it. Sheri and I were absolutely broke, our house was in foreclosure, and my BMW was about to be repossessed. I had already borrowed money from all my friends and my family, and they were fed up with me. The first few months, I called my mom and asked her to loan me the money to make the house payment. That worked a few times, but then my mom said, "Greg, if you're calling me to ask for money, the answer is 'no.' I love you, I support you, and I will pray for you. But I can't give you any more money because that will just enable you. I want you to go sign up for food stamps so you can feed your family." I said, "Come on, Mom...get real. I'm not signing up for food stamps." My mom said, "Oh, I see. You're too good to go get food stamps to feed your kids, but you're not too good to call your mom and beg for money every month. I'm not hanging up this phone until you promise me you'll sign up for food stamps so you can take care of your family." At that point, I gave in and promised my mom I'd sign up for food stamps.

We got the food stamps, which was humbling enough for me. But then things really came to a boiling point with Sheri. She was already bitter and resentful of me for hatching this crazy plan, and for convincing her to quit her job. I had basically sabotaged our entire life. One morning in the kitchen, Sheri reached her limit. She got right in my face and let me have it good. Sheri said, "What kind of man are you? You quit your job, you made me quit my job, and now look at us. I don't care if you have to get a damn job at McDonald's – but you better be the man you said you were going to be, and take care of our family!" That one hurt all the way to the bone, because everything Sheri said was 100% true. I couldn't even try to deny it. That same night, I had my men's group at the house. The guys in the group told me they wanted to come over a little early to talk to me about something. I figured maybe they had taken up a collection or something to help me out. Man, was I ever wrong.

The guys came over, sat me down, and said, "Greg, we're just gonna be straight up with you, because that's how you've always talked to us and helped us. We know you're struggling with money, and your wife is all pissed off at you, and you're losing your house. We want to tell you, you need to forget about all this real estate stuff, go and get your old job back, and get it together before it's too late for your family." I said, "Oh, so that's it. For a minute there, I thought it was gonna be something else. Well, I appreciate that - now you need to get the hell out of my house, because we're not having a meeting tonight. I don't need to hear that, so you can just go now." I threw the men's group out, and then I called Harold. I told Harold I knew I could be a superstar real estate agent, but nobody believed in me anymore, not even my own wife, or the guys from the men's group. Harold said he would help me look at the whole picture, just like he had with my sobriety. He came over to the house the next day and we laid my whole life out on paper.

When we had everything accounted for in my life, Harold spoke up. He said, "Okay Greg, here's what I see. Your wife is so mad at you, she won't even look at you or talk to you, because you've ruined her life. You're completely broke; you've borrowed money from every person you know. You tried to borrow money from me too, but I told you there was no way in hell I was giving you any money. Your house is now in foreclosure, your cars are about to be taken away, and you've screwed up your entire life. So, the way I see it, if you're not back working at your old job in two weeks, I'm gonna come back here and kick your ass myself. There's no reason in the world why you can't go get your job back and forget all this nonsense. You'll make good money again, you'll have your benefits, and you'll be back on your feet in a few months. No one will ever be able to say you didn't give real estate a good shot. You tried, but it just didn't work out. That's my advice."

After Harold left, my situation only got worse. Late that night, when I was alone, I finally broke down emotionally. I felt like I was alone on an island. My wife didn't believe in me, my sponsor didn't believe in me, and the guys in my men's group didn't believe in me. Even my own mom, who had always stood by me, thought I was crazy and refused to help me anymore. Everybody I cared about was saying, "Greg, it's over - give it up." Now it was down to me and God. I started praying with all my heart and soul. I said, "God, I just know I can be a superstar real estate agent. I just know it. Everyone thinks I'm crazy, but I know I can do it." Then God spoke to my heart, as clearly as I'm saying these words right now. He said, "Greg, trust in me, and follow through."

I got up the next morning, and I prayed again. I said, "Please

God, just give me a sign – that's all I need." I told myself, "I don't care what anyone says or thinks - I'm gonna be a superstar real estate agent. Everybody else can think whatever they want. They can say I'm hardheaded, and unreasonable, and that I won't listen to anyone. I don't care." I had asked God to give me a sign, and I had complete faith that He would do exactly that.

When I got to the office that morning, my broker grabbed me and said, "Congratulations, Greg. You just won the award for the Top Listing Agent for the month of August. You had more new listings than any other agent in the office. Nice work." Of course, I hadn't sold anything yet, or made a penny – but I had the properties in my name. I went into my office, sat down and closed my eyes, and I told God, "Thank you, Lord – that's all I needed!" I did exactly as God had told me to do: I put my trust in Him, and I followed through, all the way to the end. Before I knew it, my faith paid off and God had flipped the script on my career and my life. I won the Rookie of the Year Award for being the hottest new agent in my company, despite the fact that I had put up a goose egg in those first nine months. Over the final three months of the year, I made over $100,000 in commissions, and outsold everyone in my office. I went on to win every single sales award, first in my office, and eventually, in my entire company. It was a true rags-to-riches story. The secret of my success was simple: trust in God, and follow through. My faith got me through, because I knew I could do anything as long as I first made a plan of action, then took action, and followed through all the way to the end.

The Herald
Business Journal

Serving the Business & Technology Communities of Snohomish County
Serving the Business & Technology Communities of Snohomish County   Vol. 3 No. 4

Propelled by Faith   pg 2

**#1 Real Estate Agent again
this year**   pg 3

**Perry offers life lessons
for success**   pg 4

GREG PERRY

real estate superstar

**Once a poor kid in
south-central
Los Angeles, he's
now a 'self-made
multimillionaire'**

Cover story, pages 1-2

Cover Story: From Rags to Riches

CHAPTER 30

A REAL ESTATE SUPERSTAR

SHORTLY AFTER I got my real estate license and started my new career as an agent, the company I worked for had their annual Awards Banquet and Convention. I remember standing in the back of the room, watching as all the top agents came up onstage and received their awards. A few of the agents received these beautiful, tall, gold statues that looked like Oscars from the Academy Awards. I said a silent prayer, "God, you know what? Next year, that's gonna be me up there getting one of those awards." I didn't know what those gold statues signified, or what I had to do to get one. After all, I had only been in the business a few weeks and still had no idea what I was doing. But I planted that seed, right then and there. I had faith, I trusted in God, and I followed through to the end.

One year later, I won Rookie of the Year for the company. In one year, I went from being alone on an island, where not even my own wife, family and friends believed in me, to stepping out on faith and betting on myself. I went from being on food stamps to being able to buy out the whole grocery store. Of course, as soon as I was on my feet and making money, everyone in my circle suddenly developed amnesia. My wife, my family, my friends, Harold, and everyone else said, "We always knew you could do it, Greg – we were behind you all the way!" All the same people who had thrown me under the bus and ran me over a year earlier were now solidly in my corner. I never forgot that, but it was okay, because their doubt was part of the fuel that drove me. When I returned to my company's Awards Banquet the following year, and picked up my Rookie of the Year trophy, the owner of the company told me that everyone who ever won that award had gone on to become a top producer in real estate. I knew I was in good company, and I was determined to follow in that tradition of excellence.

At the end of my first year, I checked the scorecard, and I saw that I made a six-figure income in about three months of sales. I thought to myself, "What?! I just made a hundred grand, and it's all legit? And the cops aren't coming after me? Is this for real?!" Immediately, I started thinking, "If I can make that much in three months, I can take this even higher. If I can make $100,000 in less than one year, I know I can make $250,000 next year." That became my goal for my second year. First I wrote down all my yearly goals. Then I broke those down into monthly goals. Then I broke those down into weekly goals, and finally my daily goals. Then I wrote down my spiritual goals, my family goals, my business goals, my personal goals, and finally my goals for my whole life. I already had the desire, the faith, and the determination to be great. My goals were my plan of action; my roadmap to success.

I took some of that money I had made in those final three months of my first year, and I set it aside for my marketing budget. I realized I had already learned how to sell in the streets of L.A. You want to talk about running a business? In the business of organized crime, you can't mess up. If you messed up your business in South Central, you either paid for it with your life, or you went to jail. Messing up was not an option in the rough-and-tumble world I grew up in. I just applied all my street knowledge, all my worldly knowledge, and all my business knowledge, to my real estate business. Instead of doing the wrong thing, like I always had in the past, I did the right thing. The only difference was, in the real estate world, if I messed up, the worst thing that could happen was either my client might fire me, or I might get sued. I decided that was far more preferable than getting shot at. The rules of real estate were nothing compared to the rules on the street.

I had grown up in the fast lane, wheeling and dealing in L.A., so going into my real estate career, I decided to market myself in that same Hollywood style. One time, I was going through various magazines and publications to get some marketing ideas, and there was this high-end real estate agent in L.A. who had his own billboards. In his marketing, he was always wearing the sharpest suits, standing next to a big Rolls Royce, in front of a huge mansion. He catered to the exclusive clientele, and he had the whole package. I took one look at his presentation and said, "That's my guy right there - I'm gonna do that in my marketing." One of the smartest things I ever did early on in my career was I decided to focus all my marketing on my own backyard in Harbour Pointe. There were about 2,500 homes in Harbour Pointe, so my plan was to take over my neighborhood first, then fan out from there. I got a giant wall map with all the developments in Harbour Pointe on it, then one by one, I started walking through all the neighborhoods, knocking on doors and introducing myself to everyone. I shook every homeowner's hand and said, "Hi, I'm Greg Perry, with John L. Scott Real Estate. It's nice to meet you. Have a great day!" Then I'd give them my business card, and go on to the next house.

Next, I had my print shop design some very expensive-looking postcards, and I started sending out postcards every time I got a new listing or a sale. When I first started out, nobody knew who I was, but between the door knocking and the postcards, that changed in a hurry. I'd get a listing, and send out a "Just Listed by Greg Perry" postcard with my face on it to all 2,500 homes in the area. Then when the listing sold, I'd send out another 2,500 postcards that said, "Just Sold! Greg does it again!" The other agents in the area didn't stand a chance. I was determined that my name and face recognition was going to be unsurpassed in Harbour Pointe. Everyone would know who I was eventually, because I understood the importance of sophisticated, high-impact marketing. It didn't take long before the residents of Harbour Pointe started connecting the name and the face on my postcards to the guy who had come and knocked on their door a few months earlier.

In the beginning of my real estate career, I worked alone. I was my own listing and selling agent, and I designed all my own marketing. The office manager in the John L. Scott Real Estate office where I worked was a little sparkplug named Mel, and she used to help me with some of the administrative stuff I couldn't do by myself. I used to joke around with Mel, and tell her that someday I was going to hire her to come work exclusively for me. Mel was always outgoing and upbeat, and she could take care of some business. She supported all the agents in the office, and ran the office too. The other agents in my office would often get mad at me, because I had so much business that Mel spent the majority of her time working on my deals. Sometimes the other agents would leave anonymous hate letters in my mailbox, telling me to stay out of "their" neighborhoods. I just laughed it off, and kept right on doing what was already working so well. I wasn't about to be intimidated by some old-school agents who were upset because I had so much business. In reality, those agents didn't know what hit them once I got on the scene. Before long, I was upsetting the balance of power not just in Harbour Pointe, but in the whole county.

Every marketing piece I mailed out had my name, direct phone number, custom Greg Perry logo, and one of the many slogans I had created, such as, "One Call Does It All," "Don't Settle For Less – Hire The Best," or "One Word Says It All – Sold!" Most of the established and successful agents were still using old-fashioned, cheap-looking flyers. If they did any geographic farming at all, it mainly consisted of sending out plain black and white mailers in a generic white envelope. They'd get a new listing, stick a sign in the yard, throw some cheap-looking flyers in the box, and call it good. Meanwhile, I spared no expense: everything I did was professionally designed, full-color, and printed on high-quality paper. Everything from my personal business cards, to my flyers, to my postcards, to my listing pictures was a first-class production. I was playing the real estate game to win, and nothing but the best would do for my clients. Once the momentum started building from all my marketing, I was getting lots of new listings, and my phone was ringing non-stop. My business was taking off like a jet, and it was only my second year in real estate.

Things were changing in my office, too. Mel had been hired away, and had gone to work for a top-producing agent over in Bellevue, which was a more affluent area than Mukilteo. By then, I was doing a lot more business, and making a lot of money. As my second year came to a close, I was the #1 listing agent in my office, the #1 selling agent in my office, and the #1 agent for total commissions earned in my office. I was also the #1 agent in all of Snohomish County for John L. Scott Real Estate, largely because of my dominance in Harbour Pointe. I made over $250,000 in my second year. When I saw my sales totals at the end of that second year, I just smiled and said to myself, "This is fantastic, but if I can do $250,000 then I know I can do $500,000!" I made a mental note that $500,000 was going to be my goal for my third year. But I knew I couldn't do it by myself. If I was going to take my business to the next level, and double my income, I needed a full-time assistant. So I called Mel in Bellevue and made a date to meet with her for lunch.

When I got together with Mel, she asked me what was going on. I said, "Well, I told you I was gonna hire you to be my assistant someday, and now that day is here." Mel said, "Oh wow, Greg, I guess

I should have known you were serious!" I said, "So how much is it gonna take to get you?" I had been a master negotiator since I was a kid in South Central; I could talk my way in to, or out of, just about anything. Mel told me how much she was making with the agent she was working for. I just said, "No problem. I can beat that." Mel said, "What? Really? Are you joking?" I replied, "No joke. I told you, I'm getting ready to take my business to the next level, and I'm dead serious." Mel agreed to come back and work directly for me as my administrative assistant, but two weeks later, she still hadn't shown up. I called her, and said, "Where are you? I'm about to blow the roof off this mother – I need you right now." Mel said, "I'm sorry, Greg. I just couldn't believe you were serious about paying me like that. I'll give my notice today and be there right away."

Mel came back to our office to join me, and we blasted off. I was rocking and rolling, and honing my marketing system every day. My marketing program was powerful, consistent, and non-stop: Just Listed, Just Sold, and Greg Does It Again, over and over again. That might sound like a broken record, but in fact, I was breaking records in real estate every time I turned around. My broker started getting calls from other real estate companies, who complained that it wasn't fair how I was blanketing all the neighborhoods with my marketing and taking all the business. The management from John L. Scott came to me and said, "Greg, don't change a thing. You're doing a fantastic job. Those other agents are just jealous and upset because you're dominating them. Keep doing exactly what you're doing!"

By the end of my third year in real estate, I was earning over $500,000 annually. Keep in mind, the same houses that sell for anywhere from $500,000 to over $1 million today were only selling for $150,000 to $350,000 back in the mid-'90s. I had to sell about $17-18 million worth of real estate just to make my $500,000. In other words, I was closing eight to ten homes a month, every single month, for a year.

That's a lot of real estate! But I was just getting warmed up. I was in my element, running the streets of Harbour Pointe, and handling my business, while Mel was in my office, taking care of everything on the back end. Eventually, we were doing so well that Mel came to me and asked for a raise. I agreed to start giving her bonuses on every closing, because Mel was not allowed to receive a commission.

One day, I was picking up my office mail, and I noticed there was a commission check in there for Mel. I knew there had to be a mistake somewhere, because by law, Mel couldn't receive a commission, as she was not a licensed agent. When I checked in the deal file, I discovered that Mel had altered the paperwork, and put herself on the deal. That was not only illegal; it was dumb, because Mel knew better. I confronted her and said, "Have you lost your mind? You know you can't do that; you're not a licensed agent. You know all the deals have to go through me, and then I pay you out of my payroll. We both could get in a lot of trouble for that!"

Mel apologized, and said she had only done it because she needed the money. I forgave Mel, and told her to send the check back to our corporate office, and when corporate sent the money back to me, I would pay her properly. Mel agreed to do that, but when she went out to lunch, she cashed the check! That was beyond stupid, and I knew I had to put a stop to it. I'm all about trust and loyalty in my business, and Mel had broken my trust. I was in a real bind. I really liked Mel, and she did a great job for me, but all of a sudden, I knew I couldn't trust her. I prayed and prayed about the situation, and contemplated how to resolve it properly.

After careful deliberation, I decided I couldn't keep Mel. I told Mel I couldn't afford to keep her because Sheri and I were having a new baby. The truth was, she had broken my trust in a big way, but I didn't want to fire her or hurt her feelings. I gave Mel a nice sendoff, with a big party and lots of flowers. Once Mel was gone, I began conducting interviews for my vacant administrative assistant position. I interviewed several applicants, but nobody jumped out at me. Then a gal named Phyllis came in to see me. Phyllis was a very mature lady, and she had more hands-on experience in real estate than anyone else I had met. Phyllis had worked in title and escrow, she had run a lending company, and she had lots of management experience in her background. Phyllis was so polished and professional; she had it all together. To top it all off, I discovered in our interview that Phyllis and I attended the same church. That was like the cherry on top for me.

I told Phyllis that I thought she would be a perfect fit for the position, and I told her how much I could afford to pay her. Phyllis said she couldn't work for the salary I had offered her, because she was used to making a lot more. Phyllis asked me if there was any way I could pay her more. I said, "Phyllis, I'll tell you what. I know you want more and I respect that, but I can only afford to start you at that salary. However, I guarantee you this: when I'm done, I'm gonna be the top guy in real estate, and you're gonna be the highest paid administrative assistant. If you just stick with me, and have faith, I'm gonna take us all the way to the top." Phyllis smiled at me and said, "Okay, Greg…I trust you. I'll do it."

I hired Phyllis on the spot, and she started working with me right away. Phyllis turned out to be another one of my guardian angels, along with my mom and my wife. Pretty soon, I was telling everyone, "I am so blessed, because Phyllis is worth her weight in gold." I quickly realized that if I ever had to hire someone to replace Phyllis, it would take three people, all working fulltime, and they still couldn't do for me what Phyllis did so perfectly. That's how smart, and talented, and knowledgeable Phyllis was. Here was a woman who was like a blend of my mom and my wife, plus she had all that knowledge of real estate, running a business, and leadership skills too. I got all that and more in one package with Phyllis.

Several years later, when we were filming my Lifestyles of Success shows, the filmmakers and producers came up to me and said, "Man, where did you find that Phyllis? She'd throw herself in front of a pack of lions for you." Our relationship quickly got to the point where Phyllis was part of my family. Phyllis had the Power of Attorney for me, she could sign for anything in my name, and she was on all my bank accounts. Phyllis literally had a hand in everything I did, personally and professionally. Not even my wife had the kind of access Phyllis had to my business and my life. My work got so busy for a while that I became a workaholic, and I was spending more time with Phyllis than I did with my own family. Phyllis could practically read my mind without me needing to say anything. She knew what I was thinking, what I was feeling, and how I worked. Phyllis was such an integral part of the processes and systems I used in my business. God was definitely the key to my success, but right after God, came Phyllis.

Once I saw how valuable Phyllis was, I designed my business so that everything ran through her. I'd just check in with Phyllis to see what she needed me to do, and then I left the rest up to her. The systems that Phyllis and I created together ran so smoothly and so effectively that it allowed us to smash all the records in real estate. With Phyllis running my operation in my fourth year in the business, I became the #1 listing agent, the #1 selling agent, and I was the #1 sales associate in all of Western Washington for John L. Scott. I also achieved the Top 1% designation that year, for the first time in my career, and made well over $700,000. Reaching the Top 1% in the real estate business is like winning the Super Bowl in the NFL. When a team wins multiple Super Bowls in a short period of time, it's called a dynasty. Well, Phyllis and I were a dynasty in real estate, because together we eventually reached the Top 1% an incredible 12 years in a row!

When it comes to Marketing, no one does it better!

CHAPTER 31

MILLION-DOLLAR MARKETING

IN MY FIRST four years of selling real estate, my earnings had gone from $100,000 to $250,000 to $500,000 to over $700,000. I could sense that the next major milestone – a million dollars – was well within my reach, so I pushed all my marketing chips to the center of the table. I bought billboards all over the city. I had life-size kiosks in the shopping mall, and shopping cart ads in the grocery store. Then I bought cinema ads that ran in the movie theaters. I started buying ad space in all the real estate magazines, but unlike other agents who bought postage stamp-sized ads, I only bought the front cover, inside covers, and centerfolds for all my listings and recent sales. I bought a four-page center spread in Homes and Land magazine, and then people started calling Homes and Land, "The Greg Perry Magazine." It was nearly impossible to go anywhere in Harbour Pointe, Mukilteo, or Snohomish County without seeing my name and my face. That's exactly how I wanted it.

My listings were already being featured on the weekly Sunday morning real estate show, but I wanted to take things to the next level. I contacted KING-5 TV, the local NBC affiliate that ran the real estate show, to see about creating a customized advertising campaign for my business. When the ad execs at KING-5 heard what I had in mind, they invited Phyllis, Bobby; my buyer's agent, and myself to come downtown to the Four Seasons Olympic Hotel to hear their ideas for my campaign. I dressed up for the occasion in one of my best and most colorful double-breasted suits, and KING-5 sent a chauffeured limousine to pick us up. When we got to the Four Seasons, they took us upstairs to the penthouse suite. We were shown in, and introduced to a gentleman named Otis. Otis is the President and CEO of one of the oldest and largest commercial production and creative services companies in America. Otis and his team had been personally responsible for writing, producing, and directing music-driven commercial campaigns for companies such as McDonald's, Clairol, Sears, Proctor & Gamble, JC Penney, and dozens of other major corporate clients. To give you an idea of the caliber of talent we're talking about, Otis has won 25 CLIO awards, which is the "Oscars" of the advertising industry. Otis was so successful, and so in demand, that KING-5 had paid him a whopping $3 million to come to Seattle for just one week to consult with their VIP advertising clients.

When Phyllis and Bobby and I first walked in and were introduced to Otis, he looked me up and down and said, "Wow – now that's my kind of suit! Come here, I want to show you something." Otis took me by the arm, and led me into his private bedroom in the penthouse, where he pulled a full-length mink coat out of his closet. Otis draped the mink coat over my shoulders, and said, "Put this on and walk back out there like you own it." I laughed out loud and did exactly as Otis had instructed. As soon as I walked back in the living room of the penthouse, everyone in the room turned their heads and started hooting and hollering and whistling at me. Someone said, "Greg, you look like Superfly!" The whole room erupted in laughter, and Otis and I were instant friends. We sat down together for a few minutes, and I explained to Otis who I was, what I had accomplished in real estate, and what I was looking for in an advertising campaign. Otis listened intently, nodded his head, then got up and went in the other room. I could hear Otis playing the piano and working on a musical arrangement. He returned a few minutes later, and asked me to join him at the keyboard in the living room.

Otis said, "How does this sound?" Then he started playing and singing the custom Greg Perry advertising jingle he had just written in the other room. I was absolutely stunned, because in the space of five minutes, Otis had written the catchiest jingle I'd ever heard. He had written uplifting lyrics, a catchy melody, and a memorable rhythm track. Otis explained that if I liked what he had done, he would go back to his studios and record the song with his musicians and singers, then send me the finished product in a few weeks. When we were finished with Otis, the ad execs from KING-5 explained all the advertising packages that were available to me. The bottom line was, for the measly sum of $80,000 they could book my commercials to run for a period of 18 months. I hesitated a bit, because the cost was so high, and the TV medium was new to me. Both Phyllis and Bobby said they thought it was a great idea, so I signed up for the whole package. I had never spent so much marketing money in one place before, but it seemed like a logical next step toward becoming a household name. KING-5 sent a crew of their Emmy award-winning producers out to Harbour Pointe, where we filmed a TV commercial. A few weeks later, I received the Greg Perry jingle from Otis, and soon that was playing on TV and radio. I was a multimedia force to be reckoned with.

I didn't realize it at the time I signed up with KING-5, but that $80,000 turned out to be the best money I ever spent. Because KING-5 had booked my commercial to run for 18 months out into the future, my ad ended up running during some of the highest-rated shows on TV, including the Jay Leno Show, the 2000 Olympic Games, and numerous other high-profile programs. I became one of the most instantly recognizable names and faces not just in the real estate scene, but in all of the Seattle media. No other real estate agent could possibly compete with me after that, and I continued shattering sales records year after year after year. Before long, I was a local celebrity. Just about everywhere I went, people would wave at me and say, "Hey, it's Greg Perry!" When I took my family out for dinner, people would often stop by our table and want to shake my hand or their kids would ask for an autograph.

Looking back on it now, I realize that the marketing strategy Phyllis and I executed was so far ahead of the game, especially for a real estate agent or brokerage. We set a standard that is still unmatched for any local real estate agent or brokerage. I had so many of my listings featured on the local real estate TV show that the producers finally came to me and said, "Greg, the show is almost all your listings anyway, how would you like us to format the show?" There were other agents who had a lot of business, and who made a lot of money. But none of the other agents in the Seattle area were as committed to the marketing side of the business as I was. I knew all that exposure would open doors for me that might otherwise be closed, and my consistent high level of success proved it. Eventually, I branched out into cable TV, and my commercial was playing on ESPN, TNT, Pax TV, and The Discovery Channel, to name a few.

As my kids grew older, I started sponsoring their community sports teams. I had so many youth teams going that, at one point, league organizers called me and said, "Greg, we really appreciate you for supporting the kids, but you can't sponsor any more teams. Your name is already on half the teams' jerseys." After that, I was limited to one boys team, and one girls team per league. My Just Listed and Just Sold postcards were always a regular part of my marketing plan, and later on we started a monthly drawing where we gave away trips to Hawai'i, shopping sprees at the mall, and numerous gift cards. With all the value I was giving back to the community, the people who lived in Harbour Pointe wouldn't even consider making a move without calling me first. The agents in my area had given up even trying to compete with me. In those days, it wasn't unusual to drive down the streets in Harbour Pointe and see my For Sale and Sold signs up and down both sides of the street.

Every Christmas, I sent all 2,500 residents in Harbour Pointe a package that contained a deluxe Greg Perry daily planner, a high-end Greg Perry pen, and a color postcard with a picture of me and my family that said, "From my family to yours - thank you for making me # 1 again." I included a $25 coupon to a popular local restaurant, plus a 20% off coupon from the local dry cleaners. I would send that out in December, and by February, the listings would start pouring in. I also started the trend of sending out magnetic season schedules for the local professional sports teams, including the Seahawks, Mariners, and Sonics. The way I saw it, when people stuck those magnets on their refrigerator, I was in their home for the entire year.

Over the years, Phyllis and I had many agents who worked for us and helped us maintain such a high level of success. Shaun was the first agent to come through my system, and he stayed with me for two years. Shaun's wife, Tanya, later came and helped us out in the office before they went out on their own. Then came Bobby, who had worked at Future Shop, and Matt, who had been a valet at The Four Seasons in Seattle. Later on, I had Adrian, Debbie, and Donna. JayDee was an advertising account manager who had helped me with my TV commercials. Kelvin had worked at a car dealership. Then there was Gordon, Chuck, Jasmine, Pete, Brian, Tom, Shane, Lance, and Rick, among others.

Phyllis and I always kept a log sheet to keep track of all the clients calling in and which agent was working on which deals. I'll never forget one year, we broke the record in real estate again, and when we went back and tallied up all the calls, we discovered we had received over 900 new client calls. That's over 17 new client contacts per week, for an entire year. No wonder we set all the records! At that rate, Bobby and Matt were complaining that they couldn't keep up, and they only closed the deals that were quick and easy. The Century 21 office in town had an agent desk set up at the local mall, and they told me they didn't even get 900 calls in their whole office. We were making millions of dollars and selling hundreds of homes, and we weren't even selling everyone who came to us. Most agents would've been happy with the scraps that fell off our table, but I still wasn't satisfied. It seemed like the bigger we got, the more I wanted.

One summer, I wanted to throw a big party, but I needed a theme. Phyllis and I thought maybe a golf tournament would be fun, so we took over the Harbour Pointe golf course for a day and had the first ever Greg Perry Celebrity Golf Tournament. I invited some of my friends from the NFL and NBA, and I got the local Mercedes-Benz dealership where I bought all my cars to contribute a new Mercedes if anyone scored a hole-in-one. I sent postcards out to the local community and invited all my past clients. We had a putting contest and gave away a trip to Hawai'i. There was a real Hollywood-style buzz around everything I did, and my golf tournament was no exception.

All my success allowed me to take two months off every year, and travel with my family and spend the quality time with my kids that I couldn't spend when I was working. In the summer, I'd take off the entire month of July and we'd go to Maui and rent out a big beach house for the whole month. We did that 14 years in a row, and by the third or fourth year, all the locals in Maui knew us. In the winter, when the kids were out of school, we'd take off and either go skiing in British Columbia, or if we wanted some sun, we'd go somewhere tropical and warm. Those trips created some of the very best memories I have of my family, and it was all made possible by the success I had created in real estate. Those vacations provided the balance and the down time I needed to recharge my batteries. Sheri used to joke that she was a real estate widow for 10 months of the year, but then she'd say, "Please don't stop, because the life-long memories we create when we travel make it all worthwhile."

About five years into my real estate career, it finally hit me what I had created. I was rocking and rolling, selling houses, making great money, helping people, giving back to the community, and doing the right thing. My family was happy and healthy, I had my sobriety, and life was as good as it could be. One day, Phyllis got a call from a local reporter who said he wanted to do a story on me. For whatever reason, I wasn't all that excited about it, but Phyllis convinced me to do it. The guy came to my office and sat down to interview me. He asked me questions about my life story and my real estate business, and while I talked, he just sat there and typed on his laptop. It lasted about two and a half hours, and then he was gone.

I didn't give it any more thought, but then a few weeks later, Phyllis and I got a magazine in the mail. It was the local Business Journal, and there on the cover, was a picture of yours truly. The caption said, "Greg Perry, Superstar Real Estate Agent. Once a poor kid in south central Los Angeles, now a self-made millionaire." I sat there in my chair and stared at that cover, and it hit me. I said, "Oh, my gosh. God, you told me if I trust in you and follow through, all my dreams would come true. And now they have." I couldn't believe it, because the headline had captured the exact phrase I had said to myself, and to my friends and family, five years earlier when I left my old job to go into real estate. It was like the past five years of my life had come completely full circle. That night, when I went home, I broke down in private. For a few precious moments, I cried tears of gratitude and humility, for the way God had blessed me.

I had never been one to rest on my laurels, and as I considered everything that magazine article represented, my mind turned to the future. How could I top what I had already done? Where do you go when you've reached the mountaintop? I couldn't wait to challenge myself again, and to see where this incredible journey would take me next. Wherever it was, I knew it would be just as amazing and miraculous as my life had always been. Most importantly, I knew God walked with me every single step of the way.

CHAPTER 32

THE OFFICIAL REAL ESTATE PARTNER OF THE SEATTLE SEAHAWKS

I'VE ALWAYS LOVED professional football. From the time I was a little kid sneaking into the Los Angeles Coliseum to watch the Rams play, to later meeting the NFL players and pretending I was part of their families, pro football was always my favorite sport. After I got sober in my late-20's, I actually tried out for the NFL myself. I didn't make it, but I never lost my passion for the game. Later in life, when I had three sons, I coached all their Little League and Pee Wee league teams, and we won numerous championships together. Throughout the years, I stayed close with all my friends who played in the NFL, and I followed the league as much as possible. As my real estate career rode an unprecedented wave of success into the early-2000s, I was on the lookout for any opportunity to combine my work in real estate with my love of football.

Shortly after former Microsoft co-founder Paul Allen purchased the Seattle Seahawks in 1997, he revealed his plans to build a new state-of-the-art football stadium for the team in downtown Seattle. By the time the new stadium was ready, so was I. Before the stadium was completed, I had begun negotiating with the Seahawks' management and attorneys on a marketing deal that would blow all my previous efforts out of the water. When the team announced they were going to be the first franchise in the NFL to offer field-level red-zone suites, I seized my opportunity. I negotiated a contract to become the Official Real Estate Partner of the Seattle Seahawks. It was a three-year deal, at a cost of $250,000 per season. Now, $750,000 was an astronomical amount of money, even by my lofty marketing standards. When the management at my real estate company heard what I was doing, they tried to talk me out of it. They said, "Greg, you can't do that. It's too big. That's too much money even for you." But I had a plan, and a vision, and I was sticking to it.

I bought a field-level, red-zone suite (Suite #1, of course) that was located about ten feet from the back corner of the end zone. It was so close to the action, it was like being in the game. I always loved the NFL anyway, but my suite gave me a chance to entertain my clients like never before. As part of my contract, I also got four field passes, so I could take my clients, my family, and my friends down onto the field before the games. That was an experience my clients could never get anywhere else, and I milked it for all it was worth. I closed more big deals with high-rolling clients in that suite than I ever could have back in my office or in some conference room. That being said, my deal with the Seahawks was about more than just closing some deals. It was about branding myself at the highest level, and taking my personal and business marketing into the stratosphere. My contract included a personalized Seahawks jersey, my GP logo prominently displayed on the stadium's scoreboard and replay screen, and the largest corporate billboard in the entire stadium.

My plan from the very beginning was to penetrate the Seahawks' organization, all the way to the top, to see how a multi-billion dollar enterprise operates at the highest level. Of course there was the entertainment aspect of the game itself, which I loved. But it was also an education. When I started negotiating my contract, it was all business. When I told the Seahawks' attorneys what I had in mind for the partnership, they said, "Greg, we've never done anything like this before." I said, "Great, I'll be the first!" I was an experienced negotiator from doing so many deals in real estate, and that expertise came in handy. I convinced the Seahawks corporate attorneys to agree to let me use my suite anytime I wanted, even when there wasn't a game going on. That allowed me to take clients to the stadium for business meetings during times when I needed total privacy and a special wow factor. I also convinced the Seahawks to grant me the right to terminate the deal after the first year if I felt I wasn't getting the full value I wanted and expected.

Later, I heard from someone in the Seahawks' organization that another real estate company had tried to get their foot in the door behind me. Apparently, the company's owners called the team's office and wanted to know how a single agent like Greg Perry could be featured so prominently in such a high-profile venue as Qwest Field. The other company said they too wanted to put up a sign or a billboard in the stadium. When the team's representatives explained that the minimum cost to do that would run well into six-figures, the company said, "What? That's our marketing budget for the entire year!" and hung up the phone. Needless to say, I am still the only real estate broker or company to have been the Official Real Estate Partner of the Seattle Seahawks and the NFL. The most important aspect of the whole venture, however, was to gain access to the entire organization, including ownership, management, administrators, coaches, players, employees, and the other suite holders as well.

Me and my family, friends, and associates, up close and personal with the NFL.

Naturally, I utilized my favorite marketing tactics from real estate to woo all the potential clients my deal with the Seahawks gave me access to. During the Christmas holidays, I delivered hundreds of my packages of See's candy, GP calendars/planners, GP pens, and more. Everyone loved receiving those packages, and nobody else did anything like it.

When Tod Leiweke became the CEO of the Seahawks in 2003, my relationship with the team grew to a whole new level. It started when I went down to the team store at the stadium to pick up some Seahawks gear to outfit my suite. I was going through the store, shopping for clothing and memorabilia, when a nicely dressed gentleman came in, approached me and said, "Hi, I'm Tod Leiweke. Welcome to the Seahawks family." I didn't even know who Tod was at that point, but I figured maybe the store manager had called management to tell them the real estate broker who had just signed the big marketing deal was in there doing some shopping. Tod and I shook hands, and then Tod turned to the clerk and said, "Whatever Greg needs, give it to him. It's on me." Tod turned back to me and said, "Your money's no good in here, Greg – it's on the house." I thanked Tod several times, and after he left, I asked the clerk who Tod was. He said, "Are you kidding? That's Tod, man - he's the CEO!" I was totally blown away by that. I couldn't believe the CEO of the entire Seahawks organization would take the time to come down and meet me, and then comp me on everything in the store.

After I met Tod, and saw how cool he was, I made it my priority to connect with him whenever and wherever possible. Once I got close to Tod and we became friendly, I had an all-access pass to everything Seahawks. That year at Christmas, I called Tod to tell him I needed to deliver my Holiday gift packages to the coaches, players, and administrators. Tod gave me the green light, and the next thing I knew, I was in the locker room handing out my gift packages with the candy, calendars, and pens to the players, including quarterback Matt Hasselbeck. I was slowly making my way around the locker room when an administrator I knew from the stadium walked in with a security guard close behind. The administrator said, "Greg, you can't be in here, man. The locker room is off-limits." The security guard got up in my face, grabbed my arm, and said, "What do you think you're doing? You need to go – right now." I pulled my arm away and said, "You need to call Tod right now, because I just talked to him, and he told me it was okay." Immediately, the guard's demeanor changed. He stepped back and started apologizing, saying, "I'm so sorry, Mr. Perry. Tod doesn't always communicate with us down here, so I just didn't know. I'm under strict orders that nobody comes in the locker room. If it's alright, would you mind, please, standing right over there, outside the locker room, and then you can see the guys and give them your gift packages as they come in?" I said, "Sure, no problem."

My relationship with Tod took another big step the following year, when I was still coaching my kids' football teams. My two oldest sons, A.J. and Manny, played in the Pop Warner league, which was for 10-12 year-olds. My youngest son, Caleb, played in the 89ers league, which was for six to nine year-olds. Both teams made it all the way to the championship games of their respective leagues. That's when my problems started. It was early November, and in Washington State, we had just ended Daylight Savings Time. It was already dark by 4:30 in the afternoon, and suddenly all the sports fields were being used by soccer leagues. I was having a difficult time finding a place for the kids to practice for their championship football games. My friend Tom worked for me at the time, and one day he jokingly said, "Hey, why don't you call Tod and see if you can practice at Qwest Field?" I started laughing out loud, and said, "Yeah, right. We'll just take the kids down to Qwest and practice in the Seahawks stadium. Get real! Don't worry – I'll find a place for us." A few days passed, and I still hadn't found a field for us. The championship games were coming up fast. Then I remembered what Tom had said, and I finally called Tod.

Tod's assistant answered the phone and put me through to him. "Greg, what's going on, buddy. What can I do for you?" I hemmed and hawed for a second, then I said, "Well, Tod, I don't know how to say this…" Tod was calm, cool and collected, as always. He said, "What is it, Greg. What do you need?" Tod already knew I coached the youth football teams, so I explained the situation about the practice fields. Then I dropped the bomb and said, "Can we use Qwest Field for our practice?" Tod let out a big laugh and said, "Say what?!" My first thought was, "Oh no. I just burned every bridge I ever had with Tod." I was just about to apologize, and tell Tod to forget I had even called, when Tod said, "Hold on, Greg. I'll call you right back." Five minutes later, my phone rang, and it was Tod. He said, "Greg, I'm going to have my assistant call you back in a minute. You need to have all the kids sign our release and send them back to me ASAP. Please do not bring all the parents. This is for you and the kids. It's your practice, okay buddy?" I said, "Oh my goodness, thank you so much, Tod. I really appreciate it." Tod said, "Don't even think about it, Greg. It's my pleasure to help."

That night, a handful of the parents and I drove two football teams of kids down to Qwest Field to practice for our championship games. The stadium was lit up like there was a Monday Night Football game going on. Security guards opened the gates and let us in, while the parents sat in my suite, watching and taking pictures of their kids. I swear, those kids had never practiced so well in their lives. Unfortunately, we may have left our best work out there at Qwest Field that night, for both of my teams lost their championship games. The following weekend, there was a home game for the Seahawks. Tod stopped by my suite shortly before kickoff to see how the kids had fared. Tod grabbed me and asked, "How we doing, Greg – did we win?" I told him we lost both games, and Tod said, "What?! You came in here and practiced in my stadium and then you lost?!" Tod busted my chops good after that, but it was all in fun. The bottom line was, those kids will never forget that experience of practicing on an NFL field.

About six weeks later, I was down in Arlington, Texas with my friend, Max, who wanted me to see some property he was thinking about buying. While we were in Texas, Max invited me to go with him to a black-tie gala auction, which included some high-end sports memorabilia. I bought a few autographed pictures for myself, and then I spotted something that instantly made me think of Tod. There was a glass case containing four bronzed baseball gloves, each of which had an autographed baseball in it. The balls were autographed by Hank Aaron, Barry Bonds, Sammy Sosa, and Mark McGwire. That's four of the all-time Top 10 home run champions, all in one case. I knew Tod collected all kinds of memorabilia, and this item was truly one of a kind. I bought the gift, had it wrapped, and brought it back home with me. It was almost Christmas, so I went to see Tod in his office and told him I had something for him. I said, "Tod, you've always been so good to me, but what you did for me and those kids was absolutely priceless. I just wanted to thank you for that, so I got you a little something." Tod said, "I know you appreciate it, Greg. Don't worry about it." Tod opened the big package, and started jumping up and down like a five year-old on Christmas day. "Oh my God, Greg - I can't believe it! Where did you find this?" Tod gave me a bear hug so strong I thought he was going to break my back. Tod thanked me a hundred times, then he said, "I have to take this home right now, I can't leave this here."

From that moment on, I was golden where Tod was concerned. The administrative staff for the Seahawks was afraid to even talk to me, because they knew how close I was to Tod. I heard later that some of the people in the Seahawks offices were wondering what was going on between us, because Tod had already told everyone on the Seahawks staff, "Whatever Greg wants, make sure he gets it." The mutual respect Tod and I had for one another only grew through the years. When the Seahawks played the Pittsburgh Steelers in the Super Bowl in Detroit a few years later, Tod showed up big for me yet again. Some last-minute travel complications messed up my itinerary, but Tod graciously allowed my family and I to stay in the Seahawks team hotel - despite the fact that we didn't have a reservation, and the hotel had been sold out for several months in advance.

Unfortunately, the sense of caring and cooperation I experienced with Tod didn't always extend to everyone else in the Seahawks organization. When it came to my attention that someone was funneling my potential real estate clients to a family member of someone with the organization, I confronted the team's management and terminated our marketing relationship. I retained my red-zone suite for several years afterward, and continued to reap the rewards of the exposure I gained from my partnership with the Seahawks. My goal from the beginning of my relationship with the Seahawks was to not only market myself in a bigger and bolder way, but to get close enough to an NFL team to learn firsthand how a franchise operates. In the end, I learned an even greater lesson for business and for life: how one person, acting with intelligence, vision, and grace, can positively impact the fortunes of an entire billion-dollar organization.

Tod had seen the Seahawks backslide from a 13-3 record and a Super Bowl appearance in his second year on the job, to a 4-12 team that was underachieving, on and off the field, in his fifth year on the job. The players, coaches, and management didn't appear to be on the same page, and ownership needed someone bright enough and strong enough to clean house. My friend Harold had always taught me there was a softer and gentler way to clean house, and nobody embodied that principle in action better than Tod. When the Seahawks were at their lowest point in late 2009, Tod made a major move. In his last major act as the CEO of the Seahawks, Tod convinced Allen to hire a Head Coach that no other NFL team would have touched at the time, in Pete Carroll. Upon Tod's recommendation, Allen gave Carroll almost total control of the team by making him Executive Vice President of Football Operations. That expanded role for Carroll included the power to choose the team's next General Manager, John Schneider. The rest, as they say, is history.

Carroll and Schneider formed a dynamic duo, the likes of which the NFL had not seen in years. Together, they implemented a system of player evaluation that quickly became a new standard in the league. They completely turned over the roster within two years, and drafted and developed numerous players that no one else wanted, but who quickly became superstars and team leaders. Led by a historically great defense, and an opportunistic offense, the Seahawks won the team's first Super Bowl championship on February 2, 2014. In the afterglow of the team's big victory, Pete Carroll noted that the one person missing from the team's celebration was the same person who deserved the most credit for making it possible in the first place: Tod Leiweke. It was Tod who had brought the key pieces together four years earlier, when things had appeared hopeless.

I was humbled by my many interactions with Tod during my time as the Official Real Estate Partner of the Seahawks. I always recognized and appreciated his rare qualities as a person and as a professional. When Tod told me in the spring of 2010 that he was leaving the Seahawks to move to Florida and pursue a dream of owning a professional sports franchise, I told him how much I hated to see him go, but I understood. Four years later, as I stood with my family on the field in New Jersey and watched the Super Bowl confetti fall on the World Champion Seahawks, my mind flashed back to Tod. I remembered Tod's graciousness, and how he had always acted with dignity and respect. Tod set an example worth following in how to lead with vision and a gentle hand. In the years since then, I've incorporated those same principles in my own life, as I continue to move closer to my goals of leadership and impacting others at the highest levels.

CHAPTER 33

MICHAEL'S MIRACLE

I HAD BEEN clean and sober for several years when the opportunity to help someone very close to me presented itself. My mom had decided to sell her house in L.A. and move back to New Jersey to live with my sister, Adrienne. My brother, Michael, lived with my mom but he wasn't moving back east with her. Michael had battled a heroin addiction ever since he returned from Vietnam in the early '70s, nearly 30 years earlier. He had also battled the inner demons that resulted from being a trained assassin, and living with the insanity of war on a daily basis. In reality, Michael was a hardcore heroin addict who just happened to be a former sharpshooter with the Marines. That was a dangerous combination for anyone to try to come to grips with. But over the years, Michael had learned to wear a mask, which allowed him to go to work every day and maintain all the appearances of a normal life.

In order to handle all of the addicted troops who were returning home from Vietnam, the U.S. Government had created a program to wean veterans off of heroin by giving them methadone instead. The only problem was, the methadone solution was worse than the heroin addiction it was intended to solve. When I asked a doctor friend about methadone, he told me it was one of the worst drugs known to man, because of the way it ravaged a person's internal systems. In the U.S. Government's treatment system, the troops/addicts could walk in to a Government-run clinic and drink an oral dose of methadone to simultaneously get their fix and, allegedly, help get them off the heroin. The high produced by the methadone also helped numb the troops to the lasting effects of what we now call Post Traumatic Stress Syndrome, and hopefully pacified them to where they wouldn't act on the rage and violence they had experienced during the war.

Michael told me he had never known anyone who had gone through the methadone program and lived to tell about it. Everyone involved with it had eventually died before they cleaned up or got out. Michael believed the Government's methadone program was merely a thinly disguised way of sentencing thousands of addicted veterans to an invisible, premature death. When I came back to L.A. to see Michael and my mom before she moved to New Jersey, it was clear to me that he needed to try something different to beat his heroin addiction before it beat him, once and for all.

Over my years of being in recovery, I had helped a lot of other people get cleaned up and back on their feet. My own addiction had been such a nightmare that I was uniquely qualified to help others and I loved to do so. But Michael's case hit me right in the heart because this was my own family. I couldn't live with myself if I couldn't even help my own brother. When I first got there, Michael didn't even want to see me because he was too embarrassed about his addiction. I told him, "Michael, you're my brother and I love you. I want to try to help you. Come back to Seattle and you can live with me. We'll get you into treatment and get you cleaned up." Michael smiled at me and said, "Okay, Greg – let's do it. I'm ready."

We tried to get Michael into the methadone program at a

clinic in the State of Washington, but the waiting list was about a month long. We didn't think Michael could last the four weeks he'd have to wait just to begin treatment; he would have been dead before he even started, just from the withdrawals. Instead, we made arrangements to get Michael into the same Treatment Center in Kirkland where I had started my recovery. Michael had only been in the Care Center for about a week when the Director called me. He said, "Greg, I know Michael is your brother, and you're just trying to help him…but we can't do it. We never should have let him come here. There's no way we can get him off methadone when we're not even a methadone clinic." I told the Director, "Listen – Michael is there because he wants to get off drugs and get well. I know he can do it if you give him a chance. I would rather he die in there, trying his best to get clean, than to die out on the streets somewhere because you didn't want to help him. Let him try, and if he dies trying, so be it." The Director backed off and said, "Okay, Greg. We'll give him his chance. But that's all we can do."

Between the heroin and the methadone, Michael already had so much poison in his body, it was a miracle he was even alive. His body needed time to detoxify. But by the second week, Michael couldn't take it anymore, and he tried to escape the Center. I confronted him just as he was ready to walk out. Michael said, "I'm going back to L.A. – you can't stop me." I said, "Michael, I'm a recovering addict myself. I know how this is gonna go. You'll be dead before you know it." We started arguing and fighting. It was as if Michael and I were locked in a spiritual battle between God and the Devil. I finally broke down crying, and told Michael, "You're my only brother! If you won't do it for yourself, then do it for me! I'm your little brother and I love you!" Michael broke down and said, "Greg, why did you have to say that? I don't give a damn about my life! Why did you ask me to do it for you?" Michael agreed to stay and keep fighting his addiction.

The next time I came to see Michael, it was as if The Grim Reaper was trying to take him away. Michael was fully dressed and covered in a blanket, but he was shivering like it was the middle of winter. He was sweating and shaking, and I knew this was the moment of truth. When I came back the next day, Michael was lying quietly in his bed. When I walked in, Michael said, "Greg, it's Michael." I said, "Hey, Mike." He repeated, "Greg, it's Michael." I said, "Yeah, I see you, Mike. How are you doing today?" Again, he said, "Greg, it's Michael." I said, "Okay, Mike – I got it." Michael must have repeated those same exact words 50 times! I finally realized what he was trying to say. It was Michael - the real Michael, my big brother - back in his body, and back in his right mind. It was like he had woken up from a 20-year sleep, and the fog of the drugs had finally lifted.

Then Michael said, "Greg, take me to church – I want to get baptized right now." I said, "Okay, let's go." I put Michael in my car and we drove straight to Overlake Christian Church, where a sermon was in session. The head pastor baptized Michael right away, and when Michael came up out of that water, he was healed. His addiction was over. Done. Gone. Forever. It was another miracle, right before our eyes. Michael immediately joined my men's group, and I watched as he transformed his life in ways I couldn't have imagined. Michael not only changed his own life, but the lives of others as well, through the power of his personal story and his faith. To this day, Michael is a walking encyclopedia of history and knowledge. He loves reading and studying, learning and growing. The doctors had once told me Michael should have been dead a long time ago, because of the condition he was in when he was battling that addiction. But today, Michael is as clean, sober, happy, and together as any person you could ever hope to meet.

CHAPTER 34

HIGH ROLLING IN LAS VEGAS

THANKS TO MY booming real estate career, I had lots of disposable income. At first, I started going to Las Vegas just for the shopping. I had loved Las Vegas ever since I was a teenager. Fred had a trailer he kept out at Lake Mead, so when Keith and I were 18, we used to drive over there in our 280Zs with our girlfriends. We'd stop and see Fred, then we'd cruise over to Las Vegas and try to sneak into the casinos. I had always been fascinated by Frank Sinatra, The Rat Pack, and that whole scene with the sophisticated gangster types. Once I started making the big money myself, I started dressing like an old-school gangster, with the best suits and the finest accessories. I've toned it down a bit as I've gotten older, but I still like to dress up – that's just my personality and my style. Kelvin, one of the agents who used to work for me, called me Don Corleone, because I liked that glamorous gangster life, with the money, the clothes, the cars, and all that.

I used to go to Vegas just to shop for clothes, because the best clothing stores in the world are all there in one place. I would roll into town for a weekend, buy a couple boxes of suits, pick out all the shirts, ties, shoes and cuff links, and be back at home in Seattle by Sunday night. My colorful suits became an essential element of the personal brand I developed for my real estate marketing. People would see me driving around Seattle in my big black Mercedes, wearing a loud purple or yellow suit, and just shake their heads. I cherished my unique, colorful image, and I cultivated it every chance I got. My shopping trips to Las Vegas were part of that colorful life, and I enjoyed every minute of it.

After Steve Wynn opened the Mirage Hotel in 1989, Las Vegas suddenly became the place to go for adult fun in the United States. The whole city got re-energized after that; it was like the place was on fire. Suddenly all the big-name pro athletes, movie stars, celebrities, and people with lots of money were going to Vegas and staying at the Mirage. I started taking Sheri and the kids with me on my shopping trips, and we used to have a blast. We'd fly down to Vegas for a few days at a time, then we'd do some shopping, go out to all the restaurants, check out the latest shows, and hang out by the pool in our private cabana. We really loved the spas in Vegas, too. I'd send Sheri to the spa for a personal beauty day, to pamper her, and we used to get massages together. As for gambling, the only game I was interested in was shooting craps, because I used to throw the dice around when I was a kid back in South Central. My policy was, I never gambled around my kids. I'd hang out with my family all day, then I'd go back downstairs to shoot craps at night after the kids and Sheri had gone to bed,

I loved the whole glamorous life that Las Vegas represented; it had appealed to me from the time I was a kid growing up in L.A., with Hollywood and all the big stars who lived there. Las Vegas is simply a different kind of wheeling and dealing, because Vegas is legal. That was my kind of place. I felt like I had the best of both worlds: on one hand, I'd grown up running the streets and I knew how to wheel and deal in that environment. On the other hand, once I'd gotten sober and cleaned up my act, I learned how to wheel and deal legally in my real estate business. I had both sides covered - I knew how to step on the line without crossing the line. Once upon a time, I was King of the Street on the wrong side, and then I became King of the Street on the right side.

Everything was going great for Sheri and I, and then I got caught up playing that game in Vegas. It had all started so innocently, but the next thing I knew, I had my casino host at the Mirage and I was hanging out with celebrities. Of course, if actors, athletes, and celebrities lose a lot of money gambling, it's no big deal, because they have so much money to begin with. They can afford to lose. But I didn't have that same level of luxury. I started trying to hang at that level; except I have 7 kids and I can't afford to lose too much. Remember, I grew up as a master of disguise, wearing a mask, playing a role, and fitting in with the happening crowd. In Vegas, I found myself wearing the mask of a high roller. I got caught up living the high life, all over again.

I'd take Sheri to the casinos to meet the stars I was playing with, and after a while, Sheri told me, "Honey, I don't want to do that anymore. I don't enjoy it. It just makes me feel uncomfortable." Sheri loved me and trusted me, and she knew she never had to worry about me cheating on her. I always said, "Nobody could screw me like those dice." I made love with those dice, and that was all I wanted to play in Vegas. I never gambled anywhere else. I'd never even set foot in a casino back in Washington State. When I was gambling, it was strictly Vegas or bust for me – the stars, the lifestyle, the clothes, the shows, I loved all of that. It was bright lights, big city all the way for me. Unfortunately, the very act of gambling in Vegas was also becoming a bust for me, because I usually left all my money at the casinos when I left town.

I was high rolling back and forth from Seattle to Vegas when I slowly started to realize that the term "VIP" in the casinos is just a code word for "Major Loser." I was a VIP at the Mirage only because I gave them so much of my money. When Steve Wynn built The Bellagio, I had access to anything I wanted, any time I wanted, because I was part of the high roller clique with the big boys. Las Vegas has the best customer service in the world, because only in Vegas can they take all your money and still leave you feeling like you're the biggest winner in the world. It felt great to be there in the middle of all the action, but in reality, the casinos got all my money and all I got was their great service. The good people at the Mirage always hooked me up with anything I needed. I was losing my ass, but they made me feel great about it! Pretty soon the losses started taking a toll. It was just like my drug addiction years earlier, only now my high was gambling.

I was hitting it big selling real estate in Seattle, and my Sales agent, Bobby, was shadowing me everywhere. Bobby's father, Bob Sr., was a world-renowned, Fortune 500 success trainer. Bob Sr. was one of the best educators, teachers, and motivational speakers in the world. Bobby had grown up with a silver spoon in his mouth, and had traveled all over the world with his father. Sometimes when we were working together, Bobby and I would jump on a plane and fly off to Vegas without telling anyone where we were or what we were doing. I remember one time, we had a penthouse suite at the MGM. We took a private elevator up to our private floor, and when we walked in, Bobby said, "Oh my God! This is the baddest room I've ever seen!" We had our own Jacuzzi baths, separate masters, an elevator in the room, and an incredible view of the city.

We were caught up in the high-life trap. Bobby and I went

to all the big championship fights in Vegas, including the Tyson-Holyfield bout. I got all swept up in the excitement of being a VIP (aka, Major Loser) even though it kept hitting me upside the head. $10,000 bets were nothing to me back then...until I kept losing. My Vegas party train came to a screeching halt when it occurred to me what was happening to me. My youngest son, Caleb, was 5 or 6 years old and attending a private Christian school. One day, his assignment at school was to make a journal about his life, his hobbies, his family, his favorite places, etc. I came home from work that day and Sheri said, "Why don't you go ask your son about his day in school today. He got to stand up in front of all the students in the auditorium and talk about his life." I said, "Great!" I asked Caleb how it went, and he said, "Oh, it was awesome, Dad! They asked me about my favorite places to travel, and I told everyone I liked to go to Las Vegas!" My heart dropped. My youngest son told everyone at our private Christian school that his favorite place was not Disneyland, not Magic Mountain, not Universal Studios; no, he told them his favorite place was the MGM Grand Hotel in Las Vegas.

I had been going to Vegas for so long, and so many times, that it didn't even register to me that the whole situation was completely out of control. Finally, Sheri said to me, "Honey, I can't do this anymore. It's your thing, so you go on ahead. But I'm not going anymore." Later, when I was still taking quick trips to Vegas with my buddy Keith, Sheri would make a giant "L" shape with her arms and start singing "Loser, Loooser, Loooooser!" One night I flew down to Vegas by myself because I had an irresistible urge to shoot some dice. I got to the Mirage, and asked my host if anything special was going on that night. He said, "Well, Siegfried and Roy are having a big party for Roy's 50th birthday, but it's private – strictly invitation only." I searched around for a while, and finally found a brother who was an entertainer, who happened to know where the party was. Sure enough, just as I had done when I was a little kid sneaking in to the Rams games at the Coliseum, I worked my way into the party.

Once there, I found myself socializing with the likes of Steven Spielberg, Robin Williams, Joe Pesci, and Robert DeNiro. Later on, Joe, Robin, and I returned to the Casino while Robert left to go up to his room. I was in my element, as always, hanging with the high-rolling crowd. Little did I know it then, but some of the people closest to me had other ideas about my gambling problem. Sheri had always let me run free, because she loved me unconditionally and trusted me after I'd put together so many years of sobriety. Now however, she knew she had to take control, because I was so out of control.

One day, my longtime close friend and sponsor, Harold, called to tell me about a tremendous real estate opportunity he had just learned about, and that he thought I might benefit from. It involved a beautiful high-end home up on Queen Anne Hill in Seattle that was For Sale by Owner. Harold said he had it all set up for me to go there with him, meet the owner and likely come away with a very nice, expensive listing. I specialized in listing and selling high-end properties, so of course I said yes right away. We drove to the Queen Anne area, and Harold led me to a beautiful home on the hill. Harold and I walked up to the front door, Harold knocked and we walked right in. Once we got inside, I realized I had been set up.

In addition to Harold, there was Sheri, Bobby's dad, Bob Sr., and a counselor from a gambling rehabilitation center. My loving wife Sheri had quietly conspired with two of the men I most admired and respected – Harold and Bob Sr. - to stage an intervention on me because of my gambling addiction. The counselor was slightly shocked when I immediately copped to my destructive habit. I said,

"You got me. I can't even pretend I don't have a gambling problem, because I know I do." The counselor replied, "Oh, you're good. You're very smooth. You're using a little reverse psychology to try to take the wind out of your intervention. Unfortunately for you, the hard part is yet to come. Your wife and your friends here love you very much and they care for you. They want to help you - but you need to change."

We discussed treatment options for my gambling addiction. The most popular idea put forth by the counselor involved me going into a treatment center for a complete 28-day resident program. I knew I was sick and that I needed help. But the timing of that particular program couldn't have been any worse. Sheri and I had just returned from our family's annual 30-day vacation in Maui. I hadn't even been home to do any real estate business for an entire month, but I did have about $250,000 worth of commissions pending in escrow. I had a gambling marker for about $50,000 that needed to be paid, plus another $150,000-175,000 of general expenses from my marketing, vacation costs, and household expenses. I told the group that, and showed Harold in particular, how I couldn't afford to go away for another 28 straight days. Harold looked everything over, and agreed, saying, "Greg, you're right – you're damned if you do and damned if you don't." I made a vow then and there to Sheri, Harold, and Bob Sr. that I would change my life and stop my gambling.

I left Las Vegas in the rearview mirror after that, and started attending Gambler's Anonymous meetings. Those GA meetings helped me so much because I could be honest and open and bare my soul to the other attendees. My dad had always taught me that the truth would set me free. I confessed my gambling problem, and released the burden of my guilt. Every 12-Step program I had ever participated in had helped me change my life for the better, and

GA was no different. Before long, I was a recovering gambler, not an active gambler. I still thank God my beautiful wife Sheri had the compassion and the vision to do that intervention on me. My friends Harold and Bob Sr. stepped up for me at a time when I most needed their help. My gambling addiction was so sick that I was blinded to just how bad my disease had become. As had been the case so many times in my life, my wheeling and dealing had gotten me in trouble. With my gambling in check, however, I felt a desire to do something new and give back in a big way.

CHAPTER 35

LAWS OF THE UNIVERSE

AS I CAME through recovery, and I continued to develop spiritually, mentally, and emotionally, I realized how life really works. I discovered there are what's known as the Laws of the Universe. It doesn't matter what you believe, because the Laws keep right on working the same regardless of whether you acknowledge their truth. Here's how the Laws of the Universe work: whatever you dish out, you will receive, because life is like a boomerang of cause and effect. If you give love, you will receive love. If you lie, you will be lied to. If you cheat, you will be cheated. If you steal, you will be stolen from. That's how life really works. Everything you do comes back to you. So if you want to be successful, help someone else be successful. If you want to do great things, do great things for others. That way, all the blessings you give out will come back to you.

Now, I use the Laws of the Universe to my advantage. I bless my enemies, so if anyone tries to come against me, or tries to hurt me, love is all I have to offer them because there is no defense against love. My mom taught me that from the very beginning. She proved that to me time and time again, and I've used it. You know what? It really works! There is no defense against love. All you have to do is love someone, and that love heals them; mind, body spirit and soul. I've used that principle so many times in my life, whenever I've found myself in a hostile situation. I don't give my power away to others. I just turn everything into a positive and give love. People can't even comprehend that. Another important thing I've used every single day is the power of prayer. I honestly believe that if people only knew how much power there is in prayer, they'd be on their knees, praying all the time.

Ever since I was a young boy, my all-time favorite movie has been The Ten Commandments with Charlton Heston. That movie spoke to me as a kid, because I saw the power of God work through Moses. I saw Moses do incredible things that no one else could do. Even Moses himself said to God, "Who am I, God, to do these things?" That is still my favorite movie, and I know it from start to finish. God parted the Red Sea, and even as a kid, it made me realize that all things are possible through God.

Me and my family, living the dream and traveling the world.

CHAPTER 36

STARTING LIFE OVER EVERY DAY

I START MY life over each day when I wake up. The first thing I do every morning when I get up is say to myself, "Thank you Lord, for this beautiful day, for the beautiful sunrise and sunset, for the clouds, the wind, the rain, the fresh air, the green grass, the birds, the bees, the flowers, the trees, the mountains, the valleys, the oceans, the streams, the lakes, the rivers, the people, the places, all the wonderful things, the night, the moon, the stars, the heavens, the earth, the whole universe, everything that flies in the air, swims in the ocean, and crawls on the land. God Bless this beautiful day."

Here's another thing I say in my quiet time, because I learned that my character defects are what held me back my whole life. I say, "God, I am ready for you to remove all these defects from my character, and from my thought processes. I humbly ask you to remove all these defects from my flesh. I cast every one of these burdens on you, in the name of Jesus Christ, and I go free. I let go, and I let God have the lust, temptation, anger, bitterness, resentment, greed, envy, jealousy, sloth, laziness, gluttony, fear, doubt, worry, pride, procrastination, self-pity, impatience, lying, controlling, manipulation, exaggeration, big-ism, ego-tism, deceit, false motives, scheming, scamming, selfishness, using others, any thoughts of lack, limitation, negative thinking, false beliefs, gambling, self-justification, all of it. I give it all back to God."

Those were my character defects, the things that I used to act out and live by, and I used to think that was who I really was. But after I removed all the drugs and alcohol from my life, after I did some soul-searching, after I got honest with myself, I could see that was not who I really was. All of that came out of being in recovery and getting sober.

I've always said that the 12-Step Program is really just God working undercover. The reason I say that is because, through the 12-Step Program, God has taken all of these wonderful misfits, like myself, and turned us all into a blessing in disguise. I know I'm not the only living miracle out there. That's my interpretation of how God works through the Program. For me, it's been a combination of church, the Bible, my mother's unconditional love plus her spiritual teachings, combined with the 12-Step Program. I always believed in God, and I always prayed when I was younger. Plus my mom brainwashed me when I was a little kid, so when you put it all together, you can see I always had faith.

My Lifestyles of Success billboard.

CHAPTER 37

CREATING LIFESTYLES OF SUCCESS

I STARTED MY real estate career by stepping out on faith. I quit my job as an electrician, which was by most people's standards, a perfectly good job. Then I came home and I told Sheri, "I'm gonna be a superstar real estate agent." Shortly thereafter, I convinced Sheri to quit her job, which was also a perfectly good job. Everyone in my life thought I was crazy. When I didn't make a dime for the first nine months of my real estate career, everyone told me I needed to face reality and go get my old job back. Despite that adversity, I kept going in the direction of my dreams. I stepped out on faith in the beginning, and I never lost faith.

At the same time, I was going strong in my sobriety program. I was constantly giving back and helping others. I was changing my life for the better, I had balance in my life, and through it all, God was blessing my socks off. After one year on the job, I was rocking and rolling in real estate. I became the top agent in my office, then in my county, then in my entire company. I achieved the Top 1%

designation year after year after year. Everything I touched in real estate turned to gold. I had the background of being successful in organized crime, but to be honest, business is business. I knew how to handle my business – period. In organized crime, there is no slipping up. If you slip up in organized crime, you're dead. You have to be sharp as a tack, 24/7. I had to be on top of my game all the time, because there was no margin for error in the streets, and I was not going to be a statistic like so many others I had known.

Once I made it big in real estate, I realized how blessed I really was. I had sobriety, I had total balance in my life, God had blessed me mind, body, spirit, and soul. I had a perfect family life, a perfect work life, I was having fun, and I was making an impact in so many ways. When I reflected on what we had accomplished in real estate, I realized I was setting trends with my success. I had become a self-made millionaire, almost overnight, and my marketing was taking me places no agent had been before. By the time I reached my fifth year in my real estate career, I had reached about 10 years of sobriety. My men's group was still going strong, and I remember thinking, "If only there was a way I could somehow package everything I've learned in my life, and use it to help even more people."

Then God touched my heart, and He showed me how He had changed me. It was like God had done something to me on the inside, so that when I was helping someone out of love, with no expectation of return, I could open my mouth and His wisdom just came out of me. It wasn't me, so I can't take credit for it. I always said, if you leave it up to Greg, I'll run this train right off the tracks. But when I let the spirit of God guide me, then miracles just happened like it was nothing. God showed me that my gift in life was helping others. I had been down so many different roads in my life, and I learned so many lessons the hard way. I was the guy who always had to crash and burn in order to learn anything. But every time I crashed and burned, God resurrected me and brought me back bigger and better than ever. God pulled me out of the pits of hell so many times, that it made my faith invincible.

I believe anything is possible because I've seen it and lived it in my own life, over and over again. God showed me that the reason He gave me these gifts is to change the world and make a difference by helping others. Everything I've accomplished, any good I've ever done, was by the grace of God, not the grace of Greg. I realized the feeling I got inside when I helped someone out of love was better than closing the biggest deal, better than all the money, houses, cars, clothes, and all the other trappings of success. Helping others was better than making a million dollars, better than buying a new Mercedes, and better than traveling around the world. God showed me that giving back and helping others is why I'm here.

As I grew in my sobriety and dedicated myself to helping others, God blessed me with the gifts of insight and wisdom. Someone could come up to me and ask me anything about life, or about a problem they were having, and when I opened my mouth, the right answer would just pour out of me. I didn't even have to think about it, or analyze it, or anything. God's wisdom was just there, inside me, waiting to come out at the perfect time, and in the perfect way. I just needed to get Greg out of the way. Sometimes, I would hear the words coming out of my mouth, and it was like I was outside my own body, standing there listening and learning right along with whomever I was talking with. That's how I knew it wasn't me, because it wasn't even a conscious thing at all.

Once I recognized that, I was praying about it all the time, asking God to please show me what He wanted me to do. Eventually, God put it on my heart that it was time for me to step out on faith, once again, and start the Lifestyles of Success Institute. My mission from the beginning of Lifestyles was that I was going to change this world and make a difference. I was already so dialed in from a marketing perspective that I could've had my own business just doing that for people. But God had bigger things in mind for me. I already had all the connections, and all the resources already lined up, from everything I had been doing in real estate over the past five years.

So in 1999, I set my goal to create the Lifestyles of Success Institute. My goal was to be the #1 success trainer worldwide. Just as when I set my goal to be a superstar real estate agent, I wasn't afraid to dream big. I wasn't going to set a modest goal and hope I could maybe help one or two people in my own backyard. No, I wanted to teach everyone I could possibly reach how to live the Lifestyles of Success. My life was a complete success despite the fact that I had come out of the pits of hell. Nothing I had ever learned came from a book – it was all from my own life and the highs and lows I had experienced throughout my life. I had learned everything the hard way, but I knew I could teach others how to avoid the pitfalls I had experienced in my life. I was a living miracle, and I wanted to share that information, and inspire others to change their lives for the better. As always, I had total faith, and I knew that with God, all things are possible. I asked God to guide me with His divine wisdom, and then Phyllis and I laid out a blueprint for success.

I started doing my research in the field of success training, as it existed at that time, by going to some motivational seminars. I went to see Anthony Robbins, who was widely considered to be the #1 motivational speaker in the world at the time. I analyzed and modeled all the top people in the field of motivation and success, but I was determined that I would be second to none, just like in my real estate business. If I was going to follow through and do this at all, I was going for the gold.

Anthony Robbins figured to be my main competition, but I knew from attending his seminars that I could do my own thing at least as well as he was doing. The truth is, I had lived this stuff, from the time I was a little kid in South Central. My ideas and my teachings weren't some vague concepts I learned in a book or heard at a seminar. They were actual life experiences I had lived through. My teachings were based on the hard lessons I had learned throughout my life. It was all real, I didn't need to sugarcoat anything or dramatize it to make a point. That's the power of the whole Lifestyles program – it was real wisdom from real life.

When Phyllis and I went to see Anthony Robbins, I studied his show very intently. When we walked out of there, Phyllis and I just looked at each other and I said, "God bless him, because he's doing his thing. But Tony's got nothing on me." Part of my success in real estate came from the fact that I had great people like Phyllis helping me. Here was this very mature, professional, polished woman, who was an expert in real estate, and she was my personal assistant in every aspect of my life. That was what I had beside me, to help me, and I knew there was no way I could go wrong. When it came time to do Lifestyles, Phyllis and I just laid it all out and approached it just like we had for all those years in real estate.

Next, I hired a director and a producer, and we started filming my life story. I had a script, and everything else I needed. I contacted Guthy-Renker, the company that produced all of Anthony Robbins' work. I told them what I was planning to do, but they said, "Greg, we already have Tony Robbins. We can't bring in someone who's doing a similar thing. That would create a conflict of interest for us." After that, I decided to just set it all up myself. I knew I could take everything I had done in real estate, plug it into Lifestyles, and go from there. I had already cherry-picked the best of the best in my real estate marketing. I had Phyllis to run everything behind the scenes, I had all the media outlets I needed, the relationships, the crews, the whole works. All I really needed was the actual material itself, and that was already within me. I put everything together, edited the audio and video, and then I called Rick Cesari.

Rick Cesari was known as the infomercial king. Rick's company had produced the infomercial for the George Foreman Grill, which had made over $250 million. In later years, Rick produced the infomercial for the Juiceman Juicer. Rick's company offers a complete end-to-end solution: they do the script, the production, the packaging, the marketing, the infomercial, the shipping – the whole works. The only catch is, Rick's team commands an upfront fee of $250,000 to take over and complete a project. I had everything done first class, before calling Rick; all I needed was his help getting it off the ground. My marketing was already cruising at high altitude, as I had my real estate TV commercials playing on Monday Night Football, the NBA Playoffs, and other prominent programs.

Phyllis and I had turned my real estate business into a total marketing machine. I had grown my business from nothing, starting out at the bottom, before climbing all the way to the top echelon of the real estate industry. By the time I got around to starting Lifestyles of Success, I had spent millions of dollars marketing myself. When it came to Lifestyles, I pushed in all my chips. First I created the 12 Steps To Being Healthy, Wealthy, and Successful In Every Aspect of Life. Then I followed that up with the How To Change Your Life series. Then I created the 45-minute video for Lifestyles, and all the accompanying CD's and tapes.

I called Rick and invited him to come out to my office to see what I had put together. I planned to hire Rick's company to handle the whole thing for me. I figured they could start by simultaneously dropping my infomercial into certain select markets such as Seattle, New York, and Los Angeles. When we met with Rick and his team, Phyllis and I had everything set up to show them our program, and all the products we had created. When I finished my presentation, Rick looked at everything we had done and said, "What exactly do you want us to do for you?" I said, "We want you guys to take this program and test it out. Drop it in certain markets, and see how it does." Rick said, "Greg, to be honest, you've already done everything we would normally do for our clients, There's nothing left for us to do. Not only that, we couldn't improve on what you've done if we tried, because this is all first-class stuff. You've got it all dialed in. I'd love to tell you that you should give us your money, but I can't lie. You don't even need us." Rick and his crew walked out of that meeting in a state of shock, because I don't think they had ever seen a client that was so well prepared for success. They were the top infomercial production house in America, and they told me I didn't even need them.

After that meeting with Rick, I called up some of the local TV advertising executives who had helped me with my real estate ads, and they said they would gladly help me with the Lifestyles campaign. They agreed to drop my ads in to the late-night TV market in Seattle. We tested the 30-minute infomercial for about six months. Later on, we learned that we were up for an award at the 2000 Emerald City Awards, which was an annual event hosted by the Seattle chapter of the International Television Association. The ITA honors excellence in video, film, digital and new media production. My infomercial was one of 181 entries submitted to the ITA, and in a huge upset, the Lifestyles of Success Marketing Video won the ECA Gold Award and took home top honors. Everyone knew me as a real estate agent, but there I was winning an award like I was already a famous motivational speaker. God validated everything I believed in that night. As I went up onstage to pick up the award, I could see some people in the audience looking at each other as if to say, "Who is Greg Perry, and what the heck just happened?" It had been less than one year since Phyllis and I began working on the Lifestyles of Success project, and we had already won an award! When that happened, I knew we were ready to take off and fly.

We calculated that it would cost about $4 million to do a nationwide simultaneous launch of the Lifestyles infomercial in all the major media markets. My goal was simple: to become the most successful motivational speaker in the United States within 12 months. I already knew from my experience with real estate marketing that the best way to establish myself as a household name was to blanket a market with TV commercials, cinema screen ads, billboards, and mall ads. That way, people would see me everywhere they went, and eventually everyone would know me. We planned to start the campaign in the following markets: Seattle, San Francisco, Los Angeles, San Diego, Phoenix, Denver, Las Vegas, Dallas, Houston, Atlanta, Miami, Chicago, Detroit, Boston, New York, Philadelphia, and Washington, D.C. Once the momentum started rolling in the larger markets, the rest of the country would fall in behind, and I'd be on my way.

CHAPTER 38

PRINCIPLES OF LIFESTYLES OF SUCCESS

THE ACTUAL CONTENT in my Lifestyles of Success system was based on the experiences I had in changing my life through my sobriety. When I got deeper into the various 12-Step programs, I realized the programs were really just God's way of working undercover. I observed the people coming into the programs, and saw that, like me, their personal scorecards were reading double-zeroes. Some of those people didn't have a pot to piss in when they first walked in the door, but then I watched as God transformed their lives and healed them just like He did me. Men, women, and sometimes even young kids, had their whole lives changed by the principles and the steps in the 12-Step programs. I always thought it was a shame that the general public, normal everyday people, didn't have access to the programs, because you couldn't get in the program if you didn't have some sort of alcohol, drug, or gambling addiction.

My experience in the 12-Step programs taught me that, once

you get past Step 1, Steps 2-12 had nothing to do with drugs, alcohol, or addiction – it was really a spiritual program disguised as an addiction program. I suspected that if everyone out there in the regular world could get ahold of these principles, even people who didn't have an addiction could change their lives for the better. Unfortunately, the only way to get the wisdom of the program was if your ass was on fire and you had run out of answers on your own. Just like me, you had to have burned every bridge in the book, and exhausted every other option before you could get in to the program. Pain was the price of admission. I saw that as clear as day, and I recognized an opportunity to bring some of the concepts that had proven so valuable in my life back to the regular world.

In the early stages of Lifestyles of Success, the 12-Step program served as the basic outline, and the inspiration, for my teachings. I had radically transformed my life through sobriety, and I knew the principles were universal – you could use them for implementing all kinds of positive changes in your life. I tell people all the time, you don't have to believe in God or believe in the Devil. All I know is, I used to work for the Devil and now I work for God. I'm still the same person, but my life flipped completely from one side to the other. The reality of each side is crystal clear to me, because I've lived both sides. The transition from one to the other happened as I worked my way through the 12-Step programs and learned to utilize those principles. The principles of the 12-Step programs are actually guidelines for total life success, regardless of whether a person is trying to overcome an addiction.

The only problem is, the 12-Step programs are all called Anonymous for a reason – because what is said there, and what is heard there, stays there. We don't publicize what goes on in the meetings. That's how we create a safe environment for everyone to come clean about their problems. The spiritual aspect of the program is downplayed, because the last thing that anybody who comes to the meetings wants to hear about is some religious stuff. That would only send the people who most need the help running in the opposite direction. Besides, you can go to church if that's all you want or need. No, the real hidden beauty of the 12-Step principles is that they come from a spiritual place, and they're non-denominational. Nobody tells you to believe in this or that; it's about acknowledging a higher power and tapping into that power to change your life.

In a way, the various 12-Step programs are about people helping each other. But underneath the fellowship is the spiritual aspect. By the time you get done working the steps, and making your way through the program, you realize you've had a spiritual awakening. That was my inspiration for Lifestyles, but of course I couldn't just take the 12-Step program and copy it. So I tailored the essence of the principles, and combined them with my own life lessons; everything from running the streets as a kid to becoming a self-made millionaire in real estate as an adult. My whole life is a living, breathing miracle. Thanks to the 12-Step programs, I am now a sober child of God. The programs gave me a fresh start in life and allowed me to see the totality of my life experiences in a more profound way. Sobriety allowed me to start my life over at 25, but it really took me until I was 28 for it to sink in. Once I put it all together, I felt like a new man, and the man I am today – a living miracle. I was compelled to share my life lessons with the world in a format that would benefit others.

The first training program I created was called Lifestyles of Success. I had already learned about "The Power of 12," so I used that theme in my personal success program. Here is a summary of the 12 principles or concepts contained in my Lifestyles of Success program:

1. The Game of Life: In the first section, I teach people how to play the Game of Life, starting with the rules to the game. I used to always break the rules, so I was intimately aware of what happens when you're either ignorant of the rules, or you choose to not follow them. Once I learned to play by the rules in my own life, I could use them to my advantage. In this section, I teach people what not to do, and how to avoid going down the same dead-end streets I went down. In order to be successful at the highest levels, you need to understand that life is a straight and narrow path, and everything else is either a detour or a dead end.

2. Setting Goals: In the second section, I teach people about a powerful principle I learned in real estate. I constantly lay out my goals, in every area of my life. I have spiritual goals, family goals, personal goals, health goals, sobriety goals, financial goals, business goals, and life goals. Goals are the blueprint for building your life, just like when a construction crew builds a building. When a construction crew comes to work every day, they review the blueprints for the project they're working on. They keep doing that, over and over again, until eventually there's a completed building standing there. Just as a construction crew can't build anything without blueprints, we can't build the life we want without goals. If the crew showed up every day and said, "Let's just wing it today and see what happens," all they'd have to show for their efforts would be a useless pile of building materials. Nothing would get done, and the whole process would be a waste of time.

3. Prime Time: In the third section, I teach people that everyone has a peak time of the day, when they feel their best and are sharper and more focused than at other times of the day.

For some, it's the morning, for another the afternoon, for others it might be the evening. I'm a morning person. I get up early every day, and that's when my mind is the clearest and sharpest. I know my mind is crystal clear and focused first thing in the morning, so that's when I pray, and I read, to get my daily inspiration and sense of direction for the day ahead. That's also when I review all my goals and set my new goals. For someone else, their time might be the afternoon or evening, and that's fine. It doesn't matter which time works best for you. The important thing is to identify your time, and then set some of it aside to work on yourself.

4. Plan of Action: In the fourth section, I teach people how to make a plan of action based on the goals they already created in section #2. You have to have a plan. Once you're in your prime-time state of mind, that's when you write your daily to-do list for whatever is in front of you that day. When I had a team of people working for me in my real estate business, we had a meeting every single morning to go over our plan of action for the day. We'd review our to-do list from the previous day, to see what needed to be brought forward, and then we'd make a new list. This daily practice allows you to stay on track and maintain a consistent focus toward completion of your goals.

5. Taking Action: In the fifth section, I teach people how to follow through and actually get things done. This is where you do the things you need to do in order to get the results you want in your life. You already set your goals, you got into a peak state of mind, you made a plan – now it's time to get busy and handle your business. The to-do list you created in section #4 is crucial here because it empowers you; as you complete each task and check off the things on

your list, you get a real sense of accomplishment. You start to feel good about yourself, and it makes you want to keep your momentum going through to the end.

6. Laws of the Universe: In the sixth section, I teach people about the true nature of life. It doesn't matter whether you believe in the Laws of the Universe, because your belief isn't the point. The Laws of the Universe are constant, regardless of whether you like them or whether you agree with them. These aren't Greg Perry's laws; these are Life's laws. You need to know what they are, and how you can live your life accordingly so your thoughts, your feelings, and your actions are in proper alignment with the Laws. That's how you get on the right side of life and make things happen the way they're supposed to happen for the greatest good. One example of a Law of the Universe is, you reap what you sow. The Laws of the Universe are universal truths that I learned the hard way, from violating all of them in my own life.

7. Character Defects: In the seventh section, I teach people about the darker elements in our minds that hold us back and keep us from achieving our greatest potential. These are the personal shortcomings that sabotage our success. Here are some examples of character defects: lust, greed, anger, bitterness, resentment, envy, jealousy, laziness, gluttony, fear, doubt, worry, pride, pessimism, procrastination, self-pity, impatience, lying, controlling, cheating, manipulating, exaggeration, egotism, deceit, false motives, scheming, using others, selfishness, inferiority, thoughts of lack or limitation, negativity, and false beliefs. I teach people how to take a good, long, hard look at themselves and identify their inner negative characteristics, and then for each defect, to affirm the positive counterparts. You have to do everything you can

to root out and remove these influences from your life so you can thrive and be at your best.

8. Power of Prayer: In the eight section, I teach people about the power of prayer, and how to use it to transform their lives. I use prayer every single day in my own life, and it has made all the difference in my life. I know beyond any shadow of a doubt that it works. I pray constantly throughout the day, quietly to myself. Prayer deepens my connection to God in every moment, and allows His blessings to flow to me and through me. Prayer is an essential part of a healthy life, and it has played an enormous role in my success. It doesn't matter whether you're a Christian, or what religion you might be. Everyone can pray in their own way. The important thing is, to do it - to establish the connection with God, and talk with God about your life. Ask God for divine wisdom, guidance, love, and healing, and watch it change your life.

9. Belief System and Faith: In the ninth section, I teach people the importance of having a belief system and faith in a higher power. The Bible says, "All things are done unto a man as he believes." I know from my own life that's true. Your beliefs and your faith are what sustains you in hard times, and what helps you stay humble in the good times. The image I always draw on, and reflect on, is that of Moses parting the Red Sea. This section teaches people how to harness the power of their positive beliefs and their faith, and how to use them to their greatest advantage.

10. Relationships and Trust: In the tenth section, I teach people the importance of building trust in all their relationships. Even in my real estate business I've always said that we don't sell houses or property, we sell trust. If someone trusts you, you have a client for life. But if they don't trust you,

then it doesn't matter how slick or smooth you are, or what sales techniques you try to use – no trust means no sale, period. When someone has an excuse or a reason why they don't want to do business with you, 99% of the time, the translation is, "I don't trust you." One of the strongest personal connections I've ever had in my life has been with Mr. Li, a Chinese man who doesn't speak a word of English. By the way, I don't speak a word of Chinese, either. Mr. Li and I have to use a translator to communicate, and yet, we're connected at the heart. It's because we trust each other. Somehow, some way, Mr. Li and I built our rapport and our relationship on trust despite our communication gap. I told Mr. Li my life story, and he told me his life story, through the translator, and we became best friends. Mr. Li and I travelled the world together, and strategized in business and success, all based on a mutual trust. The universal language is love, not English or Chinese. When you can look into a person's eyes, and see their heart and soul, you can connect in love. Once you establish trust, the rest is easy.

11. The Power of Words: In the eleventh section, I teach people all about the importance of self-talk, and the words and thoughts you use to fill up your mind. It's a matter of what goes into your brain, in terms of what you say to yourself, and what comes out of your mouth, in terms of what you say to others. My mom taught me the Prayer of Protection, which I refer to several times in this book. It starts from the moment you wake up in the morning, with what you say to yourself and the world. When I wake up in the morning, I say, "Oh what a beautiful morning, oh what a beautiful day. I've got a beautiful feeling, everything's going my way." When you use positive words, loving words, kind words, you

create a positive reality. My mantra is, count your blessings. Be forgiving of yourself and others. Be kind to yourself, and to others. Be mindful of the words you use internally in your mind, and the words that come out of your mouth. Don't use negative words, or demeaning words, to yourself or to others.

12. Balance: In the twelfth section, I teach people about keeping everything in its proper place, and in its proper perspective. When life goes up, and things are great, you keep your balance and stay right in the middle. When life goes down, as it will from time to time, you keep your balance and stay right in the middle. You never get too high, and you never get too low. When you can keep yourself running on a nice even keel, it's so much easier to walk that straight and narrow path. People tend to start getting in trouble when they get too high or too low. No matter what happens in your life, you just stay humble, stay positive, and in balance, knowing that God is always working the highest good in your life. It's not about how things might look on the outside - it's all about staying balanced on the inside.

The amazing thing about the principles contained in the Lifestyles of Success program is that they are timeless - there is no expiration date on any of these concepts. They were the same yesterday as they are today and as they will be tomorrow. That's because the principles are universal. Best of all, they really work. The principles contained in the Lifestyles of Success program are so powerful that, when Mr. Li, a Chinese billionaire and success phenomenon in his own right, heard them, he asked me to be his personal success trainer and mentor his entire organization of millions of sales associates. My life as a living miracle is the ultimate testament of the effectiveness of these principles. I've used these teachings to not only turn my life around, once upon a time, but to maintain the life of my dreams on a daily basis.

I poured every experience of my life into the creation and development of these principles. The good, the bad, and the ugly – it's all there, in living color. The Lifestyles of Success program is the result of everything I've done right, everything I've done wrong, and everything I've learned in my 55 years of life. Not only that, it was all spontaneous - none of it was scripted. I prayed to God, and asked for divine guidance and wisdom. Then I opened my heart, my soul, and my life, and it all poured out of me. I created Lifestyles and offered it up to the world because I wanted others to know what I know and to live as I've lived. I wanted everyone to see that they too are a living miracle.

CHAPTER 39

REACHING OUT AND GIVING BACK

SOME OF THE most deeply rewarding experiences I've ever had were the direct positive result of my sobriety. I was committed to giving back whenever and wherever possible, and I embraced every opportunity to share some valuable life lessons and personal success principles. The whole purpose behind creating my Lifestyles of Success training program in the first place was because I wanted to make an impact and help as many people as possible change their lives for the better. My life had prepared me to be a mentor, and a high-profile success trainer. I started reaching out to schools, community groups, and various law enforcement agencies.

For the longest time, I had tried to get access to the Monroe State Penitentiary, which is about an hour northeast of Seattle. I knew my life story would inspire the inmates and help them make the best of their bad situation. My plan was to take my Lifestyles of Success film crew inside with me, film my presentation to the inmates, and then use that footage in a new program about how to turn your life around. The prison authorities quickly shot down that idea. Eventually, however, they agreed to let me come in and speak to the inmates, minus the TV crew.

I passed through four or five separate security checkpoints, where the prison guards searched me, before reaching my destination. The prison officials led me to a small classroom filled with rows of old chairs and a wooden podium. There were about 40 inmates with me in the room, and they were all brothers from the 'hood. There were no bodyguards or security guards in there to protect me. A normal man probably would've been scared to death, but to me, these were just my fellas. I'd rolled through the streets of South Central L.A. with guys just like them more than 20 years earlier. Before I started speaking, I went around the room and introduced myself to all of the inmates. I looked each man in the eye, shook his hand, and asked what crime they were in for. "Armed Robbery," said one. "Murder," said another. "Double Homicide," said a third. None of their answers even phased me, because I had grown up around gangsters and hard criminals. I knew how that life was. As a result, I felt at ease when I started speaking.

I told the inmates, "First of all, you need to know this: this was my idea to come here and speak with you fellas. Nobody invited me, nobody told me what to say, nobody paid me, and I had to practically beg the prison officials to let me in here. I'm here for one reason: because I want to give back. The truth of the matter is, the only difference between you and me is, you got caught and I didn't. That's all it is. It very easily could've been me in here listening to one of you come in and speak. It would've been me if I hadn't turned my life around."

The inmates just sat silently, listening to me talk. I wanted to reach them on their level, so I said, "Let me tell you how crazy and sick this world is. First, don't ever let anyone tell you that you're a criminal or a murderer. Don't let anyone tell you they're going to give you life, because no one can give you life. This life doesn't go on forever. I've got news for you: none of us are making it out of here alive. Second, if you kill someone on the outside, they throw you in here and call you a murderer. But if the same government starts a war, and they send you over to some country and you kill enough people, they give you a freaking medal and they call you a hero. The last time I checked, a life is a life and a death is a death. This whole world is screwed up."

I paused for a moment, and it felt like an eternity. The whole scene seemed surreal. It was quiet and perfectly still. I wondered if I was having some kind of an out-of-body experience. I felt so detached, as if I were observing myself from a higher perspective. I hadn't prepared a specific talk. I just stood there and the words flowed out of me. In those moments, it felt like God was using me to convey an important message to those inmates. At the same time, I noticed that the demeanor of the inmates had changed. The same guys who had given me the death stare when I first came in the room were now nodding their heads, and punctuating my sentences with the occasional "Amen" and "I hear that!" One inmate spoke up and said, "Man, we needed someone to come in here and talk to us like this. Someone to talk to us like men, and speak to us from the heart."

But one of the guys sitting off to the side was very slow to respond to me. He just glared at me the whole time I was talking. I found out later from another inmate that this guy's mission in life was to compile the ultimate gang anthology. Apparently, he was an expert on gangs. He knew all the sets; who they were, what era, what city, all of it. When I paused for a sip of water, he said, "So Bono, what's up? What set you from, man?" He thought he was going to expose me in front of all the fellas. I said, "I'm original OG, from the Shotgun Crips." I listed all the places we went back in the day, where we used to hang out, and how I got shot in front of the State Theater.

Suddenly, the inmate jumped out of his chair, pointed at me, and shouted, "Homeboy's straight legit! He's legit! He knows what he's talkin' about!" The most ironic part of that experience was, although it took the inmates a while to warm up to me, I felt right at home being there with them. They were no different than the guys I had run with 20+ years earlier. Their lives just took a turn for the worse that I somehow missed. When I finished speaking, I could see the obvious change in the body language of the inmates. When I came in the room, the inmates looked like vicious lions and tigers. But by the time I left, they were as tame as kittens. Everything had completely shifted, for everyone present. I walked out of there feeling spiritually refreshed, because I knew God had used me and worked through me to touch those inmates' lives. I helped them and they helped me. The prison officials thanked me and told me I could come back anytime, and that it was okay to bring my film crew next time. By then, I had realized that it wasn't about publicity, or in any way making light of the terrible environment those inmates lived in. It was about doing the right thing, giving back, and mentoring those guys. If I helped just one single inmate gain an ounce of wisdom or insight, my time was well spent.

Another time, I visited the Juvenile Detention Center in Seattle, to talk to the young kids in there. I was talking to the group, and there was one problem child who was resisting everything I said. He kept interrupting me and calling me out and cursing me, saying, "You ain't s---," and, "Why are you comin' in here talking s--- to us like you're somebody." I finally stopped and said, "Oh, okay. Now I see. Now I know why I had to come here today. It's all because of you. You know why?" The kid shot me a dirty look and shook his head. I said, "Because you're me. I was just like you. Nobody could tell me anything. I had all the answers. I came here for you, because you're me when I was your age." By the time I left the Detention Center a short time later, that kid was my best ally. He broke down and thanked me for coming and for recognizing him. Just as in the prison in Monroe, I sensed that what I was doing was important and valuable in ways I couldn't fully comprehend.

Whether it was talking to kids in school, or mentoring the teenagers in Juvenile Detention, or talking about the realities of gang life with prison inmates, I knew that God was there opening every door for me and that nothing was happening by accident. I knew I was right where I was supposed to be, every time, with God guiding me every step of the way. God always works the highest good in our lives, even if we're not consciously aware of it. He was using me to touch those people, to offer them some faith and some hope, and no one benefitted from those talks more than I did. I saw firsthand the power in my message. I didn't even bother preparing a talk when I went on those engagements. First I prayed for guidance, to let me serve the best I could, then I opened my heart, opened my mouth, and God did the rest. When I spoke, compassion and wisdom poured out of me because that's what God blessed me with after the life I've lived. Most of the time, I wasn't even aware of what I was saying.

Looking back all these years later, I think the key to my sobriety was that, about five years into my sobriety, something happened. God changed me somehow. I could be talking with someone who I had just met, just talking about life, and when the person asked me a question, or brought up a problem they had, the right answer would just pour out of me. Inevitably, the person would say, "Oh my God, how did you know that? You're right – that makes perfect sense!" I give all the credit to God for that, because I'm no psychologist. God was just using my life as a service to others. I got so hooked on that feeling of being a conduit for God that I wanted to help everyone. I opened myself up, asked God to put me where He needed me most, and I let the wisdom flow. That became a common occurrence the further into sobriety I traveled. Being real with people, and encouraging them on a heart and soul level was the best high I ever had. In hindsight, I see how God transformed my life at the same time He was using me to help others. I got hooked on helping people, and in the process, God knocked my socks off.

Mr. Li, President and Founder of Tiens, with Greg Perry, President and CEO of Lifestyles of Success.

CHAPTER 40

MEETING MR. LI

ONCE UPON A time, I had a client named Lawrence. I first met Lawrence when he hired me to sell his home in Harbor Pointe. I sold Lawrence's house to another client of mine, whose house I also happened to be selling. The transaction with Lawrence became very complicated because there were four subsequent transactions that were all dependent on the closing of Lawrence's house. In other words, Lawrence's house was the first, and most crucial, of five dominos that had to fall in order for me to pull off the entire scenario. To make matters even more complicated, Lawrence, who happened to be Chinese, had a vacation to China already scheduled prior to the closing date, and he wasn't even going to be in the country when I wrapped up all these deals. Nevertheless, Phyllis and I got everything handled perfectly, and we closed all five deals on the same day.

When Lawrence returned from his vacation, he came to see me in my office, and asked me how in the world I had managed to pull off such a feat. I explained everything to Lawrence, and when I was done talking, he jumped up and said, "You're a tiger, Greg Perry, you're a tiger!" I guess in the Chinese culture, being compared to a tiger is the ultimate compliment. I thanked Lawrence for the high praise, and we went our separate ways. A few years later, I got a call out of the blue from Lawrence. He told me he had a friend, Mr. Li, coming to Seattle from China, and that Mr. Li needed help finding a commercial property. Lawrence carefully explained that Mr. Li was a Chinese businessman with a very particular set of needs, and that it was absolutely crucial that I find him the perfect property. Apparently, Mr. Li wanted to buy some commercial land in order to relocate his manufacturing facility to the United States. Lawrence said Mr. Li needed a parcel of the very best commercial property, and that Mr. Li was sending his Vice President to Seattle to take care of everything on his behalf.

A week later, the Vice President came to town, and I blocked out an entire day to drive him and Lawrence around the Seattle area looking at commercial properties. I had already selected only the very best properties to show them. When we finished the tour, the Vice President, who didn't speak English, asked Lawrence to ask me to please show him some more properties. I carefully explained that there were no more properties to show him, because I had cherry-picked only the finest properties in the first place. The Vice President said it was very important that he find the perfect property because he didn't want to upset Mr. Li. I thought to myself, "Who is this Mr. Li, and what's the big deal?" I couldn't understand why Lawrence and Mr. Li's Vice President were so concerned about disappointing Mr. Li. I knew that Lawrence was Mr. Li's personal translator, but the whole scenario just seemed slightly odd to me. The Vice President returned to China with the property information I gave him, and I went back to work.

A few weeks later, Lawrence called me again and said Mr. Li was coming to town to see some properties for himself. I had already spent an entire day showing properties to the Vice President, and I had other business to handle. I couldn't afford to just keep driving around with these guys. I figured I'd give Lawrence and his friend from China one more shot. In my mind, they were going to buy one of the properties I had already shown them – they just didn't know it yet. When I went to pick up Lawrence and Mr. Li, there were four people waiting for me. I had to go back home and get Sheri's big Suburban just to accommodate Mr. Li's entourage. I thought to myself, "What is this guy, a Chinese rock star? Who travels with three assistants?" We got in the car and I started driving Mr. Li and his entourage around Seattle, looking at the same properties I had already shown to Mr. Li's VP. Lawrence sat in the back seat and leaned into the front seat to translate for Mr. Li, who sat beside me in the front seat. Lawrence told me that it was the first time Mr. Li or any of his assistants had ever been to the United States. At that point in my career, I had so much business going that I needed two cell phones and two pagers just to keep up with everything. As we were driving, my phones and pagers were ringing almost constantly. Mr. Li kept looking at me, and then at Lawrence, because I was on the phone every few minutes. They were all speaking Chinese to each other, which was fine with me because I had business to attend to while I was driving. One time, I had phones in both hands and was steering with my leg when Mr. Li reached over and slapped my leg and pointed at the road to get me to put my hands back on the wheel.

As we drove around the Seattle area, every so often we'd pass by one of my billboards. When we stopped for lunch, we walked by one of my mall ads. It seemed like everywhere we went, a piece of my marketing popped up, which was not my intention. We covered half of the properties that first day, and made plans to reconvene the following day to wrap up our tour. I never, ever spent two straight days in a car with a client just driving around looking at properties. I figured I was already losing money at that point, since I was missing out on all the business I could have been doing elsewhere. When we got back together the next day, Lawrence told me Mr. Li had seen my TV commercial back in his hotel room in Seattle. That was fine, but in my mind I was thinking, "I need to close this guy right now, let him go back to China, and then get back to running my business." The only reason I was even spending that much time with Mr. Li was because he was Lawrence's friend. Yes, a commercial deal of that size would be the biggest commission of my career, but truth be told, I was already losing interest with the whole thing.

We were driving down the freeway to see another property when Mr. Li turned to Lawrence and said something in Chinese. Then Lawrence said, "Greg, Mr. Li says he considers you his friend. He would like to invite you and your family to stay in his private hotel in China." I said, "Great. Tell Mr. Li I appreciate that, and I consider him my friend, too." Lawrence relayed the message, then Mr. Li said something else. Lawrence turned to me and said, "Mr. Li would like to ask you how much money you made last year." I thought to myself, "The nerve of this friggin' guy! Who does this Chinese guy think he is, asking me that? I don't discuss my finances with anybody!" I thought about it for a moment, and I realized that as soon as I closed this guy on this deal, he'd be going back to China and I'd never see him again anyway. So who cares? I figured I'd just blow him out of the water right there and be done with it.

I said to Lawrence, "Tell Mr. Li I made about a million dollars last year." Lawrence translated for Mr. Li, who nodded his head and said nothing. Then I got bold, and I thought, "I'm gonna show this guy two can play this game." I turned to Mr. Li with a smile on my face and said to Lawrence, "Tell Mr. Li I'd like to know how much he made last year." Lawrence translated for Mr. Li, then said, "Nine hundred million dollars." I almost drove off the freeway at 65 miles an hour. My brain short-circuited. After all my years of dealing, and being a self-made millionaire in real estate, I'm pretty good with numbers. I can add numbers, I can see numbers in my mind, and I can calculate numbers like nobody's business. Nine hundred million dollars. That number exploded through my brain like a bomb. Did he just say what I think he said? Maybe Lawrence misspoke, or maybe I misunderstood him. Nine hundred million dollars. The calculator in my mind was working overtime, but I still couldn't grasp that number. I tried dividing nine hundred million by 12 months to see if it was even possible to make that much. That didn't work either. I reached down and turned off both of my cellphones. Then I turned off both of my pagers. Then I shrunk down into the car seat, like a little kid driving my dad's car. All this time, I thought I was The Man, the King of the Hill in real estate. How could any person make nine hundred million dollars in a single year? I just couldn't comprehend it.

When I regained my composure, I told Lawrence, "Please ask Mr. Li, how does a human being make nine hundred million dollars in 12 months?" Lawrence translated, then said, "Mr. Li said he doesn't discuss his personal business when he's working. He only does that with his friends and family." I thought to myself, "Oh, now he's gonna throw up a roadblock and shut me down like that? Well, hold on a second, because I'm not done yet." I hesitated for a minute, then I told Lawrence, "Mr. Li said he considers me his friend, right?" Lawrence translated, and then Mr. Li nodded in the affirmative. Then I said to Lawrence, "Well, friend - please tell Mr. Li that I want to take him and the rest of my new friends out for dinner tonight, and I would like him to tell me how it's even possible for a person to make nine hundred million dollars in one year. I want to know how to do that." Lawrence translated, and Mr. Li accepted my dinner invitation.

I immediately got back on my phone and called Palisades, my favorite restaurant in Seattle. I was a regular at Palisades, and I had a special number that allowed me to call the restaurant manager directly and get any table, any time. I told the manager I was bringing in some VIP guests from out of town, and that I needed Palisades to roll out the red carpet for my friends. The restaurant always let me order anything I wanted, regardless of what was on the menu, and everything was ready for us when we arrived. We sat there for three hours, with Lawrence sitting in the middle translating every word Mr. Li and I said to each other. By the time those three hours had passed, Mr. Li and I were best friends. Mr. Li told me his life story, I told him my life story, and guess what – God connected us at the heart. Mr. Li and I were like long-lost brothers. Our life stories were really the same.

I was a poor kid out of South Central, Los Angeles, who became a self-made millionaire in real estate. Mr. Li was a poor kid out of Tianjin, China who became a self-made billionaire with his own company, which was called Tiens. Virtually every detail of our lives mirrored each other. When I quit my job to pursue my dream of being a superstar real estate agent, my wife said, "You're crazy! You ruined our lives! I don't care if you have to get a job at McDonalds, you'd better be the man you're supposed to be!" When Mr. Li quit his job to pursue his dream of manufacturing and marketing Chinese herbs, his wife said, "You're crazy! You ruined our lives! You sold our car to pay for your stupid dream! We're going to lose everything!" Mr. Li and I had lived the same life, right down to the details. God brought us together and then connected us through the language of love. Mr. Li and I had walked the same road in life, but on two different sides of the world. We couldn't speak each other's language, but it didn't matter, because we shared a bond that ran far deeper than any words.

Mr. Li needed some time to decide which property he wanted to buy for the Tiens manufacturing plant, so he and his people left Seattle and returned to China the following day. Lawrence called me a few weeks later, and said, "Oh man, Greg, Mr. Li sure loves you. He couldn't stop talking about you. But you won't believe what happened! You know the Governor of Washington State, Gary Locke? Well, he's Chinese, and when they found out Mr. Li had been here in Seattle and then gone back to China, they flew Mr. Li back over here for a meeting!" I knew the Governor, Gary Locke, was Chinese, but I still couldn't believe what I was hearing. Lawrence continued, "They brought Mr. Li downtown to the Columbia Center, and they took us up to the top for a big meeting. The Governor was in there, with the President of Seafirst Bank, and these two Chinese guys who are big shot commercial real estate brokers. They told Mr. Li they want to partner with him, and he could put his money in their bank, and they could help him with all his investments. But Mr. Li was very firm. He told them no, he only does business with one person in America, and that's his best friend – Greg Perry! Then we got up and walked out! Can you believe that?" I said, "What? Are you kidding me?" Lawrence said, "I'm serious, Greg - Mr. Li loves you!"

The next thing I knew, Mr. Li called me and said he wanted to buy a house in Mukilteo, and it had to be right by my house so that whenever he came to the United States he could be close to me and Sheri and the kids. I tried to get him into the same waterfront mansion that I eventually bought for myself, but the listing agent wouldn't let me in.

My dream waterfront mansion.

I started showing Mr. Li all the high-end waterfront homes on Lake Washington, including Kenny G's $22 million house on Hunts Point. One day I took Mr. Li out in my boat, and we drove all around the lake looking at houses from the water. I used to call Mr. Li "The Bill Gates of China," so he wanted to see where Bill Gates lived. I took Mr. Li to Medina, and we pulled up close to the shore near Bill's waterfront estate. God must have been working overtime for me that day, because as luck would have it, Bill just happened to be out in his backyard by the water. I waved at Bill and yelled, "Hey, Bill – how's it going?!" Bill saw us, waved back, and yelled, "I'm great, how are you?" Mr. Li was so excited, I thought he was going to jump out of the boat and swim to shore to shake Bill's hand.

After that episode, Mr. Li decided he wanted a house near Bill Gates. Unfortunately, there just wasn't anything good available. I showed Mr. Li several more homes after that, but eventually, he bought a house right around the corner from me. Mr. Li had the whole house furnished with beautiful furnishings, but I'd bet he never spent more than a single night there in his life. I never did sell Mr. Li any of the commercial property we had originally looked at, but by then, it didn't matter. Later on, he rented some commercial space and opened a Tiens distribution center near my house. As the months passed, Mr. Li came to Seattle more and more often to visit my family and I, and our bonds of friendship grew stronger. We were like blood brothers and best friends.

Mr. Li and Greg Perry: your winning team for Health, Wealth and Success.

CHAPTER 41

LIFESTYLES AND TIENS

MY OLD JEWISH brother Steve helped me plan everything for Lifestyles of Success, and he was also my Chief Financial Officer for the company. Steve said if I brought in outside investors to bankroll the launch of Lifestyles, they would likely want to control the project and tell me how to run it. I wasn't ready to relinquish control of something that was so personal to me, and that I'd worked so hard to create, so I had to find another way to pay for everything. I was contemplating how to proceed when it occurred to me that I could ask Mr. Li to bankroll it for me. Mr. Li was the wealthiest person I knew, and $4 million was pocket change to him. I called Lawrence, and asked him to contact Mr. Li and see if Mr. Li would be willing to loan me $4 million to launch Lifestyles nationwide in the U.S. I proposed to pay back Mr. Li's original $4 million loan within 12 months, and to pay Mr. Li an additional $2 million for interest on the loan within 24 months. Even with those overhead costs, my projections indicated I could expect to make several million dollars on the back end of the deal, once my CDs and tapes started selling.

When I spoke with Lawrence and told him my idea, he said, "Mr. Li will be here in two weeks, so you can ask him yourself." Mr. Li came to town two weeks later, and we got together so I could go over everything and give him the presentation of my Lifestyles of Success materials. I explained my whole marketing plan, and how I was going to use the $4 million loan. Lawrence translated everything for us, and Mr. Li understood what I was trying to do. When I finished, Mr. Li said he was very impressed with my plan. Then Mr. Li said he had an idea that might be even better for both of us. Through Lawrence, Mr. Li said, "Why don't you create a success training program like this for my company, for all my Tiens sales associates around the world?" Mr. Li thought his idea would serve two purposes simultaneously: first, it would launch my Lifestyles program on a much larger, global scale; and second, it would give his Tiens sales associates a valuable training tool they could use both personally and professionally.

Mr. Li's idea caught me slightly off guard, but the more I thought about it, the more I realized it could benefit both of us in a big way. Under Mr. Li's plan, we could team up to change the world and have a major impact on literally millions of people. I told Mr. Li I would think it over and let him know if I was interested in doing it his way. Mr. Li left Seattle a week later and went back to China, while I was planning to take my family to Maui for our annual summer vacation. I figured I would think it over on my vacation and then decide what to do. Right before I left for Hawai'i, I got a call from Lawrence. He said, "Greg, Mr. Li wanted me to tell you how impressed he was with your presentation, and with your Lifestyles of Success program. He really loves you, and he thinks your program is going to be very successful. Mr. Li would like to invite you to join him in Russia next month." I said, "Where?" Lawrence said, "Russia." I said, "Russia? Russia where?" Lawrence said, "You know, Russia." I said, "You mean Russia - like the Soviet Union, Russia?" Lawrence said, "Yes. Can you make it? Mr. Li really wants you to meet him there." I said, "First of all, I'm leaving for Hawai'i for a month with my family. I won't be back until the end of July. When does Mr. Li want me to go to Russia?" Lawrence said, "August 1ˢᵗ." I said, "Man, I can't do that, there's no way. I'll be returning from Maui, and then you want me to turn around and go to Russia the very next day? That's crazy."

Lawrence insisted Mr. Li was adamant that I join him in Russia. I tried to wriggle out of it, but in the end, I agreed to do it. I told Lawrence to send whatever information I would need for the trip to Phyllis, and that I would check it out when I got back from Maui. I went to Hawai'i as planned and was having a great time relaxing and playing with my family. Three weeks into my vacation, Lawrence called to tell me he was sending me all the flight information for my trip to Russia. We talked for a minute, and then Lawrence said, "Oh, by the way…Mr. Li would like to know if you could say a few words for him when you go to Russia?" I said, "Sure, I can say a few words for him, no problem. What would he like me to say?" Lawrence told me he would send me an email with some specific topics in it. The email arrived a short time later, and it said that when I got to Russia, Mr. Li would like me to speak about the following topics:

1) How I felt about Mr. Li, and myself, and how we were going to change the world and make a difference together.
2) How I felt about the Tiens Corporation, and their products.
3) How I felt about the country of Russia and the Russian people.
4) How I was going to create a success-training program that would change the world and make a difference.

After I read the email, I called Lawrence back and said, "Man, what the heck is this that you sent me? I'm not going over to Russia to give a speech. I thought Mr. Li wanted me to join him as his guest?" Lawrence said, "Oh yes, you are Mr. Li's guest, but he wanted you to say a few words." I told Lawrence I would put something together and send it back to him. A week later, I returned home to Seattle, and had a quick meeting with Phyllis before I had to leave for the airport for the flight to Russia. Phyllis gave me my passport and all my travel documents, and told me to please be sure to read the information she had received from the Russian Embassy in America. I got on the plane to Russia, and just as we were landing in Moscow, I realized I had forgotten to read the information from the Russian Embassy. I pulled out the Embassy's travel guidelines as the plane pulled up to the terminal, and here's what it said:

1) The Russians don't like black people.
2) The Russians don't like Chinese people.
3) Do not wear expensive jewelry or expensive clothing.
4) The Russian mafia is running the country, so be extra careful in everything you do.

I read the guidelines, blinked, and then I read them again. I remember thinking to myself, "Great. First of all, I look like a straight up gangster. I'm wearing a cream pinstripe suit, with tan-colored snakeskin shoes, gold cuff links, silk tie, and my gold Gucci diamond watch. I just returned from a month in Maui, and I'm as black as I can possibly be. I look like Hollywood times ten. To top it off, I'm wearing my gold-framed sunglasses. This is just perfect." I may have looked like a fish out of water, but being from South Central, I wasn't even the slightest bit worried. The first thing that struck me about the people in Moscow was the sheer hopelessness in their eyes. I had traveled all over the world with my family, but I had never seen anything like that before. It was one of the more depressing scenes I had witnessed in a while. We picked up our bags and a car came to take us to our hotel. When we pulled up to the hotel, there were international flags flying everywhere, like we were at the United Nations or something. We went inside, and there were hundreds of people in there with Tiens nametags on, milling around. It appeared that Mr. Li had bought out the whole hotel for all his international sales associates.

As soon as Mr. Li saw me come in, he came over and ushered me into a private convention room full of Tiens delegates from around the world. All of a sudden, it was lights, camera and action. Flashbulbs started going off all around us like we were on the red carpet at the Oscars. Mr. Li sat me down next to him, and someone pushed a microphone in my face. Our host introduced me as Mr. Greg Perry, President and CEO of Lifestyles of Success, and asked me why I was there. Mr. Li was clearly waiting for me to take over, so I said, "We're here to change the world and make a difference in people's lives. This is Lifestyles of Success and Tiens, teaming up, and together we're going to change the world and teach everyone how to be healthy, wealthy, and successful. That's what we're going to do, starting right here and right now." Lawrence was interpreting for Mr. Li, and as soon as I finished, Mr. Li broke out in a huge smile as if to say, "Yeah! That's my main man!" We had only been there for five minutes, and we were off and running.

After our opening remarks, we walked around to several smaller convention rooms, where there were tables and tables full of Tiens sales associates from dozens of different countries. The TV camera crews followed us everywhere we went as Mr. Li and I introduced ourselves and shook hands with everyone. I've been a lot of places, and seen a lot of things in my life, but I had never seen anything like that before. For almost an hour, we were like rock stars meeting hundreds of fans backstage. We finally took a break and got away from the crowds, and then Lawrence said we could go up to our rooms and unpack. Lawrence called to wake us up at 6 a.m. the following morning, and told us to prepare for a big day. We started out with a private international summit meeting with Mr. Li, myself, a handful of Mr. Li's closest advisors, and the top sales marketing distributors from each of the more than 50 countries in which Tiens did business. Mr. Li and I explained how Tiens and Lifestyles of Success were joining forces to create a success manual that would teach all the Tiens associates how to achieve all their personal dreams and goals. We promised to show them how to take their marketing to a whole new level, and change the world by generating health, wealth, and success for all.

I didn't realize it at the time, but Mr. Li was setting me up. Whenever we appeared together, Mr. Li was sure to place me on his right side, which I later learned is considered a position of power. The result was, the whole time I was with Mr. Li, everyone else in his organization was looking at me with a mixture of respect and fear, because they could see how much Mr. Li liked me and valued me. Keep in mind that Mr. Li didn't speak a word of English, and I didn't speak a word of Chinese. But that didn't matter, because Mr. Li and I had been joined at the heart ever since that first in-depth personal conversation we had shared over dinner at Palisades in Seattle. After that first international summit meeting, we returned to our hotel rooms to relax until it was time for the next meeting. I was always the sharpest-dressed person in the room at every engagement, and I was changing clothes three times a day, so I was always fresh. This was show time for me, and I was determined to create the best possible impression, not only for Mr. Li, but also for anyone else who was paying attention.

The next time we came downstairs, the hotel lobby was packed with hundreds of people. There were flags flying again, cameras flashing, and film crews everywhere. It was a complete circus; all that was missing were the dancing bears and high-wire trapeze artists. Mr. Li made his way to the center of the lobby and just stood there, like a regal statue. I took my usual place next to him, and for the next several minutes, we posed with our best painted-on smiles. The camera shutters were going off rapid-fire all around us, but we didn't budge. In the middle of all the hysteria, Mr. Li nudged Lawrence and told him to tell me, "Nice tie, man, nice tie!" The compliment broke up the stiffness of the situation, and helped us all relax. After posing for several minutes, we walked outside and right into another spectacle. There, lined up in front of the hotel, were over 40 brand new black-on-black BMW 5-series sedans. Each BMW had a giant red ribbon stretched across the hood, which was adorned with a 24-karat gold statue of the Tiens symbol: a golden lion standing on top of the world. The cars were gifts from Mr. Li to the Tiens elite sales associates; prizes earned for excellence in sales and marketing.

Mr. Li climbed into a white stretch limousine and emerged through the car's sunroof so he could wave to the crowds lining the streets. A police escort accompanied us as we caravanned through the streets of Moscow all the way to the Moscow Opera House. The whole scene was surreal, like something out of a Hollywood movie. When we arrived at the Opera House, Mr. Li and I were taken into a private reception room, where we were joined by the Prime Minister of China, former Soviet President Mikhail Gorbachev, and several other foreign dignitaries. When I saw Mr. Gorbachev waiting to greet us, I thought to myself, "Is this for real? Two weeks ago, Mr. Li said he wanted me to come to Russia to say a few words for him – now we're meeting world leaders. What the heck is next?!" We stood backstage at the Opera House for a few minutes, and had a very informal conversation with the Chinese Prime Minister and Mr. Gorbachev. Bodyguards surrounded us the entire time. I had no idea what was coming from one moment to the next, but by that point I was down with the program and just going with the flow. When I asked Lawrence what was happening, he just said, "It's time for the big show." I had no idea what he meant, but I was ready for action.

We walked onstage to a wave of applause, and I encountered the most amazing scene I had ever witnessed. It felt like I was at the United Nations. There were international flags draped over all the balconies, luxury boxes, and railings of the Opera House. All the seats in the audience were wired for headphones, which were connected directly to each country's interpreters so audience members could receive a simultaneous translation in their native tongues. Once we were seated, Mr. Li turned and nodded at me to begin the show. I thought, "What?!" I got up to the podium, and something magical came over me. I was in the zone. I started talking about how I was a poor kid from South Central, Los Angeles, who became a self-made millionaire in the real estate business. I talked about how Mr. Li was a poor kid from Tianjin, China, who became a self-made billionaire by creating Tiens. I talked about how Mr. Li and I had the same story, and the same background, and how God brought us together like long-lost brothers so we could change the world and make a difference for millions of people. I talked about how Tiens had the best health products and Lifestyles of Success had the best success-training resources. I told the audience we were joining together to create an unstoppable global force for health, wealth and success. I talked about how much we loved Russia, the people of Russia, and how we were going to be second to none.

I finished to a rousing ovation, then Mr. Li got up and related a similar message of well-being and prosperity. Mr. Li was followed by Mr. Gorbachev and the Prime Minister of China. After we were finished with the speeches and presentations, Mr. Li started giving away more BMW's to the sales associates. Ballerinas, ballet dancers, opera singers, and other entertainment followed that. I learned later that Mr. Li had spent millions of dollars that day just to put on that one show. After several hours of speeches and entertainment, bodyguards whisked us offstage and we went upstairs for a private reception and party that lasted long into the night. I only got a few hours of sleep before Lawrence called to wake us up. Lawrence said we had another show to get to, so we headed out to a part of town that would politely be described as the poor part of Moscow. Mr. Li had planned a smaller show for the poorest people of Moscow, and it turned out to be quite an eye-opener for me.

What really touched my heart about that particular show were the testimonials given by people when they came onstage to address the crowd. Everyone was talking about how their lives had changed as a result of using the Tiens herbs and supplements. Some people said the herbs had cured them of illnesses and diseases, including cancer and diabetes. Other people started crying as they testified about how the herbs had healed their children of various diseases. Some of the things I heard were almost unbelievable. At that point in time, I had only read about the health benefits of the Tiens herbs, and listened as Mr. Li and others had talked about them; I hadn't actually used them myself. When the show was over, I took Mr. Li aside and asked him about the herbs and supplements he was selling. Through Lawrence, Mr. Li said, "Greg, these herbs work like magic. They've been used in my culture for thousands of years. You don't know about them in America, but they're the real deal."

I told Mr. Li I wanted to try every product he had. I planned to take it all home with me and try it for myself. If I was going to stand up before audiences around the world and give speeches about how great Tiens was, I needed to be able to speak from direct personal experience. Mr. Li gave me several boxes of the Tiens herbs, and I started taking them twice a day. Before I knew what hit me, I had become a total believer in the Tiens Chinese herbs. It only took a few weeks for the herbs to transform my system, and then my body started running like a Ferrari. I learned first-hand that the real secret behind Chinese herbs is in the way they detoxify your body so its natural defenses can work properly, and then your body can heal itself. It's like getting an oil change and a tune-up for your immune system. Right away, I noticed I no longer got tired. My mind was just sharp and focused, regardless of how much sleep I got or what I ate. The herbs also trimmed me down, and I lost the extra weight I had been carrying for a few years. I started looking better, and I felt better too. My real estate business often kept me in my car for hours at a time, but with the Chinese herbs I had so much extra energy that I was ready to work strong all the time.

One of the essential beliefs of Chinese medicine is the importance of maintaining proper balance of the Yin and Yang aspects of the body's systems. Some of the herbs and supplements clean the kidneys and purify the blood. Others work on the body's cardio system, so the heart can run at its optimum efficiency. The triple ginseng supplement provides pure natural energy and endurance. Another herb acts like a cleanser to purge the body of all its toxins, while another herb contains a mixture of essential oils and fats that makes one's skin and hair silky and smooth. This was quite an education for me, and once I saw the results, I was hooked. I started taking my Tiens herbs every day, and I was dialed in. By the time we wrapped up the world summit meetings in Russia and I returned home to the States, I was a legitimate spokesman for the amazing benefits of the Tiens products.

*Greg Perry, worldwide Success Trainer for Tiens
and Lifestyles of Success.*

CHAPTER 42

SETTING UP NORTH AMERICA

SHORTLY AFTER WE returned from Moscow, Lawrence called me and said a Tiens guy from China named Ni wanted to come to America to meet me. Apparently, Ni used to be Mr. Li's success trainer in China before I came on the scene and Mr. Li made me the worldwide success trainer. Lawrence set up the meeting, and I met Ni for a private dinner with just the two of us. I got to the restaurant early, and when Ni walked in, I could see he was a pretty slick dude, with a lot of attitude. We sat down and I just listened while Ni talked. First, Ni said Mr. Li was a very powerful man. Ni told me he had made $15 million doing success training for Mr. Li in China. Then Ni said that, since I was the new worldwide success trainer, he and I could team up and make a lot of money together. Ni clearly wanted to cut a deal with me. It reminded me of when I was back in South Central, working in organized crime. I could spot a bad guy from a mile away. Ni said, "As you know, Mr. Li has a lot of money. If you and I team up, we can make a lot of money off Mr. Li. He trusts you, which means you've got the green light. You can get anything you want, and I can show you how to do it. I already made $15 million just in China, and now you've got the whole world. The sky's the limit for us if we do this together."

I just sat back and listened, and when Ni was done talking I said, "Yeah, yeah, that sounds good." Immediately after our dinner was over, I drove straight over to Lawrence's house. I told Lawrence, "That Ni guy is no good - he's corrupt. He flew all the way over here to meet me, just to tell me we can take some of Mr. Li's money. I know how guys like that think; he's rotten to the core." Lawrence said he appreciated me letting him know. The following week, Lawrence called me and said he had just picked up Mr. Li from the airport in Seattle. Lawrence said, "Mr. Li says he's really misses you, and he wants to come see you tonight. He wants to take you and your family out for dinner. He really wants to see Sheri and the kids." I told Lawrence to let me call Sheri and get everyone in the family ready. I called Sheri, and she said, "Greg, I'd love to, but I'm not ready, the kids aren't ready, and there's no way we can do it tonight." I told her not to worry about it, then I called Lawrence back and told him the news. I said, "Please tell Mr. Li I'm very sorry. We can't do it tonight, but maybe we can do it tomorrow." Lawrence said he would pass the message along to Mr. Li, and we hung up the phone.

About 30 seconds later, my phone rang again. It was Lawrence. "Mr. Li says he's very sorry for the short notice, but he really wants to see you and your family tonight. Can you please ask Sheri again?" I said I would try again. I called Sheri back, and once again she said it was just too short of notice, and that the following night would be much better. I called Lawrence back again, and told him that we'd love to see Mr. Li, but we just couldn't do it that night. Lawrence told me he would let Mr. Li know. 20 seconds later, my phone rang again. It was Lawrence. He said, "Mr. Li says he is very sorry to bother you again, but he really wants to see you and your family, and is there any way you could ask Sheri to reconsider?" I called Sheri back and said, "Look Honey, Mr. Li says he really misses us and he wants to see the kids. Just do whatever you have to do to get everyone ready." Sheri said, "Greg, you know I'd love to see Mr. Li. But I look like hell, the kids are a mess, and there's just no way. Please tell him I'm very sorry, and we can definitely do it tomorrow." I called Lawrence back, apologized again, and told him that I tried, but it was just a matter of bad timing. Lawrence said he understood, and we hung up the phone.

It wasn't 15 seconds later that my phone rang again. It was Lawrence. "Mr. Li says he is sorry to bother you again, but he would consider it a personal favor, and he would be very grateful if you and your beautiful family could please find a way to make everything work for dinner tonight."

By that time, it dawned on me that this entire episode was starting to resemble a scene from the Godfather movie, where the Consigliere (Lawrence) requests a very personal favor on behalf of the Godfather (Mr. Li). I always loved that movie, and I had seen it enough times to know that I could only turn down the Godfather's request for a very personal favor so many times before he would "insist" that I grant him his request. I called Sheri for the fourth time in five minutes, and I said, "Get your ass dressed, and get the kids ready – because we're going out for dinner with Mr. Li. I'll pick you up in 30 minutes." Sheri had seen the Godfather too. She just said, "Okay," and hung up the phone. When Lawrence and Mr. Li pulled into my driveway 30 minutes later, I jumped in the car with them. We greeted each other, then I told Mr. Li about my meeting with Ni. I said, "Look, I know Ni used to be your success trainer in China. But he's corrupt. I just wanted you to know what he's up to." Mr. Li was clearly upset, and said he had long suspected that Ni was up to no good. Mr. Li told me to stay away from Ni, and I was happy to honor his request.

Shortly afterward, Mr. Li asked me to start setting up the North American market for Tiens. I had already seen enough from my travels with Mr. Li to know that Tiens was going to be a runaway success in America. Mr. Li and I had agreed to create a global empire that combined the forces of Lifestyles of Success and Tiens, and I was already working on customizing my Lifestyles program for his Tiens sales associates around the world. A film crew followed me wherever I went to document every step of the exciting new journey we were undertaking. We scouted locations in nearby Vancouver, B.C. before we decided that Toronto provided superior access to the larger cities in the eastern United States. At the time, Tiens had 4 million sales associates operating in 50 countries. Phyllis and I hit the phones in my office back in Seattle, and within 48 hours, we had signed up 650 new sales associates up and down the west coast. I had all my friends, my family members, my old NFL buddies, and everyone else I knew on board and ready to rock for Tiens and Lifestyles of Success.

Right out of the gate, we set up Tiens associates in Vancouver, B.C., Seattle, San Francisco, Los Angeles, and Toronto. We kicked everything off with a launch party at the Meydenbauer Center in Bellevue, which is near Seattle. From there, we worked our way down the west coast. We filmed a promotional segment with Mr. Li next to the Golden Gate Bridge in San Francisco, to show the Tiens affiliates around the world what we were doing together. At every stop along the way, Mr. Li gave away new BMW's to get everyone excited about the amazing opportunities created by our joint effort. When we got to Los Angeles, we repeated the same incredible scene I first witnessed in Moscow: Mr. Li riding through the city in a white stretch limo, waving parade-style at the crowds of curious onlookers. A caravan of brand new black-on-black BMW's filled with freshly minted Tiens sales associates followed close behind.

Film crews captured every moment of our ongoing adventures as we drove down Rodeo Drive, then through Beverly Hills and Hollywood. I introduced Mr. Li as "The Bill Gates of China." As far as I was concerned, Mr. Li was an international superstar who would eventually have his own star on the Hollywood Walk of Fame. Everywhere Mr. Li and I went, we preached our mantra of how Tiens and Lifestyles of Success were changing the world and making a difference. Mr. Li and I were off to a flying start, and it looked like nothing could stop us from achieving all of our shared dreams and goals. Several of the distributors that Phyllis and I had originally signed up had hit the ground running, and were making a lot of money. Mr. Li had given me my own line in the company to make sure we got North America established quickly, and it worked. Some of my distributors were making anywhere from $5,000-$14,000 per month within the first several months of selling Tiens. Even the people who were only doing it part-time were often making $500-$1,000 per month. It was a great business, with great products, and a lot of great people. I was enjoying myself, and was busily preparing all the Lifestyles and Tiens success training tools. Lawrence had since been promoted to Executive Vice President of North America, in part as a reward from Mr. Li because it was Lawrence who had introduced us in the first place.

CHAPTER 43

GOING INTERNATIONAL

AFTER THE FIRST five U.S. markets were up and running, Mr. Li and I resumed our international travel. We went to Thailand, and I brought a group of 35 of my best friends, family members, a handful of my NFL guys, and as many of my top distributors as could make the trip. Once we got there, I was running with Mr. Li, and meeting with dignitaries, including the Prime Minister of Thailand. As always, there were paparazzi following us everywhere we went; it was like traveling with a movie star or a rock group. We were treated like royalty, and I quickly realized that was a common occurrence with Mr. Li. That whole scene back in Moscow had really blown me away, but when we were in Thailand, I saw that the Moscow spectacle was no fluke. Mr. Li only knew one way to do everything: first class, all the time. Money was no object, and there was seemingly nothing Mr. Li's money couldn't buy. Mr. Li's modus operandi was simple and straightforward: his #3 guy, Mr. Di, would go into a country ahead of us, and set everything up for our arrival.

Usually, Mr. Di would make a substantial donation to the country or some noteworthy local cause. Then once he had their attention, Mr. Di would give them lots of the Chinese herbs for free, and find a meaningful way to help many of the local poor people. By the time Mr. Li and I and the rest of his crew got there, the local political leaders were ready to roll out the red carpet for us. No expense was spared, and that's exactly how Mr. Li liked it. In one city in Thailand, we pulled into town and there on the beach waiting for us were about 30 banana-style speedboats. Mr. Li had ordered them for our entourage, and all we had to do was jump in and take off. We all went out parasailing and cruising around the ocean. In another city, our hosts took us to an animal park, where we posed for pictures with trained tigers, played with monkeys, and watched a group of trained elephants play soccer. The crazy thing about that was, those elephants could actually play! Later, we held a Tiens Worldwide Summit in Toronto, which we had set up as the company's primary distribution center for the eastern half of North America. In Toronto, we got to go up in the CN Tower, which is over 1,100 feet tall. It reminded me of the Space Needle back home in Seattle, only the CN Tower is nearly twice as tall.

Everywhere we traveled, we were greeted by the upper crust of that country's political structure. I grew accustomed to accompanying Mr. Li at private receptions with Kings, Queens, Emperors, and Prime Ministers. I was just a poor kid from South Central, but as Mr. Li's worldwide success trainer, I found myself consulting with world leaders. Sometimes I would sit down with a foreign dignitary for a private conversation about life or global business, and it would suddenly occur to me where I was and what I was doing. It was all happening so fast. Mr. Li would often push me out in front of our Tiens group and let me do all the talking, just as he had done when we were in Moscow. I was a very confident and relaxed speaker, and I think Mr. Li knew I could convey our shared message of health, wealth, and success even better than he could. It was a match made in heaven. When we weren't enjoying receptions with dignitaries, or sightseeing in the countries we visited, Mr. Li and I were strategizing for the future global empire of Tiens and Lifestyles of Success.

While we were in Thailand for the Tiens Worldwide Summit, Mr. Li reminded me of the offer he had made me the day we first met, when we were driving around looking at commercial property together. Mr. Li had invited me to bring Sheri and the kids to China, as his personal guests at his hotel. But after that initial invitation, we had both gotten so busy with Lifestyles and Tiens that it had slipped our minds. We agreed that after Thailand, we would carve out some personal time together. When I got back to Seattle, my kids were just about to go on Spring Break, so Sheri and I packed up the family and flew to Beijing. Needless to say, Mr. Li rolled out the red carpet upon our arrival. A stretch limo picked us up at the airport, then we stopped off at the Henderson Centre, which housed Tiens' Beijing headquarters. Mr. Li had purchased an entire floor in a state-of-the-art building that wasn't even available to the public. Then we headed out to Tianjin, the home of Tiens' global headquarters. When we arrived in Tianjin, Mr. Li put us up in three beautiful rooms at his private hotel. This trip had nothing to do with Lifestyles, Tiens, or a success seminar. We were simply there to spend quality time with my main man. Mr. Li had always loved my family, and this time together gave us an opportunity to bond on an even deeper level.

As always, Mr. Li only knew one way to roll, and that was first class all the way. My family and I were treated like VIP's the entire time we were in China as his guests. When we got up the first morning, the hotel had prepared a beautiful American-style breakfast buffet with everything we could possibly want. It was the best of everything, like you'd find in a 5-star resort. After we ate, it was time to start creating some special memories. Mr. Li had assigned us our own private tour guide, to take us everywhere and see all the sights. The limo picked us up again, and we started at the Great Wall of China. It was funny at first because, when we were walking along the Great Wall, there was a mob of about 50 people following us. The law in China was that you could only have one child, and there I was with seven kids and my wife. It was like the Chinese people thought we were the Jackson 5 or something. At one point, the crowd was so close to us, taking pictures and everything, that Sheri got a little unnerved by it all. She told me, "Honey, I'm really uncomfortable. These people are getting too close. They're way past my comfort zone." I told Sheri, "It's okay. That's just the Chinese culture. They like to touch and get close and take lots of pictures. It's no big deal." Mr. Li had made me a bit of a celebrity in China, from being so close to him, and my family and I were seeing the effects of that firsthand.

As we walked further along the Wall, my kids started enjoying the attention. They were taking pictures with all the tourists, and having a great time. We continued walking along, and there was a Chinese man with a beautiful white horse. My two-year old son, Caleb, said, "Dad, I want to ride that horse." I talked to the man and set it up, and the next thing you know, my baby boy was up there riding that white horse on the Great Wall of China. That was a sight I will never forget as long as I live. At the top of the Wall, there was a shrine with pictures of all the world leaders and famous people who had been through the Great Wall at various times. They also had a lot of traditional Oriental costumes there, and we took a bunch of family pictures with all of us wearing the costumes. From the Wall, we went to Tiananmen Square, and then to a tour of the Forbidden City. I had seen the Forbidden City before on TV, but to see it up close and in person was absolutely amazing. My whole family was just in awe of everything, and our personal tour guide made it even better.

We went back to Tianjin, and had a wonderful private dinner with Mr. Li. The next day, Mr. Li had us all set up to go shopping. You really can't drive a limo through the streets in the shopping district, because the streets are so narrow, and there are so many bicyclists. Our guide split us up into smaller cars, then we were on our way. Sheri had her own personal shopper, who helped her pick out everything to try on. They didn't have dressing rooms where we were, so instead, four or five ladies formed a circle around Sheri and held up a big sheet, and then Sheri went inside the circle and changed her clothes. It was a little strange for Sheri at first, but after a few minutes, she said, "Hey, I think I like this – they're all waiting on me!" The whole shopping experience was fabulous for my wife and my kids. Another day, Mr. Li had it set up for us to take the kids to an amusement park. We got there, and the kids were going crazy having so much fun, because there were no lines, and they could go on the rides as many times as they wanted. It turned out later that Mr. Li had rented out the whole park, and we were really the only people in there. The kids had a blast, and when they saw Mr. Li again, they couldn't stop thanking him for giving them their very own amusement park for the day.

We went back over to Tianjin, and our guide took us up to the top of the big radio tower there, where we could see all over the entire city. The view was simply incredible. No matter where we went, or what we did, Mr. Li made sure my family had the best of everything all the time. Every night we came back to the hotel and shared a beautiful private dinner with Mr. Li. We didn't use an interpreter at that point, because Mr. Li and I were so connected at the heart that we could just talk to each other and communicate with the tone of our voice, our gestures, and our eye contact. It might be hard for people understand how we could relate to each other like that, but when God connects two people through the heart, and you have a rapport, and you love each other, and you're cut from the same cloth, you can communicate perfectly. The universal language is love, and Mr. Li and I shared a love so deep and strong. We had traveled around the world together, working and sharing with people from different countries, and we knew what each other was thinking without even saying a word.

I've been a lot of places, and done a lot of great things in my life, but that whole week in China with Mr. Li and my family was one of the most beautiful and memorable experiences I've ever had. I know it was special for Mr. Li too, and I realize now that what made it special for him was that he got to share in something he didn't have himself. My kids, my wife and I surrounded him with so much warmth and love that he couldn't get anywhere else. We took hundreds of pictures on that trip, and when I look at those pictures today, I see how joyful and blessed Mr. Li looked in all of them. It was an amazing time for all of us, and one we'll never forget. My kids still talk about that trip from time to time, and I know one boy who will always have a special memory of riding a white stallion on the Great Wall of China.

CHAPTER 44

STORM IN SAN FRANCISCO

THE BUZZ FROM my family's trip to China stayed with me for a long time, and I was grateful for that once in a lifetime experience. None of it would have been possible without my dear friend, Mr. Li. Unfortunately, not all of the people involved with Tiens were enjoying the ride. Mr. Li had brought one of his VP's from China, Miss Fi, over to America. After my team got the San Francisco market set up, Miss Fi stepped in and said she wanted to take it over for us. Apparently, Miss Fi figured that since she was Chinese, and San Francisco had a large Chinese population, it would be easier for her to capitalize on that market. Miss Fi mistakenly assumed that her native Chinese heritage was some great advantage that would allow her to succeed on her own terms, without having to utilize the same success principles we were applying in all the other U.S. markets. What Miss Fi failed to realize was that there's literally a world of difference between being Chinese in China and being Chinese in America. Her act didn't fly in San Francisco, and the first round of sales numbers proved it. Vancouver, B.C., Seattle, Los Angeles, and Toronto were all setting sales records straight out of the box, while San Francisco was dead last in North American sales.

Because Miss Fi was Mr. Li's VP in China, the poor performance in San Francisco was a very bad reflection on her. She simply couldn't afford to fail; it would have been career suicide for her to disappoint Mr. Li by blowing her opportunity in San Francisco. What I didn't realize at the time was that my old pal Ni was the mastermind behind Miss Fi. Ni hatched the whole San Francisco plan to make Miss Fi look like a hero, so they could take credit for it and continue with his plan to get more of Mr. Li's money. That became crystal clear to me after I got a call saying Miss Fi and her crew from San Francisco wanted to meet with me to discuss how they could get that market going. When they first called, I just assumed that since I was the worldwide success trainer, they wanted me to help them improve their sales. I agreed to meet with Miss Fi, and she brought her team to town to have dinner with me.

As soon as we sat down, I saw what their plan really was. Miss Fi laid it all out for me. "Greg, here's what we want to do. We want you to get San Francisco up and running strong, like the other markets. Then we're going to get Lawrence out of the picture, and take over the rest of North America." Those fools had no idea that Lawrence was my real estate client from so many years ago, and that he was my friend, and that he was the one who had introduced me to Mr. Li. Their plan was to blame Lawrence for San Francisco's poor performance, then take all the credit for making North America a success. I sat there and listened to Miss Fi's grand scheme, and I just nodded my head and rolled with the punches. Those clowns must have thought I was some dummy who had never done any business before. My mind flashed back to all the times I had to think three steps ahead of some brother in South Central who thought he could outsmart me. I thought about all the times in real estate when I had to know the answers to the questions someone was going to ask me before they even thought of the question in the first place.

As soon as my dinner meeting with Miss Fi was over, I called Lawrence. I'm old school all the way; true blue and loyal to those who do me right. I wasn't about to stand by and watch as Miss Fi and her crew threw Lawrence under the bus for something that was all her fault. I said to Lawrence, "I got news for you, buddy. Miss Fi and Ni are coming for your head. That meeting had nothing to do with San Francisco. They want you out, then they're gonna take all the credit for the success of North America. They're afraid they're gonna upset Mr. Li by blowing it in San Francisco, because they know that would be the end of Ni's whole game." Lawrence said, "Okay, Greg. Thanks for letting me know. I'm not going to let that happen."

The next time Ni and Miss Fi came to visit the North American headquarters and distribution center we had set up in Everett, Lawrence snapped and lost his mind. He called the U.S. Immigration Department, and told the officials there that Ni and Miss Fi were in the country illegally. The Immigration Department came in and scooped up Ni and Miss Fi and threw them all in detention. When I heard what Lawrence had done, I went to see him right away. Lawrence told me he did what he had to do to protect himself and Tiens. I told Lawrence he had made a huge mistake. I said, "What were you thinking? Have you lost your mind? That's like calling the FBI on your own company. You just can't do that." It turned out that Ni and Miss Fi did, in fact, have some problems with their paperwork, but that was beside the point. Regardless of how wrong Ni and Miss Fi were, what Lawrence did was just bad for business. And it quickly blew up in his face.

As soon as Mr. Li heard about the Immigration fiasco involving Ni and Miss Fi, he called me and told me to be on the next plane to

China. I was planning to leave that next day for Hawai'i to spend spring break with Sheri and the kids. I had our trip all set up, so I told Sheri to go ahead without me, and that I'd catch up with her and the kids as soon as I was done in China with Mr. Li. I flew to Beijing, where Peter, who was Mr. Li's new translator, greeted me. Peter was clearly excited about his new position. Little did he know that Mr. Li changed out his people every two years because he couldn't trust anyone. With all the infighting and backbiting that was going on in America, it was easy for me to see why Mr. Li ran his business that way. Peter took me to Tianjin, where I joined Mr. Li at his private resort.

Mr. Li was visibly upset when I met with him. "Greg, I trust you. Tell me the truth – what is going on in America?" I gave it to him straight. "First of all, like I told you before, Ni is corrupt. He's behind everything Miss Fi is doing. Ni is masterminding her plan to take over North America. Miss Fi told me she wants to fix San Francisco, but it won't work. America is a different game than China. The strategies that work in China won't work in America, plain and simple. Miss Fi came to see me, and the truth is, her and Ni are going to cut Lawrence out and then take over North America. They're afraid to disappoint you, so they're going to take Lawrence out and then take the credit for everything after I fix it. They came to the office in Everett, and Lawrence called Immigration and had them all thrown in jail. The whole thing is a big mess, and there's all this backstabbing going on." Mr. Li just sat there, listening and shaking his head.

I continued, "There's another thing. I'm tired of Ni going around telling everyone he's the success trainer for Tiens in America. You told me I'm the worldwide success trainer. That's why I've been doing all this work, getting North America all set up. It can't be both of us - it's one or the other." I pulled out a contract I had prepared and laid it on the table. I said, "I need to protect myself here. If I'm your success trainer, then you need to sign this contract so I know I'm not wasting my time trying to make this thing in America a success." Mr. Li didn't even hesitate. He pulled a pen out of his jacket and signed the contract on the spot. After he signed the contract, Mr. Li said, "You are the success trainer for my company, and there is no other. You don't have to worry about any of these other people." That was all I needed to hear. I left the meeting with Mr. Li and flew to Hawai'i to meet up with Sheri and the kids.

By the time I got back home from Hawai'i several days later, changes were already underway in the North American operation. Ni and Miss Fi had been released from Immigration detention and had gone back to China to get their paperwork in order. Unfortunately, Lawrence also got caught up in the storms of change. Lawrence broke Mr. Li's trust the moment he called Immigration on Ni and Miss Fi, and it cost Lawrence his position as Executive Vice President of North America. Lawrence still came to the office, and he tried to carry on as best he could. But the damage was already done. I pleaded with Mr. Li to give Lawrence another chance, but Mr. Li was adamant - he was done with Lawrence. Before long, Lawrence stopped showing up entirely, and Ni and Miss Fi were back in town and running their same old game like nothing had ever happened. It seemed like the more things changed, the more they stayed the same. I guess I should have known the real drama was just getting started.

CHAPTER 45

TIENS TURNING POINT

MY NEXT WORLDWIDE Summit for Tiens was in Saint Petersburg, Russia. I didn't fully recognize it at the time, but my relationship with Tiens was moving steadily toward a point of no return. Lawrence had been bumped aside after the Immigration fiasco with Miss Fi and Ni. Miss Fi had taken her bold power play to a whole new level by producing a letter which she claimed proved that Mr. Li had stepped down as the President of Tiens, and that she was now the running the company. I knew right away that the letter was pure bull----, because there was no way Mr. Li would ever give up control of his business, least of all to someone like her. Miss Fi had always been afraid of me, because she knew I could see right through her. With Lawrence out of the way, and Mr. Li a million miles away in China, Miss Fi's letter was enough to fool most of the people in the North American market. I had been around too many con men in my life to fall for that kind of trick. The truth was, Ni was still working behind the scenes with Miss Fi, scheming new ways to get their hands on even more of Mr. Li's money. After the debacle with Miss Fi in San Francisco, Mr. Li had taken my advice and brought in an American guy to be the face of North American sales. Miss Fi wasted no time convincing him that she was the real power of the North American operation.

I had recently brought in a new success trainer, a doctor named Steve, to help us out in North America. Steve was a real go-getter, who had over 6,000 distributors in his down line. Miss Fi had convinced Steve that she was running everything, by claiming that she had control over the corporate bank accounts. Steve had no way of knowing what was really going on behind the scenes. I flew over to Saint Petersburg for the Worldwide Summit, and I had a private meeting with Mr. Li. I told him, "Look, Miss Fi has a letter saying you stepped down as President, and that she's now the President of Tiens Corporation. I'm calling bull---- on all of this stuff. So let's get it straight right now: who's running the show?" Mr. Li looked me in the eye and said, "Please, that's crazy talk. I will never step down, and if I did, you would be the first one to know." I said, "That's what I thought, but I needed to hear it directly from you." Mr. Li said, "Here's the bottom line: I told you before, no one will ever come between me and you. No one. My people are so envious and scared of you, it's ridiculous." I said, "That's all well and fine, but I'll tell you what I'm gonna do. When I get back to Seattle, they're finished – all of them. Their new front man over there, he's gone. Steve, he's gone. As for Miss Fi, I don't care what you do with that mess. I'll leave her up to you. But I'm done with these people."

When I got home to Seattle, we had a series of shows set up for Tiens and Lifestyles. I rented out several hotel ballrooms for events featuring me and my top distributors. At one event, I was onstage speaking when one of the guys I had told Mr. Li about, the front man for North America, tried to make a big scene and embarrass me in front of everyone. He came running in and started calling me names, and saying I had ruined his life. Some of the guys on my sales team wanted to take him apart, but I told them to let him be. Apparently, Mr. Li had already made the call to the U.S. and cleaned house before I even got home. When I got to the office the next day, Steve was sitting at my desk like he owned the place. Steve saw me come in and he looked like he had just seen a ghost. He said, "It wasn't me, Greg – honest. I didn't know what was going on behind the scenes." I just said, "Get out of my chair, and get out of my office – you're done."

I was putting the finishing touches on the Lifestyles/Tiens video training series, making some last-minute edits before we launched the success training program worldwide. We had hours and hours of film from events all over the world, including Russia, China, Thailand, Canada, and the United States. I had my contract with Mr. Li to sell videos, CDs, tapes, training manuals, and we were almost ready to go. Then I got a call from Miss Fi, who said, "When you bring all the materials to the corporate distribution center, can you please bring all the original hard copies, so we can have them here for safe keeping?" I thought, "Yeah, right. Like I'm some friggin' idiot who doesn't know the score." I realized then that Mr. Li had no idea what Miss Fi was really up to, and the lengths she was willing to go to in order to perpetrate her plan with Ni. The whole scene was just so dirty and filthy and corrupt. Mr. Li was fine when it was just he and I together. But Tiens was an enormous, multi-billion dollar global empire, and behind Mr. Li's back, the inmates were running the asylum.

After the call from Miss Fi, I had a moment of clarity. I realized that there was so much money on the table in Mr. Li's business that it brought out the absolute worst in everyone. I had always known that when the money comes out, that's when everyone's true colors come out as well. The greed factor kicked in hard, and it was just never enough for some people. There was backstabbing and infighting and scheming and scamming, all day every day. It reminded me of when I was running in the gangs in South Central. Back then, I'd come home and take a shower to try to wash off the ugliness of life in the streets. But no matter how hard I scrubbed, I just couldn't get clean. I felt that old familiar ugliness starting to stick to me all over again with Tiens. Some of the people in the organization were just so corrupt. They would lie to Mr. Li and act like everything was on the up-and-up, but as soon as he turned his back, their dark side took over.

The whole situation was spiraling out of control, and I saw where it was heading. But it wasn't just everyone else who was losing their minds. I took a good hard look at myself, and I realized I was changing too. I looked at my friends and the people around me in the organization, and sure enough, the same thing was happening to them. Everyone was making big money, and driving a new BMW, and all of us were stuck in that mode of always wanting more. No matter how much flowed to us, it was never enough. It was as if we could see how much more there was still to be had, and we lost all perspective. I guess that's what happens when you start running with a guy who had made $900 million in a single year – you lose all sense of perspective.

One day when I came to the corporate office we had near my house, I felt God condemning my heart once again. I was the #1 Tiens distributor in North America, and to be honest, I wasn't even trying to be a distributor. I was there to be the success trainer and teach others how to be successful. But because I was at the top of the totem pole, with a huge down line, everything flowed up to me. I came in to work one day, and it occurred to me what was happening. I still had my real estate business, plus Lifestyles, plus Tiens. That's three full-time jobs, on top of my wife, my kids, my sobriety, and my God. I was stretched out like a rubber band.

Phyllis and I were doing real estate during the day, then Lifestyles and Tiens at night and on the weekends. As if that wasn't enough, there was the constant travel for seminars, shows, and whatever else came up. Oh, and don't forget the occasional Tiens worldwide summit meetings around the world. I was going full blast, 24/7.

I was chock full of the Chinese herbs, and those things make you run like a finely tuned sports car. I barely had time to sleep, and I rarely had time to eat. It was lights, camera, action, all the time. It was beyond ridiculous; it was insane. I had smashed all my personal records in real estate by August, and I wasn't even working at it all the time like I had in the beginning of my career. I had 30 billboards scattered around the Seattle area, and I was spending over $100,000 per month on marketing and business expenses alone. I was about to get an American Express Black Card, and the threshold for that was $200,000 a month. I was in Seattle one day, then Los Angeles the next, then Beijing or Tianjin the next. I was accustomed to wheeling and dealing from my days in South Central, but this new life was insane even by my crazy standards.

As I stood there in my Tiens office, contemplating what had become of my life, I heard God's voice in my head, and I felt Him condemning my heart. God said, "Greg, what are you doing?" My goal in the beginning with Mr. Li was to change the world and make a difference in people's lives. Now, I saw myself in a different light. I had changed, and things were different – but not in the ways I once imagined. I realized it had become all about me: what do I want, what do I need, and what do I have. I had a guaranteed contract with Mr. Li that would pay me $350 million over three years. My Lifestyles of Success training program for Tiens was done, in English and Chinese versions. I already had my Lear Jet picked out. I already had my white Bentley picked out. But something just wasn't right. I thought about my $900 million man, Mr. Li.

I realized that, in one sense, he had it all. But in another sense, he had nothing.

First of all, Mr. Li was one of the loneliest people I had ever known. He was on top of the world, but he couldn't trust anyone. Mr. Li had no place to lay his head, and no room to rest, because he was so alone in this world. He couldn't stop moving for even a second, and he could never let his defenses down. Mr. Li changed out his top people every two years, because he didn't think he could trust them. He figured after two years, they'd know too much. His closest people were like actors, playing roles. The #2 guy in Tiens was Mr. Li's cousin, Mr. Yin. He was the handsome face, and the well-spoken gentleman of the whole Tiens organization. Mr. Yin was the smooth, polished, charming guy everyone liked, who could get everyone working hard and feeling good about themselves and the business. Then there was the #3 guy, Mr. Di. He was the one who applied whatever pressure was needed to make sure everything worked exactly the way it was supposed to. I recognized that role from my days in organized crime. Every big organization needs a guy to play the heavy, and to clear the roadblocks; whatever they may be.

All these thoughts were flashing through my mind, and it was wearing on my conscience. Then God said, "Greg, you sold yourself out. You sold out for everything. And it's going to cost you everything you have. Are you ready for that? Are you willing to pay the price? You sold your soul to the world, and you've got it all now. But you're going to lose it all. How does it feel?" I realized there was a price tag on the life I was living. There are no free lunches in life. There's a price you pay for everything you do in life. How much are you willing to pay? If I kept going down the path I was on, it was going to cost me my wife and my kids, first of all. I'd always said that Bill Gates isn't the richest man in the world, I am – because I have my God, my sobriety, my wife, and my kids. I realized that I would lose all of those things in my new life centered around me, me, me, and me. I was The Man. I was invincible. Nobody could tell me anything. But God condemned my heart in a powerful way, and suddenly I knew that I wasn't spiritually, mentally, or emotionally mature enough to handle what was happening to me. I knew I had sold out my family for my success. Did I honestly believe I could run all over the world, chasing all this fabulous success and all these millions of dollars, and still be there for my family? I knew I had to choose between God and my family on one hand, or my personal success and financial independence on the other. I knew I couldn't have both, no matter how hard I tried to rationalize it and convince myself otherwise. It was decision time, and the ramifications were going to alter the course of my life. I remembered that day at Fred's house, when I walked up to his front door and saw my life pass before my eyes. The same thing was happening all over again, and it hit me hard. I already knew what I had to do. I told God, "Okay, I got it now. I see how it is. I'm done. It ends right here, right now."

CHAPTER 46

FACING THE FALLOUT

ONCE I MAKE a decision, it's final. I accept the consequences of my decision, and I don't go back. But when I made the decision to end my relationship with Tiens, there was a lot of cleaning up to be done. When I told my Lifestyles CFO, Steve, of my decision, his response wasn't quite what I expected. Steve said, "What do you mean, you're quitting? You've got a contract for $350 million. You can't quit." I said, "I've made a decision, and I'm sticking to it. I'm done with it." Steve said, "Well, I've got news for you - you can't be done. You have to follow through on this, because the truth is, you're broke." I said, "Broke? How can I be broke?" Steve said, "Greg, you paid for everything upfront. You have to fulfill that contract just to get your money back out of this." Everything I had done to create the Lifestyles program, in terms of all the development costs, the legal fees, and everything else, had been paid for out of my own pocket. The Lifestyles brand was copyrighted, and I was the sole owner of it. But once I decided to end my relationship with Tiens, and walk away from all the money that would have been generated by the sales of the Lifestyles program, I was in big trouble.

Steve got me on a conference call with a bankruptcy attorney, Kevin, and the two of them staged a pseudo-intervention for my financial situation. Steve said, "Greg, you've got three choices: door number one, you follow through with the contract, and you get paid." I said, "You didn't hear me - that's not gonna happen." Steve said, "Okay, door number two, you go back to Mr. Li, and have him reimburse you the $3 million for your hard costs to develop the program." I said, "That's not gonna happen either. The costs of the program are on me, because I was gonna do it anyway, with or without Mr. Li. So I can't ask him to pay for something that was mine all along." Steve said, "Alright, then your other choice is door number three, you file bankruptcy." I said, "Bankruptcy? Why would I file bankruptcy? I'm a million dollar, top-producing agent, year in and year out. I'm not filing bankruptcy." Steve said, "Now you're the one who didn't hear me. Those are your only choices. You're out of money. There is no more money for anything. You took all your real estate money and poured it into the Lifestyles and Tiens program. You were running all over the world, spending money like you had a money tree growing in the backyard. There is no money tree. There's nothing left, Greg – nothing. You're $3 million in the hole."

I told Steve I wasn't interested in any of the three options he gave me, and then Kevin jumped in on me. He said, "Listen, Greg – Steve laid it out for you. You either fulfill the contract and get paid, or you get the money from Mr. Li, or you file bankruptcy for $3 million. That's all there is to it. There are no other options here. None." I didn't like any of those options. However, I had already made up my mind I was not going to sell my soul and lose everything that I valued most in my life to chase the money that I knew would only ruin me. In the end, I agreed to listen to Steve and Kevin's advice, and on December 21st, 2001, I filed bankruptcy. I called my friend Lennox, who was the Owner and CEO of my brokerage, John L. Scott Real Estate. I told Lennox what I was doing and why, and Lennox said he understood. The next day, when I woke up in the morning, God said to me, "I just wanted your attention, Greg. I just wanted you to see where you were headed and what you were doing to yourself." I knew instantly what that meant, because I saw that I had gone off the deep end of seeking fame, fortune and success in worldly terms, and not in spiritual terms. That $350 million was signed, sealed and delivered to me. I didn't have to go out and run around and try to sell the Lifestyles program – it was set up automatically through the Tiens system. I just had to flip the switch, and all that money would have been mine. But I saw through it, and I pulled myself out of it in the nick of time.

My head had gotten so big, and my head was so hard, that no one could tell me anything. I had my Lear Jet and my Bentley picked out, and I was on my way to the top of that mountain, baby! When I think back on it now, I realize that I had to get right up to the edge of that mountain and look over the edge, before I recognized what was happening to me. Thank God I figured it out before it was too late. A few days later, Lennox had Jerry, the President of the company, call me. Jerry said, "Greg, I understand you've filed bankruptcy. If that's the case, we can't allow you to keep any of your employees. You'll have to let everyone go, including Phyllis." I said, "Listen, Jerry – if Phyllis goes, I go. Period. You have to let me keep Phyllis, or I'm done." Jerry allowed me to keep Phyllis, but I had to let all my sales agents and my other administrative help go.

Jerry told me to come to his office for a face-to-face meeting so we could discuss my future and figure out a plan for getting me back on my feet. I sat down with Jerry, and we looked at every aspect of my business. Then Jerry said, "How much do you think you'll make this year?" I said, "I'm gonna make about $900,000." Jerry said, "You think you're going to make $900,000? Let's be realistic, Greg. You just filed bankruptcy, and all your people are gone, except Phyllis. How in the world are you going to make $900,000?" I said, "Jerry, I'm telling you, I'm gonna make $900,000 next year. You can count on it. Write it down and put in the bank." I'm sure Jerry thought I was crazy, but I didn't care. I set my goals, I stayed focused, and I followed through. At the end of the year, when we looked at the scorecard, I had made just over $900,000. Is that amazing or what? That's how awesome my God is – He blesses me over and over again, despite myself.

Periodically, after the bankruptcy was in works, my attorney would call and say I needed to pay $10,000 for this, or $25,000 for that to balance everything out. One time, Kevin called me and said I needed to pay $75,000 to settle an account. I called John L. Scott's corporate office, told Jerry I needed $75,000 to pay a creditor, and because I was closing so many deals again, Jerry just said, "You need $75,000? No problem, Greg – come and get it." Lennox and everyone at John L. Scott had always been faithful to me, and supportive, and that loyalty meant a lot to me.

The fallout from my Tiens decision continued on for several weeks. After I filed bankruptcy, I called all my creditors and explained the situation. Then I called my vendors and the companies that helped me with all my marketing. I had billboards around town, mall ads, TV commercials, the whole works. I told my account reps what happened, and promised them I would be back on my feet in no time. To a person, they all said they weren't very happy about the bankruptcy, but they appreciated me calling and owning up to it. They agreed to continue working with me, and they said they would help me get back on my feet. For a while, I had to buy all my marketing on an a la carte basis. But that was a huge victory, because it allowed me to continue my marketing as I earned money throughout the year, without starting all over again. Without that, I would've been dead in the water.

Within 24 months, I had broken all my personal records in real estate all over again. Within 36 months, I had purchased my dream house on the bluff in Mukilteo for $3.8 million. Ironically, I bought the same house that I had originally wanted to sell to Mr. Li. My strategy for getting back on top after all that adversity was the same as it had always been: I set my goals, I made a plan of action, and I followed through to the end. It wasn't easy to get my business back on track after I left Tiens and filed bankruptcy, but eventually I got it done. The fallout from my life-altering decision affected me in a personal way as well, because I still had to deal with all my friends, family members, and associates who were connected to me through Tiens. When I told them of my decision, I got a lot of resistance. In a way, I understood. After all, everyone underneath me in my down line was making a lot of money selling Tiens. Some of my friends had even traveled with me and Mr. Li, and they had grown accustomed to living the good life because of their work with Tiens. Many of them were driving the new BMW's that Mr. Li had given them, and they weren't very happy with me when I told them I was done with it. I must have heard the same protest a hundred times. They all said, "Greg, have you lost your freaking mind? You can't quit now. Nobody in their right mind walks away from hundreds of millions of dollars. Are you feeling okay? Man, you just need a vacation or something, because what you're doing isn't right."

Like I said before, when I make a decision, it's final. Just like that day at Fred's house, I walked away, and I didn't look back. Eventually, hundreds of people who came in underneath me gave up and walked away too. Tiens' North American sales started slipping across the board, until the whole operation just dried up. One by one, all the corporate offices started closing. Seattle was the first market to hit bottom, then California, and eventually Vancouver and Toronto shut down too. Miss Fi, Ni, and their crew tried in vain to keep everything going without me, but they never could make it work. The truth of the matter was, I had started North America from scratch, and when I left, it was like someone popped the drain and let out all the bathwater. Lawrence left Tiens for good, and the new management team in the Seattle office couldn't do it without us. At the very end, Mr. Li came to America to work out a final severance package for Lawrence. Phyllis and I went to visit Mr. Li at his hotel, to say our final goodbyes, but when we got there, Lawrence told us that Mr. Li's mom had just died, and Mr. Li was very distraught. It didn't feel right to pile on top of my dear friend when he was already reeling emotionally, so we just let him be. I called Mr. Li later to tell him that I loved him, and that I couldn't go on with the work we had planned. That call was one of the most difficult conversations I've ever had, but I never doubted my decision to walk away. To this day, I believe that decision saved my family, and probably my life.

CHAPTER 47

RAQUEL'S FIRST MIRACLE

AS IF MY life wasn't proof enough, here's a great example of the power of God, faith and prayer. About 10 or 11 years ago, I was asleep at home when I got a call at 4:30 in the morning. It was my daughter, Royale, who told me that my oldest daughter, Raquel, was in a coma from a drug overdose. Royale said Raquel was in Intensive Care in a hospital in Cherry Hill, New Jersey. I'd never been to Cherry Hill, New Jersey in my life; I didn't even know where it was. Royale was hysterical, crying and screaming on the phone. Then my ex-wife Rae called to fill me in on all the details. Rae had also been addicted to drugs while we were married, but unlike me, she had never gone into rehab. Raquel had been staying at Rae's house, and as I'd always said, nothing good ever happened when those two got together. Rae was crying on the phone, saying Raquel was going to die. Rae told me where Cherry Hill was, so I immediately got on a plane and flew back to New Jersey to see Raquel. While I was traveling, everyone was calling me to express their concern and to see how Raquel was doing. I told everyone, "Don't worry, she's gonna be alright. Just pray for her."

I got to New Jersey, found the hospital, and went to check on Raquel. I walked into her room, and Raquel was lying in her bed looking like the Bride of Frankenstein. Raquel was in a coma, and the doctors had her on life support, with all these machines running and keeping her alive. They were pumping charcoal and all kinds of drugs into Raquel. It was a nightmare. I huddled with Raquel's doctors, and told them I had family friends who were doctors, and to please just give it to me straight. I told the doctor, whatever the truth was, I could handle it. I just needed to know straight up what the situation was. The doctor said, "Okay Mr. Perry, here's the honest truth. We have the best facilities here; the best doctors, the best neurologists, and the best of everything. We have done everything medically possible to help your daughter, but…" The doctor's voice trailed off, and I said, "So what you're saying is, we need a miracle. Is that right?" The doctor said, "That's right. I'm sorry, Mr. Perry." I said, "Well, you don't need to apologize, because you don't know my God."

I walked back into Raquel's room, where she was still lying in a coma, and I said to her, "Look, little girl…I told you, if you go back to New Jersey to your mother's house, you're gonna wind up in a body bag. You're lying here right now in a coma, and the devil is trying to take your life. You're gonna have to fight, Raquel. You're gonna have to fight for your life with everything you have. Your dad loves you, Sheri loves you, Royale loves you, A.J. loves you, Manny loves you, Dominique loves you, Janaye loves you, and Caleb loves you." When I said Caleb's name, I saw a single tear come out of Raquel's eye and slowly trickle down her cheek. I saw that tear come down, and I said, "Alright, here we go. You're gonna have to fight! You can do it, Raquel – fight for your life! The devil wants your life - don't let him get you! Keep fighting!" The doctors just stood there looking at me, with no emotion or expression. It was dead quiet in that room, except for me talking to Raquel. I was praying, "Dear God, in the name of Jesus Christ, bring my baby back."

Later that night, I left the hospital and went down the street to the Hilton hotel. I didn't even know where I was, but here is how awesome the power of God is. I walked into that hotel, and they were having what is called an AA (Alcoholics Anonymous) retreat, or convention. There were several groups from various 12-Step recovery programs all together in one place. I went in there and told the group that I was in the program myself, and that I had 17 years of sobriety. I told them my daughter had just OD'd and she was in a coma, on life support, fighting for her life. There were over 500 people in that room. Right away, they all joined hands, and started praying for Raquel. What are the chances there would be an AA convention, full of people from all over the state, meeting in my hotel, right when I walked in?

The next day, I went back to the hospital, and Raquel came out of the coma. But there was one problem – she was paralyzed. I'll never forget - the nurse told me to get some tennis shoes and put them on Raquel's feet because her feet would start balling up as a reaction to the paralysis. I went and got Raquel some Nikes and put them on her feet while she was lying there in ICU. The doctors and nurses were working with Raquel, and she was like a little infant. It was almost like a toy when the batteries die. One side of Raquel's body was completely paralyzed, and simply wouldn't work. Every day, I'd go talk to Raquel, and tell her how much everyone in the family loved her, and to stay strong and keep fighting. I kept her pumped up, but Raquel was like a little baby at that point; she couldn't speak or move or do anything. I didn't even know how much she was aware of, so I put pictures of everyone in the family up in Raquel's room to remind her who she was.

Little by little, one day at a time, Raquel started to wake up and come back. I'd show her pictures of us, and all she could say was, "Ahhh…Greg Perry." Then I started showing Raquel pictures of our family, and slowly, she started to remember who everyone was. I showed Raquel pictures of herself, and said, "This is you." Every single day, I told Raquel what day it was, and where she was. That went on for several days, while I camped out in ICU with her. Raquel kept coming back a little bit more each day, and slowly but surely her mind was awake again. The doctors and nurses had Raquel working around the clock, with physical therapy and other recovery programs.

One day, I questioned Raquel to test her memory. Raquel remembered who she was, she knew where she was, and she knew why she was there. I said, "Do you know what happened to you?" Raquel said, "Yeah, I overdosed." I said, "That's right. Do you remember what I told you about going to New Jersey?" Raquel said, "Yeah, you said I'd be in a body bag." I said, "Oh, good…so you remember all of that. Are you ready to go home?" She said, "Yeah, Daddy, I'm ready to go home." I said, "Okay, then get up out of that bed and I'll take you home. Let's go."

I knew one side of Raquel's body was completely paralyzed and wouldn't work. Raquel's brain was telling her body to get up, but only one side of her body worked. She pushed and struggled, and her one good leg was kicking like a bronco against the surface of the hospital bed. Whack! Whack! Whack! Raquel's leg kept smacking the bed as she struggled to gain enough leverage to get out of the bed. I just kept saying, "Let's go. Get up." Raquel was sweating like she'd just run a marathon. Finally, after 10 minutes of Raquel's leg smacking the bed, I told her to relax. I said, "Good – you see that? God isn't gonna make it so easy on you. You're gonna have to work, little girl. God isn't gonna let you off the hook. You almost took your life, but God brought you back. Now you're gonna have to earn everything from here on out." Raquel just sighed and said, "Awww, Daddy, I know."

I was sitting there in the hospital room with Raquel, and it occurred to me what had happened. I had watched as, right before my eyes, God had resurrected my daughter from the dead. I'll never forget when I first checked into my hotel, I opened my Bible, and said, "God, give me a word." The first verse I laid eyes on said, "The effectiveness of a righteous man's prayers can do many things." I also remember that when Raquel first came out of the coma, I was so happy I was just beaming. Late one night as I was coming through the emergency room to go visit Raquel, I ran into the security guard, who noticed I was excited. He asked me why I was so happy, and I told him that my daughter had just come out of a coma. The security guard had a strange look on his face, and he said, "Is your daughter that pretty little girl that came in here in a coma?" I told him it was, and the guard said, "I was here when they brought her in. To be honest, I thought she was dead. The doctors were doing everything they could to jump-start her, but I thought she was gone. I'm so happy for you. God bless you, brother."

Meanwhile, throughout the process of being in ICU with Raquel, Sheri and the kids kept calling me and asking when I was coming home. I told them I wasn't coming home without Raquel, no matter how long it took. Raquel kept improving, and eventually I made arrangements to transfer her to a hospital in Seattle as soon as we got back home. Right before we were going to leave New Jersey, the doctors there wanted to do a procedure where they would insert a tube into Raquel so they could look at her heart and make sure it didn't have a hole in it. Raquel was doing great at that point, so I wasn't thrilled about the test, but the doctors assured me it was a necessary precaution.

Unfortunately, it turned out my intuition was on target, because when the doctors sedated Raquel for the procedure, it knocked her stupid again. Raquel had drug addiction in her DNA from being my daughter, because I was still using when she was born. Her body just couldn't tolerate hard drugs, and the heavy sedatives set her back in her recovery. We got Raquel going again, and we prepared to return to Seattle. Before we left New Jersey, my sister Adrienne brought my mom to see Raquel in the hospital, and together we celebrated my mom's birthday right there in Raquel's hospital room.

When I got back to Seattle with Raquel, Sheri and the kids were there to meet us. I don't think anyone in the family had any idea what to expect. Raquel had always been a gorgeous, healthy young girl, and had even been a model in her younger years. When the family saw her looking like she'd come back from the dead – which she had - with only half of her body working, they couldn't deal with it. Raquel was still strapped to a hospital gurney when we got off the plane. Sheri took Raquel into a restroom to help her get cleaned up after the long cross-country flight, and Sheri just about had a nervous breakdown. It was all too much, seeing this beautiful girl in such a sad state. We all did our best to get through a difficult situation, and then we took Raquel to the local hospital to continue her recovery in Seattle. At that point, it had only been about three weeks since Raquel had overdosed in New Jersey.

A few days after we got Raquel into a hospital in Seattle, we had a meeting with her team of doctors to assess her situation and to discuss her recovery goals going forward. I could tell right away that the lead doctor hadn't even looked at Raquel's charts, because none of the things he had written for her goals sheet were realistic. When I objected to the goals, the lead doctor said, "Mr. Perry, we never should have admitted Raquel into our program here, because our program is too aggressive. We might need to look at some alternative living situations to try and find a better fit for Raquel." When I asked him what that meant, the doctor said, "We don't know if Raquel is ever going to come out of this." I told the doctors I had already heard enough of that kind of talk from the doctors back in New Jersey, and that I had brought Raquel to that hospital because I heard from some friends that it was the best. I also told them I was going to pull Raquel out of there and take her over to another hospital the following week. Before I left, I said, "Raquel is going to throw that wheelchair out the window and walk right out of here when we leave next week. You don't know my God, or me, or my daughter." You could have heard a pin drop as the team of doctors and technicians just stared at me. Then I went out of town for a few days to get the rest of the family set up on a trip they had planned.

A few days later, I got a call from the same doctor. I answered the phone and said, "What do you want?" The doctor said, "I don't know quite how to say this, Mr. Perry, but Raquel is standing up in her room. We're going to reevaluate this whole situation, and in the meantime, we'll just keep Raquel here in this program." I hung up the phone and I didn't know whether to start laughing or crying. Raquel stayed in the program at that hospital for a month, and before we left, the doctors told me they had never seen anyone who had been in Raquel's condition recover that quickly. I neglected to mention to the doctors that in the four days between the assessment meeting and the phone call from the doctor, I had Royale go visit Raquel twice a day and give her Chinese herbs. I'd been taking Chinese herbs myself for several years, and knew them to be a tremendous health benefit. Between the Chinese herbs, the endless prayers of our friends and family, and the power of my faith in God, Raquel couldn't help but set the record for the fastest recovery time. Raquel walked out of that hospital after a month and never needed a wheelchair again.

Raquel had to endure numerous therapy programs in her recovery, including physical therapy and speech therapy. Raquel had to learn to walk, talk, and eat again, among many other basic daily functions. It was almost like Raquel was the new baby in the family. For six months after her stay in the hospital, we had Rehab Without Walls come to our home and work with Raquel. If you saw Raquel today, you wouldn't believe she's the same girl who almost died in ICU back in New Jersey. Raquel is a personal trainer now, and she looks even more like a model than she did when she was younger. She's drop-dead gorgeous, totally healthy, and in incredible shape. Raquel loves mentoring others and teaching them how to be their very best not just physically, but in all aspects of their lives. She is a living, breathing miracle herself, and a faithful child of God.

Throughout that process with Raquel, even when I was with her in the hospital in New Jersey, my friends would call and say, "Greg, are you okay? How are you holding up?" All I know is, I witnessed another miracle in my life. I watched as God resurrected my little girl from the dead, brought her back to life, and then gave her a new life. Raquel literally had to start her life over, like a baby learns to walk, talk, eat, everything. It wasn't easy, and it didn't come overnight; she had to work hard for it. But I had complete peace, because I never doubted for one single second that God would come through for me. When Raquel was lying there in a coma, and I was in that hotel room in New Jersey, I got on my knees and said the most powerful prayer I've ever said in my life. I pleaded, "God, I'm calling in all my favors. Everything I've ever done for anybody, every person I've ever helped. I'm pushing all my chips to the center of the table, because I need a miracle, Lord. You bring my baby back. I'm taking her home. You bring her back." I never let one bit of doubt enter my mind after that, because I knew the grace of God would come through for me. And guess what – He did. Again. Just like He always has. My family has always been so blessed, and my life is so full of miracles that I never doubt Him, ever.

CHAPTER 48

MIRACLE ON THE MOUNTAIN

SEVERAL YEARS AGO, I took the whole family up to Whistler, in British Columbia, for a mid-winter ski vacation. My mom came with us, my sisters Adrienne and Angela brought their families, and Keith, my best friend from childhood, brought his family. Altogether, there were 22 of us, and I put us all up in six suites at the Pan Pacific Hotel at Whistler. One beautiful sunny day, a bunch of us went out snowmobiling. Our group was so large that we split up into two smaller groups. Before we left, I said a prayer, just like my mom had always taught me. I said, "Lord, I ask that you put a web of protection around everybody and keep us all safe." Then I repeated the full Prayer of Protection for us:

The light of God surrounds us
The love of God enfolds us
The power of God protects us
The presence of God watches over us

The mind of God guides us

The life of God flows through us

The law of God directs us

The peace of God abides with us

The joy of God uplifts us

The strength of God renews us

The beauty of God inspires us

Wherever we are, God is

My daughter, Dominique, was riding on a snowmobile driven by my sister, Adrienne. They were running second in the long line of snowmobiles behind the instructor, who had my youngest son, Caleb, riding with him because Caleb was so young and small. All of my kids have grown up as thrill-seekers. They've been cliff diving and rock diving in Maui, and they've been riding jet skis since they were five or six years old. They've been water skiing, wake boarding, snow skiing, snowboarding, surfing, body surfing, snorkeling, you name it. They've done all that and more ever since they were in grade school. My kids have always had a tremendous sense of adventure and high-energy fun. They like to go fast, and they are fearless. Dominique was about seven or eight years old, riding with her aunt Adrienne, and she kept telling her aunt, "C'mon, go faster!" The snowmobiles can reach speeds of over 70 miles per hour, so you're supposed to keep a safe following distance behind the person riding in front of you. Dominique told Adrienne, "Stop for a minute and let them get further ahead, then we can go really fast and catch up to them."

Adrienne stopped for a few moments and let the instructor and Caleb go until they were out of sight. Then Adrienne hit the gas, and she and Dominique took off at full speed to catch up. The instructor had pulled ahead, but when he looked back and didn't see Adrienne, he figured there must be a problem. He rounded a bend in the trail, stopped, and got off the snowmobile. Caleb was still sitting on the snowmobile while the instructor waited for Adrienne and Dominique to show up. The girls were flying down the hill at warp speed, when they came around the bend in the trail and saw Caleb right in front of them, like a sitting duck. That trail was designed to be driven single-file, with no shoulder or room on the side to maneuver around. Adrienne told me later she only had one thought when she rounded that corner and saw Caleb. She said to herself, "I am not hitting Caleb - no matter what." If Adrienne had run into Caleb with her snowmobile, he would have been killed instantly, and Dominique and Adrienne probably would have died in the collision.

Instead, Adrienne yanked the steering wheel to the left, and she and Dominique flew off the path, and then off a cliff that was on the side of the hill they had been riding down. They flew over the trees, and were literally flying through the air just like the people in those extreme sports videos. On the other side of the cliff was a rock formation and some trees. Adrienne somehow managed to hit the only patch of deep snow within 50 feet. The snowmobile crashed into a hillside, flipped over, and was totaled. Dominique was thrown off somewhere in midair, and landed on the rocky ground below, while Adrienne landed in the deep snow and was buried like a javelin. The rest of the family was riding behind Adrienne and Dominique and saw them go off the cliff, so they ran down the hillside to find the girls. They got down to where Adrienne was buried in the snow and dug her out. Adrienne was understandably upset by the whole experience, but she wasn't injured. Dominique sustained some bumps and bruises from her fall, but she came out of it okay and even went skiing with me later that same day.

When Adrienne tells that story today, she says, "I don't know how Dominique and I didn't die on that mountain that day." The instructor told me that when he saw the snowmobile fly off the cliff, he got on his radio to call for the Rescue Patrol and told them, "It isn't going to be pretty." He said that snowmobile was flying through the air like Evel Knievel jumping over a canyon. It's a miracle no one was hurt that day. That doesn't surprise me, though, because I'm so used to it. I've seen so many miracles in my life, and God always watches over my family and me. All I know is, my guardian angels were working overtime that day to protect my sister, my daughter, and my son. I still pray the Prayer of Protection every time I go somewhere, especially with my family, and I swear to God it works. It's amazing to think of all the miracles I've experienced, plus Michael beating a heroin addiction, plus Raquel surviving an overdose and being in a coma, plus Adrienne and Dominique crashing on the mountain that day.

Another time, I was driving Angie's husband's 280Z home from Canada one night when I hit some loose gravel going around a curve and spun out in total darkness. The car slammed into something hard and metallic, and I was pinned inside. I couldn't even open the driver's door - I had to crawl out through the passenger window. It was pitch black outside, so I couldn't see what I had hit. I ran all the way back to Angie's house and explained what happened. I apologized to Patrick for getting in an accident in his car, and I told him I would gladly buy him a new car. The next day, we went back to the crash scene and surveyed the damage. We discovered the car had slid off the road and crashed right into the bucket of an enormous earthmover that was parked on the side of the road. The sharp metal edge of the earthmover bucket had sliced the back of the car almost in half, and the edge of the bucket had stopped just a few inches from my head. The car was completely destroyed. A few inches more, and I would've been done too.

CHAPTER 49

AN OLD FRIEND RETURNS

ONE AUTUMN DAY, I was coaching my son's peewee football team in Mukilteo, when I got a call from China. I recognized the number right away. It was Robin, Mr. Li's latest protégé, and Mr. Li, on a three-way call. As soon as I picked up the phone and heard that familiar voice speaking to Robin in Chinese, I said, "Hey! Mr. Li, how are you? It's so great to hear your voice again!" I hadn't really spoken to Mr. Li or seen him since I'd left Tiens almost a decade earlier. Mr. Li said he was building a brand new, state-of-the-art campus in Tianjin, and it was almost done. It was an enormous complex, complete with a college, office buildings, a hotel, spa, and nine Presidential suites. Robin said they would be sending me the renderings so I could see how it looked. Mr. Li invited me to come to China to see it in person. As happy as I was to hear from Mr. Li, I really didn't want to go to China to see him. I already knew that what he really wanted was me, his homeboy, to come back to him. Mr. Li fed off my energy and my charisma, but as I said when I left Tiens: when I make a decision, it's final. I saw no reason to believe that any of the chaos had changed in the years since I had left.

I told Mr. Li I had been branching out from real estate and getting involved in some new kinds of business opportunities, and that I'd love to share more information about them with him. I talked about my venture with Liquid Cable, and how I thought he could make some serious money if he wanted to get involved as an investor. I told him I would send him the details and the prospectus, but he kept turning it around and talking about me coming to China to see his new campus. Right after we got off the phone, we sent each other all the information we had promised one another. A few weeks later, Mr. Li called back, to reiterate his invitation for me to come to China to see the campus, and I reiterated my invitation for him to consider becoming an investor in Liquid Cable.

Mr. Li and I kept going back and forth like that for a few months. I'd send him information on Liquid Cable or some other investment, in hopes of getting him to buy in, and then he'd send me information about his ever-expanding campus, in hopes of getting me to go to China to see it. Neither of us would budge and give the other what they really wanted. Finally, I got another call from Robin, saying "Hi Greg, Mr. Li says he misses you very much, and he would like to know if you could meet him in Los Angeles in a few days. He is launching a brand new line of Tiens products, and he would like to show them to you and see what you think of them." I told Robin I would be happy to meet Mr. Li in L.A. for a day. I arrived in Los Angeles a few days later, and checked into the hotel where Mr. Li was staying. We went out to dinner at Morton's Steakhouse. It was wonderful to see my old friend again after so many years. Mr. Li asked about Sheri and the kids, and we reminisced about the good old days of travelling the world together.

Mr. Li showed me the new line of Tiens products he was planning to launch, and I offered him some success strategies. When our waiter brought the bill for the $900 dinner, I quickly grabbed the check and paid it. Mr. Li was furious, and tried to strong-arm me into letting him pay. Some things never change. The Godfather of Tiens had always paid for everything, and it drove him crazy whenever I turned the tables on him. But he was very pleased when he saw the special gift I had brought for him: a beautiful collage of pictures taken when we were travelling the world together. Some of my favorite pictures of us were taken when Sheri and I accepted his invitation to visit him in China and stay at his private resort hotel. Mr. Li had always loved Sheri and my kids, and I know that picture collage meant a lot to him.

After dinner, Mr. Li and I headed back to our hotel to get ready to leave town. Mr. Li was on his way to New York, and I was on my way back home to Seattle. We had only been in the car for a few minutes when Mr. Li directed Robin to translate. Robin said, "Greg, Mr. Li says it has made him very happy to see you again. If it's not too much to ask, Mr. Li would like to know if there's any way you can stay over for one more day and take him shopping tomorrow in Beverly Hills?" I said, "Sure, I can do that. Tell Mr. Li I'll take him shopping like he's never shopped before in his life." I met up with Mr. Li and Robin the next morning, and we got started on some serious power shopping. For all the years I had known Mr. Li, he had always worn the same old tired style of clothes: a sort of modern version of traditional Chinese formal wear. That was a pretty boring fashion statement for a guy with so much money. Since Mr. Li had always admired my taste in clothes, I decided it was time for a makeover for my billionaire friend.

We started our day at the Beverly Hills Hotel, where there was a custom suit shop that catered to a very exclusive clientele, including famous actors and entertainers. Mr. Li bought a couple nice suits, but the selection there wasn't quite what I was hoping for, so we quickly moved on. I knew exactly where we needed to go next to give Mr. Li a clothes shopping experience like no other in the world, and one befitting a man of his financial stature. Our destination was an appointment at the legendary Bijan, the world-famous boutique on Rodeo Drive in Beverly Hills. Bijan has been described as the most expensive store in the world. Bijan himself was an extravagant fashion and fragrance designer from Iran, whose by-appointment-only showroom caters strictly to society's wealthiest and most elite members. The list of influential men that Bijan has clothed reads like a Who's Who of the Rich and Famous, including current and former Presidents, Prime Ministers, politicians, billionaires, athletes, actors, and entertainers.

When you have an appointment at Bijan, it's a completely private experience. They close down the entire store just for you, while four staffers wait on you simultaneously. We got in there, and I went crazy for several hours. Mr. Li completely trusted my judgment, so I just pulled suits as fast as he could try them on. Those four staffers were running in circles trying to keep up with us. By the time we were done at Bijan, Mr. Li had spent about $200,000 on suits, shirts, ties, and all the accessories. In addition to his one-of-a-kind shopping experience, Bijan was also famous for his incredible collection of luxury cars. His yellow Bugatti was parked out front, and his custom yellow Rolls Royce Phantom Drophead Coupe was in the back. When I told Mr. Li how much I liked that Phantom Drophead, he said, "I have one back in China. Come back to China with me and you can have it." I said, "That's okay, someday I'll buy my own."

When we were done at Bijan, we headed over to an upscale silver antique store, where I helped Mr. Li pick out several collections of beautiful silver furnishings for the nine Presidential suites he had built in his campus in China. Mr. Li explained that he had built nine separate Presidential suites so that whenever world leaders and dignitaries came to visit him, there would always be enough space for everyone and no one would ever be offended that another visiting party had better accommodations. Mr. Li bought several sets of beautiful estate-style silverware, platters, plates, and other furnishings that he wouldn't be able to find, let alone buy, anywhere else. After that, I took Mr. Li over to Santa Clarita Studios in Valencia, so he could see where I planned to film my Dream Life television show. We met up with my good friend and producer, Romeo, and I showed Mr. Li around the studios. Santa Clarita Studios is home to many famous TV shows, including the hit series, CSI. We wrapped up our day with another posh dinner in Beverly Hills, then we jumped in the Mercedes I had rented and I drove us back to the hotel. It was Robin, Mr. Li's daughter, Mr. Li, and myself. When we got back to the hotel, we said our last goodbyes. Mr. Li and I shared a big warm hug that lingered for a few special moments. I told Mr. Li that I loved him, and he reciprocated. No translation was needed to convey the depth of the love and respect we felt for another.

Finally, just as we were completing the final edits of this book in May of 2015, I looked up and saw my main man, Mr. Li, making global headlines yet again. Apparently Mr. Li had celebrated the recent 20th anniversary of his Tiens Group Company in typically grand fashion, by rewarding over 6,400 of his top-producing employees with a luxurious, all-expenses-paid French vacation. Mr. Li rented out 140 hotels in Paris alone, and 4,760 more rooms in plush hotels in Cannes and Monaco. French authorities said it was the single biggest vacation booking ever in France, and the cost of Mr. Li's gesture was estimated at $15-20 million. But that's nothing to Mr. Li. I saw him do it time and time again, when we were working closely together, laying out our game plan and strategizing the future global success of Tiens and Lifestyles of Success.

Greg on top of the real estate world.

CHAPTER 50

THE RISE AND FALL OF GREG PERRY REAL ESTATE

BY 2008, THE real estate market was starting to collapse. At first, it appeared that Seattle might be spared the agony that was hitting so many other major markets across the country. States such as Florida, Arizona, Nevada, and California were hammered especially hard, but the local economy in Seattle looked to be stronger than in most other places. In reality, it just took a while longer for the tsunami to hit here. When it finally reached Seattle, the results were devastating. Seattle lost over 30% off its peak real estate values, and that crushed the successful business I had built over my 15-plus years. I had been rolling hard for a very long time. I had made tens of millions of dollars, and I had spent millions on my marketing. As my career had gone on, and as my reputation as a top producer had grown exponentially, I had gradually moved into the higher price ranges. By the time the market crashed in 2008-09, I was known mostly for selling million-dollar-plus homes, and I had sold countless listings in the $3,000,000-5,000,000 range.

When the market in Seattle first started declining, a lot of the high-end agents couldn't afford to keep their highest-priced listings, because of the high marketing costs. But I always believed in my ability to market and sell homes that other agents couldn't. So even when the million-dollar listings started slowing way down, I went in the opposite direction – I doubled down. I scooped up as many of them as I could, thinking that if I sold even a few of them, the huge commissions would more than make up for the lack of quantity. I had a meeting with my sales agent, Gordon, and I told him, "We're gonna go after all the high-end listings and own the top-end market. None of these other agents can afford to compete with me in that segment of the market." Gordon and I went after all the multi-million-dollar homes we could find, and within 30 days, I had added $15 million worth of high-end listings to my inventory. In one high-end neighborhood alone, I added $10 million worth of the most expensive properties. Unfortunately, when I looked up a few years later, I saw that 90% of those listings ended up going back to the bank as foreclosures. The banks had stopped the risky lending practices that had contributed to the real estate bubble in the first place, and that spelled death to the high-end market I had previously dominated.

As if the real estate market crash wasn't devastating enough to my business, an old legal matter reared its ugly head at the worst possible time. I had always been squeaky clean in my real estate business, which was quite an accomplishment in itself, given my high profile and the number of agents that would have loved to see me go down. There wasn't a lot of gray area when it came to Greg Perry – you either loved me or hated me. My clients loved me and my marketing, but a lot of agents resented me for it. In any event, I had always kept out of trouble, which really wasn't that hard to do with Phyllis taking care of my business in the office. One day, I got a letter from my corporate office, to notify me that I was being charged with a zoning violation by the State. I didn't even know what that meant. Apparently, one of my clients from about five years earlier had a complaint about the house we had sold him. It was a young guy who wanted to run his landscaping business out of his house, and he needed to build a shop for all his equipment. I was in Australia at the time, and apparently my sales agent told the guy there was no problem having a home business or a shop. The guy bought the house and we thought everything was fine.

It turned out that when the guy went to build the shop, he had a hassle with the city. He loved the house, and even though he was able to finally build the shop, he turned it back around on me and my company. Somehow, the State got ahold of it just before the Statute of Limitations was going to expire, and someone decided to come after Greg Perry. Our John L. Scott attorneys got on the case, and in the depositions, it was determined that I didn't have anything to do with it. Even the other agent told the State it was him and not me. But the State didn't care about the details - they said that since the agent was working for me, they wanted me to admit I was wrong. I refused to settle on their terms, so the State said they were suspending my license for one year, with nine months forgiven. That left me with an actual suspension of three months. I'd been in real estate for 15 years, closed thousands of transactions, earned tens of millions of dollars in commissions, and I'd never had a single legal problem. The State didn't care about that, and suspended me for three months anyway. I always joked that I'd be in trouble if I ever went a month or two without a deal, and suddenly I was looking at three months of no deals in a dying housing market. That was more than I could sustain, and it stopped my business dead in its tracks.

The State also forced me to immediately stop every aspect of my marketing. That meant no mall ads, no billboards, no magazine ads, no commercials, no marketing at all. Then came the killer blow. I had about $900,000 in commissions pending in escrow, but the State said I couldn't have any contact with my clients, or any contact with the employees in my office. They made it clear they would be checking up on me. That meant I couldn't even hand my deals off to another agent to finish them for me. I lost all those deals in escrow, because my clients couldn't put their deals on hold until my suspension was over. I was up a creek without a paddle. It reminded me of the old days in organized crime, because the whole thing felt like a setup. It was a helpless feeling. By the time the State reinstated my license three months later, the damage was already done. I was always the king of cash flow, but three months without any business was more than I could handle.

During my three months off from real estate, I scrambled around trying to find a way to make some money. I needed an outlet, and something to do, or else I would've gone crazy sitting around the house. I hooked up with some friends who had invented a technology business related to Internet bandwidth. They estimated the business could be worth as much as $4 billion within 36 months. We met every night to put the business together, and I was advising them on how to restructure the business to make everything work. They gave me a 33% share of the business, and made me a Vice President. I put my friend Romeo in as President, and brought in another friend from New York to help with the technical side of everything.

We started running meetings with investors, and I set it all up. We met in Las Vegas to prepare for the technology conference with all the big guys in Hollywood. I was borrowing money left and right to try to keep the business afloat until we could convince some heavyweight investors to get involved. We had attorneys advising us on the stock allocations, copyrights, etc. Liquid Cable was going to be my home run, the biggest thing I had ever done in my life. At the very last minute, the whole thing blew up, because that old familiar greed factor kicked in, and the backstabbing and infighting tore it apart. I tried my best to hold it together until we could sell off the concept, but it was too late. Liquid Cable died, and I was left even more in debt than I was when it started.

By the time the smoke cleared after the Liquid Cable implosion and my three-month suspension from real estate, I had racked up $7 million in debt. I had also started gambling again when I was in Vegas with the Liquid Cable crew, to try to raise some extra cash, and I had to once again face the truth about that old bad habit. I called the casino and basically turned myself in. I told them I recognized I had a gambling problem, and that I was done with the whole thing, once and for all. I told them I wasn't coming back, and that they needed to close my credit line. The casino bosses said they would work something out for me, so I could pay back the $150,000 that I owed them. I said, "You don't understand – I'm done. I'm not coming back." They said, "Well, we can close your credit line, no problem. But if you're done, and you're not coming back, then you'll need to pay off your balance, in full, right now, today." I said, "Are you crazy? I can't do that!" I got an attorney from Las Vegas who specialized in casino debts. He educated me on all the legal tactics the casinos use to go after people who don't pay off their markers. We fought with the casino for about a year and half, then the casino sent me a notice saying that, with the interest on the debt, I actually owed them $450,000. The casino said that if I didn't pay the debt once and for all, they were going to seek a warrant for my arrest for defaulting on a personal debt.

I was just about at the end of my rope with the casino and the threat of the rising debt, when the attorney said, "Greg, I don't understand why you don't just file bankruptcy. I'm looking at your financial picture, and you're a bleeding corpse. You're down $7 million, and you've got nothing. If you file bankruptcy, you can clear the deck, start all over again, and this will be gone forever." It had been about 10 years since my first bankruptcy, and there I was staring at another one. I had worked so hard to get everything straight and get back on my feet after that first bankruptcy, and yet, for all the success I'd had since then, I had to start all over yet again. I filed Chapter 7 again, and eventually, my case was moved up into Federal Court. It turned out the Trustee used to live just down the street from me, and they knew all about me from living in my neighborhood. I was already behind the 8-ball before we even got started. It only got uglier from there. I had to turn over thousands of pages of legal documents, pertaining to my life, my real estate business, and my other business ventures such as Lifestyles of Success and Liquid Cable.

When the Trustee saw that I had almost a million dollars of deals pending in escrow, and the old corporate documents from Liquid Cable that said it could be worth as much as $4 billion, the red flags started flying. They immediately assumed that I must have had money hidden somewhere in the world, and that I was concealing significant financial assets. A few months before I filed my bankruptcy, the State and Federal court system in Seattle had been turned upside down by what has been called the largest personal bankruptcy case in the history of Washington State. Michael Mastro was a prominent local real estate developer who filed bankruptcy for debts of over $500 million. According to local news reports in Seattle, Mastro and his wife were suspected of committing massive bankruptcy fraud, and later fled the country to avoid compliance with the judge's orders to turn over some significant assets.

As my case unfolded, and the Trustee grew increasingly hostile toward me, I couldn't help but believe that there was a connection between the Mastro case and my own. I wondered if maybe the high-profile embarrassment inflicted upon the local legal system by the Mastros had caused the courts to cast an increasingly suspicious and vigilant eye toward every multi-million dollar bankruptcy case. Throw in my larger-than-life visibility factor, with my TV ads and billboards, and it seemed like I was a convenient target. The attitude of the Trustee seemed to be, "We may have missed on the Mastros, but we can damn sure nail Greg Perry." The sad truth of the matter was, I had no money. I had borrowed money from everyone I knew, just to keep gas in my car and groceries on the table. As a friend of mine said at the time, "You know, Greg, if they'd just ask all your friends, we'd tell them you spent every dollar you ever made – five times over!"

The local bankruptcy Trustee referred my case up to the Federal level, and they came at me with both barrels blazing, trying to charge me with 98 separate counts of bankruptcy fraud. They were on a mission to take me down and throw me in jail. Even my attorney said, "Dang, Greg - I've never seen anything like this. They're coming at you hard." But I never wavered one single bit. When the court asked me to provide documents, I did. When they asked me how I spent this money or that money, I told them the truth. The Trustee couldn't seem to grasp the fact that I could spend so much money in so many different ways. I told them straight up that I had gambled away some money, I had spent hundreds of thousands on my real estate marketing, and I had spent millions more on maintaining a lavish lifestyle. I had nothing to hide, but it never seemed to be enough for the Trustee. The Trustee came out to my house with the same appraiser from the Mastros' case, and they started going through my sports memorabilia, putting price tags on everything. They dug into the background information on the used cars I had purchased for my kids. They scoured every inch of my house – which was deep in foreclosure, by the way - trying to locate the secret wall safes where I had supposedly stashed all my millions of dollars. Sheri was so stressed out by the whole process that she almost had a nervous breakdown.

Early on in the bankruptcy process, I sat all my kids down and told them what was going on. I let them know in no uncertain terms that they were going to hear all kinds of rumors and allegations about their dad being a fraud and a criminal. I instructed them to keep living their lives and block out the noise. I told my friends to cooperate with the Trustee and give them anything they wanted, because they weren't going to let up on me anyway. I submitted three thousand pages of records and documents, covering every aspect of my life. No matter how aggressive and belligerent the Trustee got with my family, my friends, and me, I just blessed them in my prayers and complied with whatever was asked of me, day by day. My case slowly worked its way through the court system, and within a year, I was looking at a slate of trial dates running six months out into the future. Through it all, I just stayed humble, stayed faithful, and kept praying to God that the truth would finally win out.

One February day, Sheri and I were driving around in southern California, helping my daughters, Dominique and Janaye, look for a college to attend. My cellphone battery had died in the car, but when we got back to our hotel, I discovered I had several urgent voicemails from my bankruptcy attorney. I figured he was probably relaying another in a seemingly endless series of requests from the Trustee. When I called my attorney back, I was once again reminded of my favorite scene from my favorite movie, The Ten Commandments. My attorney answered my call and said, "Greg, I don't know how to tell you this, but I just got a call from the Federal prosecutor working your case. They're dismissing all 98 counts against you, without prejudice. That means they can't come back and pursue you again for this matter. It's over, Greg. Your bankruptcy has been approved."

I just sat there, stunned for a moment. When I told Sheri the good news, she immediately burst into tears. I was in absolute awe of how great and powerful my God is. Just as He had done so many times in my life, He had parted the Red Sea and worked another miracle for me. My faith had once again seen me through a crisis that might have killed a less faithful man. Several of my friends told me that they didn't know how I could survive the stress of that whole process. After that episode, I knew beyond any shadow of doubt that God was always working the highest good in my life. I knew if He could pull off a miracle like that for me, then His plan for my life must be beyond even my wildest imagination.

12 months after my bankruptcy was approved, I was back on my feet and a self-made millionaire all over again. As was the case with all the other adverse situations I had faced in my life, when I looked back on them later, I saw the life lessons that each one contained. The Federal bankruptcy case was really an opportunity for me to practice my faith, on the deepest levels. For example, I believe in forgiveness. God knows, no one needs forgiveness more than me. Through that case, I had the chance to work at forgiving those who would do me wrong. I never held a grudge against that Trustee, even though they came at me with both guns blazing for over a year. When I prayed during that case, I prayed for them to find peace within themselves.

I believe in faith, hope, and optimism. Even during the darkest hours of my case, I never lost my faith. I never stopped believing in the power of God to work miracles, not only for me, but for everyone involved. I never lost my hope in the best possible outcome for my family and me. I never stopped looking forward to each day with a renewed sense of optimism that any day could be the day when my miracle would unfold. I truly believe my faith, hope, and optimism is what got me through that ordeal. There is also the power of prayer. I prayed nonstop through that entire experience, and in the end, all my prayers were answered. The whole ordeal turned out to be a huge blessing in disguise. I always said that pain is the admission price you pay for new life. I paid the price, and in the end, I got to start my life over again.

My all-time favorite picture of my beautiful, blessed family.

CHAPTER 51

MY BLESSED FAMILY

FIRST OF ALL, I just want to thank God for my beautiful family. As I've said so many times before, Bill Gates is not the richest man in the world; I am. My wealth has nothing to do with money or possessions. My personal wealth starts and ends with the four main blessings in my life: my God, my sobriety, my wife, and my children. I've been blessed with such a wonderful family. It starts with my beautiful wife, Sheri, and includes all seven of my children: Raquel, Royale, Abraham, Immanuel, Dominique, Janaye, and Caleb.

When I was younger, before I had children, I always thought that I'd like to have four kids: two boys, and two girls. In my first marriage, to Rae, God blessed me with my two oldest daughters, Raquel and Royale. Raquel was my first daughter, and was always my little princess. We named Raquel after the famous actress, Raquel Welch. My Jewish mom, Margy, came up with the name for our beautiful and healthy second daughter, Royale. Later, I married Sheri, and we made plans for a family together, too. I still wanted two more kids, hopefully two boys, to go with the two girls I already had.

God blessed Sheri and I with our first boy, whom we named Abraham John Perry, or A.J. for short. I prayed about naming my first son, and God spoke to my heart, and said, "Abraham." We added the middle name in honor of my father. The next time, God blessed us with our fourth child, and our second son, Immanuel. We thought Immanuel Isaiah Perry was a beautiful name for our son, and it has special meaning too, since the first two names came from my favorite book, the Bible.

After A.J. and Manny, God blessed us with Dominique, who was like my second little princess. Dominique was always a smart and happy child, with big beautiful eyes, and a great disposition about her. About a year or so later, God blessed us with another beautiful little daughter, named Janaye. Sheri picked out that name herself, and I always loved it.

A few years later, God blessed us one last time, with our seventh child, a beautiful boy named Caleb. After Caleb was born, Sheri said to me, "Thank God for Caleb, because now we actually have eight kids. Nobody's a bigger baby than you - so you can be number eight, and I'm done having babies." I knew better than to argue, because Sheri was right; I am a big baby.

So we stopped right there, and the Perry Crew was complete: four girls, three boys, Sheri and myself. That was all we needed to create a lifetime worth of love, fun, and togetherness. Those seven kids have enriched my life in countless ways and they have meant everything to me. Every one of them was born healthy and happy. Over the past 33 years, my kids have made me the best father, the best husband, and the best child of God I could possibly be. My family is what gives me my drive and my motivation to provide for them and take care of them. Somehow, God saw fit to bless me despite myself with seven beautiful children.

As my kids got old enough to start getting out and going places,

I started planning to travel with them so we could see the world together. By then, our family had been blessed in so many ways; spiritually, financially, with my sobriety, and every aspect of our lives. I decided I would take off two months every year to travel and be with my wife and my kids. I took off the entire month of July to go to Hawai'i or another tropical paradise, and then in the month of December, I would take my family on a winter vacation. With each passing year, when I set my goals, I would set yearly goals based on working for 10 months, not 12 months, because I knew I was taking two months off to travel. That gave me all the hunger and drive I needed to succeed at the highest levels in real estate. Many of the biggest and best adventures in my family have occurred during our vacations. Those are the best memories a family could ever possibly have. The travel time we've all shared together is what created the perfect sense of balance that contributed to my success.

As my kids continued growing up, we began taking our annual family vacations to Maui. At one point, we had a streak of 14 straight years of staying in Maui. Each year, I rented out a house on the beach for a full month and invited all my friends, my extended family, and all their kids to join Sheri and I and all of our kids. It's not really fair to call those trips a vacation. Let's just say we lived in Maui for a month every year. We had a non-stop, 31-day party by the ocean, with the whole group together. My kids all grew up in the ocean: surfing, swimming, snorkeling, cliff diving, boogie boarding, and boating. I chartered a boat and we went fishing, water-skiing, jet skiing, and wakeboarding. I rented bikes, and we rode all over the island together.

We knew all the locals by about the third year in a row of going to Maui. The locals knew all my kids and they always welcomed us with love. When we weren't sharing in a family adventure, I turned the kids loose and let them run free. All seven of my kids had an absolute blast when we were in Maui. It was such a blessing for me to be in a financial position where I could unplug and get away with my family like that. Some years, we couldn't wait until our summer vacation, so we traveled on Spring Break. We rented a beach house in Cannon Beach, Oregon a few times. Other times, we took trips to Australia, The Bahamas, or Florida. We've been all over the continental United States, from Disneyland to Disneyworld, Universal Studios, Las Vegas, and California. We've travelled internationally to the Bahamas, all over the Caribbean, St. Thomas, St. Maarten, the Grand Caymans, and Bermuda. We've had so much fun together over the years, and it's because my kids are my pride and joy, my drive and my determination. The way I roll, I might be dead by now if it wasn't for my kids keeping me grounded and connected to life.

I've always been a big kid myself, so being a dad with a big family and having lots of fun with kids always came natural to me. I used to say kids are smarter than adults, and given the choice, I'd rather hang around the kids. When we went on our larger family vacations, sometimes I'd leave the parents at home and just take the kids. I knew the kids and I would have more fun without their parents than we would if the parents were there with us. I remember one time, Keith and I took about a dozen of the kids from my extended family to Disneyland for a day of fun. The kids were asking me how long we were going to stay, and I told them we'd stay until they shut down the park for the night. I think the park closed at midnight, but by 10:30 the kids were saying they were tired, their feet hurt, and they wanted to go home. I gave them all a hard time for being the only kids in history who ever wanted to leave Disneyland early. We stayed all the way to closing, and by then the parents were calling me and wanting to know where the kids were. I brought them all home, safe and sound asleep in the car after a full day of fun. That's just one small example of the kind of fun I've been blessed to have with my big beautiful family.

Another time at Christmas break, we took all seven kids skiing at the resort at Whistler. I taught all my kids to swim before they could walk, and they knew how to ski before they could ride a bike. Raquel and Royale were both in their late teens and they knew how to ski well. A.J. was probably eleven, and he was a good skier. I was still working with Manny, who was about ten, teaching him to ski. Then I had Dominique and Janaye, they were maybe seven or eight, and they could ski a little. Caleb was about two, and I had him in my backpack. We went all the way to the top of the mountain together, and then we came down. As we took off together, I paused and noticed I had Raquel and Royale out in front, with A.J. and Manny behind them, and Dominique and Janaye on either side of me. I saw my kids skiing together and I said a quiet prayer, thanking God for my blessed family. It was all about spending quality time with my family, and showing them some of the best things in life.

I got to a point in my real estate career where, after I had consistent success, I could afford to put my kids in one of the top private Christian schools in Seattle. Because of that, all my kids had a great quality education. I've been so incredibly blessed to be able to afford a quality of life that most people only dream about, and to share that abundant life with my kids. I make sure my kids know that all the blessings we enjoy as a family come to us by the grace of God, not by the grace of Greg. God has always watched over my family, and guided us and protected us every step of the way. There have been many times in my life where I knew my guardian angels were keeping my family blessed and safe in all kinds of dangerous or difficult situations. I'm not smart enough to do anything on my own, but with God's wisdom I can make things happen and be a powerful force for good. God has blessed me with seven beautiful healthy children, and they've made all the difference in my life.

CHAPTER 52

COACHING UP KIDS

THROUGH ALL THE time I spent traveling and playing with my kids, I always remembered what I learned from my Jewish father, David, when I was a kid. David was like a second father to me after my dad died, and he also coached me in Little League baseball. David showed me how to bond with my kids and love them through youth sports and coaching. I first got involved in community sports when my oldest son, A. J., was six years old, and wanted to play Little League football. I sponsored A.J.'s team his first year, but unfortunately, the team was poorly coached, to put it politely. The following year, I jumped in and got involved in the coaching. The rest is history.

When I retired from Youth coaching after 14 years, my scorecard read: 14 seasons, 13 playoffs, 10 championship games, and 4 championships. But that can't compare to the way all the kids I coached over the years changed my life. We never recruited anybody, and we never cut anybody. We taught all the kids how to play the game of life, and how to win. Our number one goal was having fun and enjoying the camaraderie of playing together. My role was simply to get the kids into championship shape, and let the results speak for themselves. I coached all three of my boys, starting when they were just six years old. I coached them all the way up to when they were 15, and entering High School. Then I stepped back down into the younger leagues and started over with my next son. The truth of the matter is, the whole time I was coaching, I was really just teaching the kids the principles from my Lifestyles of Success program.

I taught the kids to protect the family, so that when they grow up, they always take care of their families. Over the years, I found that when a kid is having fun with other kids, and they're in top physical shape, winning takes care of itself. I taught my teams the three basic tenets of football:

1) If you can't run, you can't play football. First, I made them run until they cried, and then I made them keep running until they loved running and they never got tired. They ran until they were in the best shape of any team in the league.

2) The fundamentals of football, including how to tackle, how to block and how to play properly so they wouldn't get hurt, which would take the fear out of hitting, and allow them to play at full speed. If you can't hit, you can't play football.

3) Sometimes playing football hurts and a boy feels like crying. I taught the kids that crying is a part of football. I told the kids there's nothing wrong with crying, as long as it doesn't stop you from playing. If you're injured, then you can't play. But if you're not injured, and you just hurt, you can still play football and play it well. That's called toughness, and being willing to go the extra mile that your opponent isn't willing to go. That's how championships are won in every sport.

The real key to building the team concept was getting everybody together after the games for a big tailgate party. I'd buy a few hundred pieces of fried chicken, and a bunch of food and drinks for everyone. Then we'd hang out and celebrate with the players so they could enjoy the fruits of their hard work with their teammates and their families. Those parties after the games, where the parents could tell their kids how proud they were, and support them, created a real bond not only in the team, but also in the community. Some of the other teams used to hate us because we always won, and then we'd have a big party; but that's exactly why I was there. We didn't always have the most talented team, but we always had the best team and the closest team. Our players and families would do anything for each other, and our bond was second to none. One of my mottos in life is, "The key to living is giving." The teams I coached embodied that great principle to the fullest.

Winning in any field of endeavor in life is about putting your heart and soul into whatever you're doing. I truly believe that if you do your best, God will do the rest. I taught that to all my players over the years. We used to say the Lord's Prayer before every game, and then we'd go out there and have fun together. We rarely lost, and when we did, it was only by a few points here or there. Working with all those kids for all those years in football gave me a sense of balance in my life like I'd never known before. It felt so good to impact young people in that way. Football season started in early August, right after I returned from Maui. My teams always made the playoffs so we'd end up playing into November. The parents used to have a running joke about which suit I'd be wearing when I showed up at practice. I'd come straight to practice from my real estate business, wearing my trademark GQ suits. I'd take off my snakeskin shoes, put on my football cleats, grab my whistle, and I was ready to coach. When practice was over, I'd change back and go right back to work at the office.

I always told the boys, "Once you become a champion, you're

a champion the rest of your life." I taught them how to apply the wisdom they learned from winning football championships over to the rest of their lives. All the life lessons my coaches and I taught the boys could be translated from football right into their daily lives, if the boys chose to do so. My goal was to mold young boys into young men, and I believe we succeeded. Some of the kids I coached went on to star in high school and college. First and foremost, coaching was a way for me to mentor my own boys, and show them how to impact others in a positive way. My three boys have grown up knowing what it takes to win, and knowing how to win. In the end, that may be one of my greatest gifts to them.

My kids and my grandson on our annual vacation in Maui.

CHAPTER 53

MY KIDS

RAQUEL

MY FIRST CHILD was my daughter, Raquel, who was born in August, 1982. Because she was my first baby girl, Raquel was always my special little princess. I'll never forget those first few moments after Raquel was born, and the doctor put that beautiful baby girl in my arms. In an instant, I felt and understood everything I took for granted when I was growing up, with my mom and my dad. It all made perfect sense to me in the blink of an eye. We named Raquel after Raquel Welch, the famous actress. Of course, I spoiled my Raquel rotten when she was a little girl. For the first five years of Raquel's life, we lived in a waterfront condo on Alki Beach in West Seattle. We loved living on the water, going boating, and having fun with all our friends and family coming over all the time. Raquel got used to that fun-loving lifestyle as a little girl.

Because I gave Raquel everything her little heart could desire, she was always dreaming her big dreams about having even more fun. I remember one Christmas in particular, when Raquel was about seven years old. She marched into the room one day and handed me her Christmas Wish List. There was exactly one item on Raquel's list: the Toys 'R' Us store. Not a toy from the store, or a shopping cart full of toys. No, Raquel wanted me to get her the entire store for Christmas. Like I could just empty out the store and have it delivered to the house. But that's how Raquel thought. Raquel has the same boldness I have, of believing in herself, and being willing to dream big and not settle for less than what she really wants.

Raquel and I have a very different and special kind of relationship than I have with my other six kids. Raquel was born into our lives when I was still using drugs and living that whole lifestyle on the dark side. Then over time, Raquel saw me get clean and move over to the light side. Raquel saw up-close the whole dynamic of me going through all those personal changes. Raquel was also there when I went from rags to riches, financially and professionally. Once I hit it big in real estate, our whole lifestyle changed radically. Raquel was riding in limousines when she was 12, and we were travelling around the world by the time she was in high school. Raquel got exposed to a way of life when she was just a teenager that most people only see on TV, and it made an impression on her. I spoiled Raquel enough when I was working my regular old job; having lots of money in the family only made it worse.

Coming up through school, Raquel was always a fantastic athlete. When she was just a freshman in high school, her freshman track team was already faster than the senior team. I remember one time, Raquel's team had a big track meet coming up to determine who would go to the State finals. Raquel was babysitting her friend's young daughter for a day, and she took the little girl to the mall. While she was at the mall, Raquel shoplifted something from one of the stores, and got caught. The police came and arrested Raquel and took her over to the police station. My real estate office was right down the street from the police station, and everyone in the city knew me from all my billboards and marketing. The police called me at work and told me what happened with Raquel. I told the police I would come to get her, but in the meantime, I was going to scare the crap out of her. When I got to the police station, I sat Raquel down and let her have it. I said, "Are you friggin' kidding me with this? First of all, you have everything in the world you could ever want, and we have the money to buy anything you don't have. You go to the mall and you steal some stupid little cosmetics thing? Have you lost your mind? And the worst part of all, is you do it while you're supposed to be babysitting a little girl! Do you have any idea how bad you made yourself look?"

When I finished chewing her out, I took Raquel back to the mall and the store she had shoplifted from. I made her apologize to the manager, just like my dad had done with me when I shoplifted as a kid. The next day was the big track meet. I told Raquel, "Guess what – you're not runnin' in that track meet." Raquel threw a fit and said, "Dad, no! You can't do that! I've been working all season for this meet, and we're gonna win the whole thing!" I just said, "Well, you should have thought about that when you had the bright idea of stealing some cosmetics." Raquel begged me over and over, but I held firm. I said, "Absolutely, positively, not. You're not runnin' track after that little episode at the mall." I took away the most important thing in the world to Raquel, and I didn't even think twice. I had to do it, because Raquel needed some tough love to balance out all that spoiling I had done. Raquel's track coach even called me and pleaded with me to let Raquel run. He said, "Mr. Perry, I don't know what happened with Raquel; that's none of my business. But Raquel is our fastest girl, and our star relay runner. We need her badly, and we would really appreciate it if you would reconsider your decision." I told the coach, "Fair enough. I'll tell you what: you ask Raquel what she did, and if she's willing to own up to it, and tell you why I won't let her run, then she can run in the meet."

Raquel came home crying a short time later, and her track team lost at the meet. The girls on her team were so mad at Raquel for not running that day, I don't think they ever forgave her after that. It turned out my daughter didn't have the courage or the nerve to face what she had done, so she didn't run. I knew my daughter all too well; I knew she was so prideful that she would never give up the truth of what she had done at the mall. My pretty little princess couldn't face the ugly truth of her own behavior, and it cost her and her teammates everything they had worked for all season. As Raquel got older, I started taking the family to Overlake Church in Kirkland. One of Raquel's girlfriends from church was Emmy, who used to babysit our boys when they were little. Emmy attended a private Christian school, and she thought it would be great if Raquel could go there too. Sheri and I looked into it, and we agreed it would be a good move to have Raquel at a new Christian school.

Raquel had only been at the new school about a week when I came to pick her up from school one day and found her crying hysterically. Raquel was crying like I had cried at my dad's funeral. I just thought, "Oh my God – what happened?" Raquel got in the car, bawling her head off, and I kept asking her what was wrong. Raquel said, "I can't do this! This school's too hard! There's no way I can do it!" I said, "Hold on - stop right there. Let me get this straight. You can't do this school because it's too hard? What about all these other freshmen in here that get dressed and come to school every day, just like you? You're telling me God hasn't blessed you with enough wisdom, intelligence, and understanding, and that you can't make it? Please. That's just a copout. Listen to me, little girl: life is what you make it. It always has been and it always will be.

You need to look within yourself, and realize that God has blessed you with everything you will ever need to do anything you want in this world. You better wake up and dry your eyes, because I don't want to hear any more about it." I took Raquel home that day, and we never again talked about school being too hard for her. Raquel re-dedicated herself after that episode, and she ended up becoming an Honors student, which made me so proud.

When Raquel turned 17, I bought her a brand new Volkswagen Jetta for her birthday. Raquel had graduated with Honors, and I wanted to reward her for her effort, and for setting the bar nice and high for the rest of my kids, who also went to the same school. When I gave Raquel the car, I told her to not let anyone else drive it. Of course, the first time Raquel let her boyfriend drive her car, they got into a head-on accident and totaled it. I didn't even bother replacing the car, because Raquel had already proven she couldn't follow my instructions. Unfortunately, after the accident, I had a much greater concern. Raquel had broken her arm in the accident, and when she went to the hospital, the doctors gave her some very powerful painkillers. Because Raquel was conceived when I was still using drugs, she already had the potential for drug addiction in her DNA. Those painkillers were the worst thing to ever happen to her. The next thing I knew, Raquel was getting high with her friends, and taking prescription pills. Raquel started living life in the fast lane, and staying out late. I used to tell all my kids they had to be home by midnight, because nothing good ever happens after midnight. When Raquel would come home late, I'd use reverse psychology. I turned up all the lights, nice and bright, and I told her, "If you wanna stay out late and smoke pot and party with your friends, go ahead. I'm already set, so if you wanna be a loser and throw your life away, be my guest."

Raquel probably hated it when I did that, but I had to let her know the road she was going down wasn't a good one. Years later, my daughter Royale said, "Dang, my dad's not playing with the kids on this drug stuff. I don't need to keep hearing my dad talk about me being a loser." But it took Raquel longer to figure it out. Raquel was always a beautiful girl: tall, slender, and athletic. She looked like a model, and she had a very charismatic personality to match. Everyone loved Raquel and wanted to be around her. But Raquel became a party girl, and it cost her dearly later in her life. Eventually, Raquel got hooked into the high life, the Hollywood life, of running with the wrong crowd and doing all the wrong things.

One July, Raquel returned from visiting her mom in New Jersey just as we were getting ready to leave for our annual Maui vacation. I knew Raquel was having some serious challenges with her drug problems, and I didn't trust her to stay out of trouble for a full month without any adult supervision. Raquel probably thought she was going to Maui with the rest of us. Instead, I drove her over to the treatment facility in Kirkland and dropped her butt in rehab for the whole month, while the rest of the family went to Hawai'i and had fun. Raquel was furious with me after that, but I didn't care. I told Raquel I wasn't going to put my life and our family's lives on hold because of her bad habits. That was just the first of many trips to rehab for Raquel.

The challenges with Raquel only intensified over the years. Sometimes she didn't get to go with us to Maui; other times I sent her home early because she was acting up and being a distraction. Eventually, Raquel's high-life ways caught up with her. Just as had been the case with me in my own addiction, Raquel reached a point where the drugs were using her, and she no longer had a say in the matter. When that happens, the addict must surrender and give themselves up for treatment. It's the only way to stop the downward cycle. Raquel's cycle of addiction lasted about 13 years, and it robbed her of any hope of a normal life from the ages of 18 to 31. I knew exactly where Raquel was heading, and I understood her problems better than anyone because of my own drug experiences. My family never gave up on Raquel, never stopped loving her, and never stopped believing she could turn her life around. We needed a miracle to bring Raquel back from the dead once before, but even then, she returned to her old using ways. My faith never wavered, but even I couldn't have foreseen the second life-saving miracle that God pulled off to rescue my princess from certain death.

Raquel was staying at my house, and starting to get her life back on track after her previous trip to rehab. One day, Raquel told me she had met some guy from Texas, and that they were in love, and they were going to move back to Texas together. I put a stop to that talk, but then I helped Raquel and her new boyfriend get set up in a house together, just on a short-term basis. Raquel kept insisting that she and her boyfriend were going to get married. I kept telling Raquel to slow down, and get to know this guy before they ran off together. Around the same time that Raquel was letting me know she was destined for Texas, Royale announced to the family that she was marrying her longtime boyfriend, Ryan, and that they were planning a move to Louisiana for his job. As soon as Royale left for Louisiana, Raquel followed suit and took off for Texas with the love of her life. I didn't approve of Raquel's move, but I figured at least she was relatively close to Royale's home in Louisiana.

Before I knew it, Raquel got into a big fight with the guy and got herself arrested on domestic violence charges. Apparently the domestic violence laws in Texas were different from where we lived in Washington State. The fact that the guy was from Texas probably didn't help matters for Raquel, and she ended up taking the fall for the fight. To be honest, I wasn't all that surprised by the news of

Raquel's arrest, since I knew how violent Raquel could be when she lost her temper. Raquel has always been a fighter, and she's super-strong for a slender, wiry girl. I could imagine what the fight must have been like if Raquel was the one that got arrested. The situation only got worse after the police discovered that Raquel had several outstanding warrants from her old drug days of running all over the country. Because Raquel couldn't afford to bail herself out, she had to spend nine months in a small Texas jail. In a way, I thought Raquel going to jail for a while was actually a good thing, because at least I'd know where she was, and she'd get three square meals a day. There was also a female chaplain in the jail, and Raquel had lots of free time to read and discuss the Bible.

By the time Raquel was released from jail, all of her warrants had been cleared, except for one in California. I told her to come back home and I'd put her to work in my real estate office. Raquel agreed, but said she wanted to stop in California on the way home and clear up that last warrant, so she could move forward with a clean slate. Raquel had an attorney friend in California, named Robert, whom she knew from being in the treatment program together. I knew Robert mostly as Raquel's sugar daddy, because he always gave her money when I wouldn't give it to her. Robert called me and promised he would set Raquel up with an attorney to handle her warrant situation in court. Then he promised to send her back home to Seattle in a few days. I told Robert that was fine, and I hung up the phone thinking I'd be seeing Raquel very soon. I already knew I couldn't let Raquel stay in California for too long, because it was so easy for her to get into trouble down there. Raquel had nine straight months of sobriety at that point, but I knew that could change in an instant.

Meanwhile, the other attorney had taken up Raquel's case, and he promised to handle everything for her. Raquel met him for dinner to sign some court papers, and apparently the guy bought her a drink. I called Robert the next day to see when Raquel was coming home, and Robert said the attorney had taken care of the outstanding warrant. I told Robert to put Raquel on the phone, but I heard Raquel yell, "I don't wanna talk to my dad!" I thought, "Uh-oh. What happened to mess her up like that again?" I told Robert I needed to talk with Raquel, but a moment later, Robert said, "Greg, Raquel just took off out of here – I'm going after her." I tried to call Raquel, but she didn't answer her phone. I knew right then that Raquel must have used drugs again, because she always did a Dr. Jekyll/Mr. Hyde personality thing when she was high. By the time I got through to Raquel, she was at the UCLA hospital in Los Angeles.

Raquel said that after she left Robert at the hotel, she called the other attorney from court. He picked her up, and took her out to eat. She said she couldn't remember what happened after that, but when she woke up the next day, all her stuff was gone. Raquel had no purse, no ID, no credit cards or bankcards, nothing. Raquel thought the attorney might have slipped a date-rape drug into her drink when she went to the restroom during dinner, and that she had been drugged again and didn't know what had happened. Raquel had lived in California for a while during her 20's, and she had lots of rich boyfriends and sugar daddies down there. I knew all about those days, but now it looked like that old pattern of drug use and sex abuse was rearing its ugly head again. I told her I was sick of all her game playing and drama, and I hung up the phone.

By the time I came to my senses and called her back, Raquel was out of the hospital and looking for a place to stay. Raquel told me then that she wasn't coming back to Seattle. There was a guy Raquel knew from the program who ran a charity in Venice Beach, feeding homeless people and serving the community.

Raquel said she was going to see this guy in Venice Beach and help him. I didn't think Venice Beach was the best environment for Raquel while she was battling sobriety, but she was an adult, and I couldn't force her to come home if she didn't want to. The guy called me later and said he had been in the program with Raquel, and that he would gladly help her out. We talked for a long time, and I was okay with the situation. I called Raquel every single day to check up on her, and everything seemed to be going well. One day, right around Christmas time, I called to check on Raquel again, and the guy from the charity told me Raquel wasn't there. He said Raquel had gone out for a walk on the beach with some guys, and that she would be back in a little while. Instantly, the alarms in my head started going off, because I knew how crazy that whole scene was at Venice Beach. There was no telling who Raquel might be with, or what she might be doing. Sure enough, my darkest fears came true, as Raquel never came back from that walk on the beach.

Days passed, then weeks, then months, with no word from Raquel. Every single morning when I prayed, I put a prayer of protection around Raquel, and asked God to help her, wherever she was. One morning, as I was saying my usual prayers, God spoke to my heart and said, "Get Raquel." I said, "Okay, Lord." I called my good buddy Keith in L.A. right away, and explained the situation to him. I told Keith I had no idea where Raquel was, but the last time I talked to her, she was in Venice Beach, working with the guy helping homeless people. I sent Keith a picture of the guy with Raquel. Keith said his printer wasn't working, but he had a friend coming over later to fix it. A few hours later, Keith's friend came over to fix the printer, and as soon as Keith printed out the picture, the friend said, "Hey, I know that girl – that's GP's daughter. I used to see them all the time in Maui. GP don't play." It turned out the guy had lived in Hawai'i for a while and he remembered me and my family. Keith asked his buddy if he knew where Raquel was, and the guy said, "Yeah, I just saw her recently. But she's part of a real bad scene, man. It's like in that movie, 'Taken.' You don't wanna go over there. If those guys knew I was talking about it with you, they'd kill me." When Keith called me back and told me that, I knew what he meant. The villains in the Taken movie kidnapped young girls, then got them hooked on drugs and turned them into sex slaves. It was any father's absolute worst nightmare for his daughter.

Keith filled me in on the situation, and said, "G, you're gonna have to come down here for this. I know the area where Raquel is, but my homeboy says it's like Beirut over there. You gotta come down here tonight, and we'll go get Raquel." Keith and I had been down this road before, in our gang days, and we knew what to do. Keith told me he was going to put on his black gear, get his 9-mm, and drive over to the area in his old truck to survey the situation before I got there. I told Keith I had to go to an AA meeting, but to call me as soon as he got there to let me know how it looked. Then I went to my AA meeting, which was in a local church. When it was my turn to share with the group, I talked about Raquel, and the situation I was facing in California. I told the people in the meeting that Keith wanted me to come down and help him rescue Raquel, and that I didn't want to step back into that old world of violence because I knew what I was capable of. I asked everyone in the group to pray for me and my daughter, and they did. When the group took a smoke break, I walked over to the chapel, got down on my knees and prayed as hard as I could. I said, "Dear God, please help me. I need a miracle right now, Lord. Please God, bless this whole situation. I know if I go down there to get Raquel, I'm gonna open up that dark part of me again, where I have to do something crazy to save my little girl." It occurred to me at that moment that this very same day had begun at 6:30 a.m. with God telling me, "Get Raquel."

When the meeting was over, I jumped in my car and drove home. Keith called me just as I was walking in the door. Keith said, "G, I got her!" I said, "What? You got her?" Keith said, "I got her! I just drove over there to check it out, and Raquel was standing out there, so I snatched her up and took off!" Keith said that when he saw Raquel, he rolled up to her and said, "Hey cutie, what's going on? Jump in here with me." As soon as Raquel got in Keith's truck, he floored it and took off out of there. Of course, Raquel started screaming bloody murder, until Keith took off the baseball hat that was pulled down over his eyes, and said, "Raquel, it's me – it's Keith!" At that point, Raquel realized she was safe with Keith and everything was going to be alright. The next day, Keith and I made arrangements to bring Raquel home to Seattle. She had no ID, and she was in terrible condition. Keith had known Raquel since she was born, and he told me, "G, she's in bad shape, man. She's pretty beat up." We finally got Raquel home safe and sound the next day.

When I picked Raquel up at the airport, she could barely walk out to the car. She walked like a zombie, and she looked like one too. It was tough to see Raquel in that condition, but I knew the worst was finally over. I was going to get my little princess back on track, no matter what. After Raquel got home from California, the gut-wrenching detox process began. Raquel needed several surgeries just to drain her body of all the poisons from the drugs she'd been taking. After that, it was back to rehab yet again. I stopped counting Raquel's trips to rehab back when her scorecard was a perfect 13-for-13: she'd been in rehab 13 times, and she'd been kicked out of rehab all 13 times. It took Raquel 12 years to get one year of continuous sobriety. But I see now that Raquel just wasn't ready yet. After all, it took me four calendar years just to get one year of continuous sobriety, so I could relate to Raquel's challenges with addiction. I never gave up on my beautiful daughter, and she eventually rewarded my patience in the best possible way. Today, Raquel is living proof of what is possible when you let go and let God heal every aspect of your life: spiritually, mentally, emotionally, and physically.

As I write this, Raquel has recently passed her two-year anniversary of sobriety. She's a certified personal trainer now, and a success mentor in her own right. If you saw Raquel today, you would never in a million years guess what she's been through in her life. Raquel is as much of a living miracle as I am, and she knows it. Through all of her struggles with addiction and living on the dark side, Raquel has never lost her faith in God, or her belief in the power of prayer. My faith and belief in prayer has always been strong. But when it comes to miracles, I simply go back to that incredible day when I was praying and God told me to "Get Raquel." What are the chances that, after not hearing from Raquel for nearly three months, God would tell me that morning to find Raquel and bring her home? Did God know Raquel's time was almost up? Her doctors told me later that the toxins in her body would've killed her within a few days if Keith hadn't found her. What are the chances that the same guy who came to fix Keith's printer also happened to know me and Raquel from when we had vacationed in Hawai'i? What are the chances that the same guy also remembered seeing Raquel in the same area as the drugs and sex ring operation? What are the chances that, at the exact moment Keith drove by in his truck, Raquel happened to be standing there on the sidewalk so Keith could pick her up and save her life?

It doesn't matter how miraculous it was for any of those things to happen, because God made all of them happen. The truth is, God resurrected Raquel from the dead, and brought her back to

me and my family. In the space of 18 hours, we went from having
no idea where Raquel could be, to finding her like a needle in a
haystack in a city like Los Angeles. Like I've said before, God has
worked so many miracles in my life, I just expect it now. When God
speaks to my heart, I listen. When God tells me to do something,
I do it. When I pray, like I did that night in the chapel at the AA
meeting, I know God hears my prayers. When it's the last moment,
of the last second, of the last minute, of the last hour, and I need a
miracle, I just pray with everything I've got. It doesn't matter how
unlikely it is, or how many impossible things need to line up to
make it happen. God just makes it happen, every single time, over
and over again. I wouldn't even be alive today if God hadn't worked
so many miracles in my life. I know for a fact that Raquel wouldn't
be alive today if God hadn't worked some amazing miracles in her
life, too. When I look at my beautiful princess today, so strong and
sober, and so full of life, I thank God for the miracle of keeping my
whole family alive and together.

ROYALE

My second child was my daughter, Royale, who was born in
February, 1984. The day Royale was born, Rae and I still hadn't
chosen a name for her. We had been through all the baby name
books, but we just couldn't find a name that we both liked enough
to commit to. I called Margy to see if she had any ideas. I considered
Margy my second mom, because she had co-raised me from the time
I was eight until I was 14. Margy suggested the name Royale, and
we instantly fell in love with that name because it just sounded so
classy and unique. To this day, I still haven't met another girl named
Royale. If you've seen a picture of my family, you know that, more
than any of my other kids, Royale is my spitting image. Beyond
her appearance, Royale also inherited some of my boldness and

slickness. The GP DNA served Royale well in her younger years. Royale grew up watching her older sister, Raquel, and emulating everything Raquel did. I'm sure Royale could see how spoiled Raquel was, and it didn't take Royale long to figure out how to play the game in order to get everything she wanted. Like her older sister, Royale was a superstar athlete in school, and she particularly excelled in volleyball and track.

I'll never forget when Raquel and Royale were little girls, about seven or eight years old, and I used to tuck them into bed at night. The girls would always beg me to tell them stories about my old life growing up in the 'hood in South Central, L.A. Sheri and the girls and I lived in Harbour Pointe, which is a very nice upper-middle class neighborhood about 30 minutes outside Seattle. But my little girls wanted to hear about the time I got shot when I was 13, or when I was in jail, or some of my many other questionable exploits. I was always 100% honest with my kids when it came to talking about everything I had experienced in my life. I always told my kids the truth, even about the negative stuff, because I didn't want them to make the same mistakes I had made. I figured my kids needed to know the reality of my life story so they could avoid the wrong roads I went down.

I used to have so much fun playing with my two little girls when they were younger. I loved to chase them around the house and have pillow fights with them. I had custody of the girls from the time they were very young, and Sheri and I took Royale and Raquel everywhere we went when they were little kids. When we went back to L.A. to visit my family, we took the girls to Disneyland, and then around to some of my favorite places in the old neighborhood so they could see where I grew up. Even at home, there was rarely a dull moment. Royale was very tender-headed as a young girl. She was fine when Sheri was around to help with all her girl stuff.

But when Sheri was gone, we had some issues. I'm the best dad in the world in most ways, but when it comes to doing Royale's hair, "Daddy can't comb no hair." That's pretty much how Royale used to say it when she dismissed me from hair-styling duties. I used to try to cover it up and get by with cocoa butter and whatever else I could find, but Royale wasn't having it. She'd throw her hands up and say, "No, Dad - just...no."

Royale was always very active and athletic, and she loved to ski; whether it was water-skiing or snow skiing. One of the things I always loved about Royale was that she was so smart, and such a fast-learner. She was sharp and two steps ahead of the game, kind of like I had to be when I was running the streets as a kid. Royale grew up and matured the fastest of all my kids, because she could experience something once, and then figure everything out so quickly. I remember a little incident we had when we were living in Harbor Pointe. I built a really nice suite for Royale and Raquel in our basement, and the girls loved having their own space away from the boys. One night, I had to put Raquel in checkmate for something bad she had done. I thought I had handled my business just fine, but apparently Royale didn't see it that way. I was done with Raquel when Royale decided she was going to take up the fight for her big sister. Royale jumped right into my business, and Raquel's business, but the problem was, Royale had no business. Meanwhile, I had all five of the other kids standing there watching me, as if to say, "Let's see how Dad's gonna handle this!" I've got seven kids of my own, and I grew up in a family of six. I learned early on from my family, that if you let one kid get away with something, you might as well give the rest of them the green light too. I knew I had to set the table for the whole group, right then and there.

Royale jumped up in my face and said, "You can't tell me what to do!" I said, "What did you just say?" Royale cocked her head and repeated herself with a little extra emphasis, "I said, you can't tell me what to do." I looked her in the eye and very calmly said, "Listen, Royale. I want you to go downstairs right now, and pack up all your stuff. Get everything you've got…empty out your dressers, your closet, all of it. Right now – get moving." Royale turned and stomped off toward the basement. My other six kids stood there, wide-eyed and frozen in place. A little while later, Royale emerged from the basement, dragging her suitcase and clothes bags, and wearing an angry scowl. Royale probably thought I was staging some kind of dramatic parental prank to try to scare her. But she quickly learned that, in the immortal words of my man James Brown, "Papa don't take no mess." I rolled Royale out of bed early the next morning, threw her clothes in the trunk, stuck her in the car, and drove her straight to the airport. I bought Royale a first-class, one-way ticket to New Jersey. Royale didn't know it yet, but she was done living at my house, and was going to live with her mother.

For the next year, Royale begged me repeatedly to let her come back home to live with us. Even from New Jersey, Royale could see that our house in Mukilteo, with six other kids and a cool big sister, was the place to live. Sheri said, "Greg, you have to let her come back. She really wants to be here with us." I said, "Nope. That's not happening." I must have said that to Sheri and Royale a thousand times. Whenever Royale called to beg me again, I said, "Don't you remember? I can't tell you what to do. What you do is none of my business. So that's fine. Do whatever you want to do. You don't need a dad telling you what to do. See ya! Wouldn't wanna be ya!" Then I'd hang up the phone. That used to drive Royale crazy, but that's where I left it, for a long time. I think that whole episode was a huge blessing in disguise for the whole family. First of all, it taught all my other kids that Dad don't play, so don't test me. Thankfully, none of them did after that. As time went on, Royale's pleadings grew increasingly apologetic. One day, Royale said, "Dad, I'm so sorry. I didn't mean it." I said, "I'm sorry too, Sweetie. But this is what happens when you tell me I'm not the boss in my own house. Because I am."

The following year, Royale came back and resumed school at the high school near our house in Mukilteo. She had a lot of friends from the neighborhood that went there, so Sheri and I didn't force Royale to go back to the private Christian school with the rest of our kids. She was happy to be back with us, and it showed in her new-and-improved attitude. But even a bright and happy demeanor wasn't enough to save Royale and Raquel from their near-constant flirtations with danger. Now, I'll be the first person to admit that I've needed a whole crew of guardian angels to watch over me with the dangerous situations I've gotten myself into in my life. But Royale and Raquel just couldn't stay on the straight and narrow road when they were teenagers. By that I mean, those two little girls couldn't drive a car straight down the road to save their lives. Thank God I always had safe vehicles for them, because those girls tested my limits and the limits of German engineering.

For many years, I had an old Mercedes station wagon that was like a warhorse vehicle for me. I used that car for all my dirty jobs, like hauling all the boys around during football season, going on skiing trips, etc. That car had withstood lots of long hard miles over the years, but it couldn't withstand the driving of two teenaged girls who struggled with radical concepts like braking and steering. I used to say my girls had fulltime jobs – in the car-crunching business. Mercedes was always my favorite car, not just for the style or the luxury, but because they were safe. I always knew if my kids got in an accident in a Mercedes, the car could get totaled, but the kids would walk away without a scratch. I've seen it with my own eyes too many times to believe anything else. One time, when

Raquel was 16, I let her and some friends take the Mercedes wagon down to the Oregon coast. They were coming home on I-5, driving through downtown Seattle when, somehow some way, that car got up in the air, turned all the way around, and wound up in the other lanes going the opposite direction. I had trained Raquel to always call me first whenever she had an accident. She called, and said, "Dad, I had an accident. I don't know what happened, but the car is smashed up." I asked her, "Is the car still drivable?" Raquel said, "I think so. The bumper is smashed, and the lights are broken because we hit that concrete thing on the side of the freeway."

I told Raquel to drive the car over to the nearby Mercedes dealership where I had bought all my Benzes over the years, and to leave it there. I told Raquel I would meet her there to pick up her and her friends. The next day, I got a call from the dealership. The Service Manager said, "Uh, Mr. Perry? I'm not sure what your daughter hit last night, but whatever it was, she hit it pretty hard. The frame of the car is actually bent. You're looking at about $10,000 to straighten it out." Keep in mind, the car was a 1989 model, with a lot of miles, and it wasn't even worth the price to repair it. My insurance company totaled out the car, and paid me for it. I turned right around and bought the car back and had it repaired. There was no way I was letting that car go after all the kids in the car walked away from that bad accident.

The next episode of "Driving with the Perry Girls" starred Royale. I had sponsored an And-1 basketball game in Portland, Oregon and we were coming late at night. I was driving my 600SL, following Royale and her girlfriend, who were in the Mercedes wagon. We were driving along, in the pouring rain, and the girls were right in front of me. I got on my phone and started talking, and after a few minutes, I noticed I didn't see the wagon in front of me. I couldn't figure out how they got away from me, because

I was going pretty fast myself. I drove ahead to try to catch up to them, but I still didn't see them. I remember I passed the Federal Way exit, when I got a call from Royale. She said, "Dad, we flew off the freeway! It's dark, and we flew off the freeway!" I said, "You what? What do you mean? Where are you?" Royale said she didn't know where they were, but that she remembered seeing a sign for Federal Way. I immediately exited the freeway and headed back toward Federal Way.

I reentered the freeway going in the original direction, drove for a minute, then I saw the flashing lights of a State Patrol car on the shoulder up ahead. I pulled up behind the Trooper and stopped. There was no sign of the Mercedes or Royale and her friend. When I got closer, I saw Royale and her friend in the backseat of the Patrol car. Royale said, "Dad, I wasn't speeding. I swear I wasn't speeding." Royale said she and her girlfriend were fine, with no injuries. I said, "Where's the car?" Royale pointed over the embankment next to the freeway and said, "It's down there - we hit a tree." I couldn't even see a tree, much less the wagon. I approached the Trooper, introduced myself, and then he pointed down into the darkness. He said, "Your car is down there, wrapped around a tree. I'm not gonna give your daughter a ticket, because I have no idea how that car got down there." The State Patrol had to shut down I-5 to allow a tow truck to straddle the freeway lanes sideways and retrieve the Mercedes from where it had stopped, about 50 yards down the embankment in the mud and the trees. That car must have taken flight in order to get so far off the road and down into the trees. But those girls walked away without so much as a scratch. Once again, the insurance company totaled the car, and once again, I bought it back. I continued driving that car for many years - and my girls continued driving me crazy, too.

As Royale and Raquel were getting older, my ex-wife, Rae, used to play these little mind games with my girls and me. Rae would stir up a bunch of drama and then use Raquel and Royale to try to get to me. Rae knew how to manipulate the girls to turn them against me and Sheri. There was a time when everything was going smoothly for our family, and Raquel was doing great with her sobriety, and everyone was happy. But Rae couldn't stand it when all of us were happy, because she was miserable. Raquel had been with her mom that night in New Jersey when she overdosed, and I had warned Raquel about how trouble seemed to follow her mom around. I had custody of the girls, but whenever Rae came around, things got dramatic. Sure enough, out of nowhere, Rae decided to move from New Jersey to Mukilteo, to live in Royale's boyfriend's apartment. It's difficult to imagine a more awkward scenario, but leave it to Rae. We tried, in vain, to figure out what Rae was thinking. Ryan was Royale's boyfriend in high school, and he had his own apartment, which just happened to be right around the corner from Raquel. It turned out that Rae moved to Mukilteo to get closer to Raquel, because she wanted to see Raquel more often. I made it clear to Rae that if there were any more incidents with her and Raquel, Rae could forget about any future visitation rights.

We had already needed one miracle to bring Raquel back from the dead after her overdose in New Jersey. She was getting back on a good track and doing well with her sobriety. One time, Raquel wanted to go visit her mom after Rae had moved to a house in Mill Creek. I didn't know exactly where the house was, but it was close enough to my house that I didn't worry too much. I was at a Seahawks game, while Raquel went over to her mom's. When I left the football game, I had to go pick up Raquel, because I didn't want Raquel spending the night at her mom's house. I called Royale to ask her for directions to Rae's house. Royale stalled for a few minutes, then she said, "Uhh…I'm not supposed to tell you where she lives." I said, "Look Royale, I couldn't care less where your mom lives. I'm just going to pick up Raquel. Where is the house?" Royale said, "Well, my mom told me not to tell you." I said, "Listen to me, little girl. This isn't about your mom, or me, or you. This is about Raquel. What is the damn address for the house?" Click. Royale hung up the phone. I tried to call her back, but she didn't answer.

I called Royale back again, and left a voicemail. I said, "Royale Perry. You better hear me loud and clear. I'm gonna give you five minutes to call me back and give me that address. I don't play these games, least of all with my kids. If you don't call me back in five minutes, you're gonna see the price you're gonna pay. I'll tell you right now, you're not gonna like it." Five minutes passed, and Royale hadn't called back. I was getting close to Mill Creek, so I called Raquel and got the address to Rae's house. I picked up Raquel, and took her home. A little while later, after Royale heard that I had already picked up Raquel, Royale called me back like everything was cool. She said, "Hey Dad, sorry about that." I said, "Me too. I want you to bring that brand new convertible I bought you over to my house with all the keys and everything, 'cause you're done driving that car. It's over." Royale said, "What? That's my car!" I said, "No it's not – it's in my name. That's my car. Bring it over here first thing tomorrow morning." The next day, Royale showed up at my house with that beautiful black-on-black Volkswagen convertible. Royale was crying and complaining, trying to manipulate me again. I snatched the keys out of her hands and put the car in my garage. I love my daughter, but I've occasionally had to remind Royale not to test me when I put her on the spot.

For some odd reason I can't explain, there were always issues with my oldest girls and their cars. It seems like Raquel and Royale were always getting in accidents or having their cars taken away from them. Raquel totaled the first car I ever gave her, the

Jetta. Then she wrecked the Mercedes wagon on the freeway. In California, Raquel was driving a BMW I had given her, but then I took it away from her as punishment. Raquel totaled yet another brand new Volkswagen convertible. Royale forfeited her first car, the Volkswagen convertible, for getting a little too sassy with me. Then she totaled the Mercedes wagon when she flew off the freeway. Finally, just a few months ago, Raquel totaled her latest Mercedes, which I had just bought for her a few months before.

Another time, I took the family to Las Vegas for Spring Break. Raquel and Royale were running a bit behind and weren't quite ready to go when the rest of us left the house. I got them set up to catch a later flight, and didn't give it another thought. As soon as I got to Vegas, I got a call from Raquel and Royale. They said, "Dad, we missed our flight." I said, "You missed your flight? How did that happen?" The girls said, "The car overheated or something, we don't know why." I said, "Okay, so you missed your flight. Where's the car now?" Raquel said, "Oh, it's still on the freeway." I said, "On the freeway?! You left my car on the freeway? Where on the freeway?" Raquel said the car was parked on the shoulder in north Seattle. I called the Mercedes Roadside Assistance program, told them where the car was, and asked them to pick it up and tow it to the shop. Mercedes took care of my car, and that left my two girls for me to contend with.

I said, "Wait a second – if the car is at Northgate, how did you get to the airport when you don't have any money?" Royale said, "Oh, we flagged down this taxi and we told him we were Greg Perry's daughters, and to just bill you for our ride, because the guy knew who you were from your billboards and TV commercials." I said, "Let me get this straight - you burned up my car, left it on the freeway, and I'm paying for your cab ride?" When I got back from Las Vegas the following week, the Mercedes Service Manager said, "Mr. Perry, I want to tell you something. Our technicians said that, in the history of repairing cars, they've never seen a Mercedes engine burned up like this. I don't know what your daughters did, but you need a new engine."

Royale learned some valuable life lessons from all her adventures with cars, and her mom, and her big sister. When she started to mature and figure things out, Royale became a real source of pride for me and Sheri. I used to take Royale, and her group of friends, and her boyfriend Ryan, up to Vancouver, Canada in my boat, and we had so much fun together. But in high school, the party was on for all those kids. One night, Royale and Ryan came home really late and I was waiting for them. I sat them down, and I said, "I don't even want to hear what you've got to say for yourselves. If you don't get off the road you're on, you're gonna get in more trouble than you can handle. I've been down that road, and I'm telling you to watch yourselves. Ryan, you're done. You're never coming over here again." The kids listened intently, and didn't try to argue. Ryan apologized and said, "Okay, Mr. Perry. You're the boss, you don't have to tell me twice." I loved all those kids, and I honestly didn't want to see any of them get hurt. But just like back when I was running the streets as a teenager, life was weeding people out. Pretty soon, some of Royale's old friends with bad habits started falling by the wayside. Fortunately, Royale and Ryan both changed their ways, and they matured a lot in a very short time. Later on, Ryan came back around to Royale, and they got serious about each other.

Ryan came to me one day, and said, "Mr. Perry, you know I've always loved Royale. My father died when I was young, and you've been like a father figure to me. I think I want to get certified and be an underwater welder, working on oil rigs and things like that." I thought that was a great idea, and pretty soon, Ryan had a good job working for one of the oil companies in Louisiana. A little while later, Ryan came back to see Royale, and he really had his life together. I had always loved Ryan, and I could see that Royale was in love with him. Ryan sat down with me, and said, "Mr. Perry, I need to talk with you. You know, I've loved Royale ever since we were little kids in middle school." I said, "I know, Ryan. You've always been the guy she loved, too. I'm proud of you for the way you've grown up and really become a man. You've done well for yourself." Then Ryan said, "Mr. Perry, I want to marry Royale, and take care of her for the rest of her life." I said, "Well, let's see what Royale says about this." Royale said, "Dad, I love Ryan. I want to marry him and have a family and everything."

At that time, Royale was working in Bellevue, doing property management. Raquel and Royale had worked for me off and on over the years, and they always did a great job for me. They knew if they messed up, they'd get fired, so they always did a great job of helping me out with my organization and marketing. One time, I had a big investor client who owned a huge apartment complex that was being converted to condos, and he was having lots of problems with property managers. I sent Royale up there to check it out. A week later, my client called me and said, "Greg, I have to tell you, Royale is an administrative superstar. She's got this whole thing figured out in a week." I said, "Well, she learned by seeing how I run my business – which is, like a machine." Royale just had a natural ability for business, even when she was younger. I hated to see Royale go away, but I knew her heart was with Ryan and that they'd be happy together. Ryan said he wanted to take Royale to Louisiana, where he was planning to buy a house and settle down. I gave Ryan and Royale my blessing, and a few weeks later, they were on their way to Louisiana. What a tremendous blessing it turned out to be for everyone.

Royale and Ryan have a great marriage, and Ryan has been a

great son-in-law. They've given me three beautiful grandchildren: Cameron, Carter, and London. Ryan now works for Chevron Oil, while Royale is an executive assistant for a big company. They live in Houston, and have a big beautiful house with a swimming pool, right on a golf course. I'm so proud of both of those kids. Royale and Ryan have matured so well together, and it shows in every aspect of their lives. They're both strong, loving parents, and they're ideal partners for one another. Ryan and Royale have earned a lot of respect in our family, because of the tremendous example they've set as role models for the rest of the kids in my family.

A.J.

My third child was my son, Abraham, who was born in April, 1992. I remember I was driving down the freeway one day, thinking about potential names for my first son. Of course, my first thought was the selfish one, "Maybe I should name him Greg Perry, Jr." I prayed about it and asked God what I should name my first son. God spoke to my heart, and said, "Abraham." I heard that name, and I said out loud in the car, "What? Abraham? Are you kidding me?" But God wasn't kidding. That's how Sheri and I welcomed our first son, Abraham John (after my father) Perry, to this world. We've always called him A.J. for short. One interesting note about A.J. is that he shares a birthday with my longtime best buddy, Keith. When A.J. was born, I was so proud of my first son, and I took A.J. everywhere with me. As a result, A.J. grew and developed very quickly. He started walking when he was just seven months old, and by eight months, he was jumping off the coffee table into a pile of pillows like a miniature gymnast. A.J. was always really strong as a baby. I used to make him hang by his hands for as long as he could. I'd put A.J. up on the monkey bars at the playground, and tell him to just hold on tight and don't let go. The other parents around me would be having a panic attack, and telling me to take A.J. down, but I just stood there watching A.J. I'd tell the other parents, "Don't worry, he'll be fine." A.J. could hang there for several minutes at a time.

I taught A.J. how to swim before he could walk, and he was always very athletic. I pushed him hard, even as a little kid, and made him dig deep inside for his greatness. A.J. responded well to my training, and when he turned six, I got him into Pop Warner football. I sponsored A.J.'s team and was an assistant coach that first year, but the team lost all their games but one. The next year, I took over as Head Coach. A.J. was seven by then, and my son Manny was six, and they played together. We won our very first championship that season, which started a long run of football success for my sons and me. To this day, I still have hanging in my office the picture of me and my two boys posing with that first championship trophy. A.J. was my star running back, and a great all-around athlete. When he got to high school, A.J. played for his school's football team. A.J.'s school was known for its basketball success, and in reality, they had no business trying to play football. One night, the football team went somewhere for a road game, and they brought my little prince home with a broken ankle. I couldn't believe it. I was in shock for a few days, because as long as I'd been coaching, none of my kids ever had an injury like that. I had always coached all the kids on the fundamentals of football, and how to position themselves properly so they wouldn't get hurt. A.J. had always been the hammer, not the nail. A.J. was only 15 when he broke his ankle, and that injury ended his playing career.

From that point on, A.J. became my assistant coach for my offense. A.J. was and is an excellent offensive coach, and it wouldn't surprise me one bit if he ended up getting a good coaching job someday. A.J. was right next to me on the sidelines while his

younger brothers came up through the ranks of youth football, and
A.J. learned all the tricks of the trade. We took kids that weren't
the most talented players, and we won championships. We took
the kids other teams didn't want, and we won championships. We
didn't recruit anybody, and we didn't cut anybody. We coached
up those kids, and taught them how to play not just the game of
football, but also the game of life. We taught them to trust each
other, to play for each other, and we brought out their best. We
molded kids into being winners in life, and the results speak for
themselves. A.J. played from ages six to 15, and then coached with
me for another five years after that. I swear right now, A.J. could
take a high school team or a college team that was struggling and
turn them into winners. He knows the game inside and out, and he
knows how to get through to kids.

I'll never forget, for A.J.'s 15th birthday, I gave him the BMW
325i I had originally gotten from Mr. Li and Tiens. When I first
got the car, I gave it to my mom, who was living in New Jersey with
my sister, Adrienne. But after my mom complained about the car
having too much power, I had it shipped to my house and gave it
to A.J. for his birthday. Of course, since he was only 15, A.J. didn't
even have a driver's license yet. I didn't care about that, because
A.J. was a great kid, and I wanted him to know that car would
be waiting there for him when he turned 16 and got his license.
Caleb was only eight years old when A.J. got the BMW, and as
soon as Caleb saw the BMW with a big bow on it, he pulled me
aside and said, "Hey Dad, I've been thinking. I want a Ferrari for
my birthday." I just smiled back at him and said, "Yeah, right. I'll
remember that." A.J. also worked for me in my office, like Raquel
and Royale had before him. A.J. was sharp as a tack too, and he
could get stuff done. When I did all my big marketing campaigns in
Harbour Pointe, I had A.J. round up a bunch of his friends to help

us out. We'd have pizza parties in the office, and the kids would do all the packaging, and then I'd send them out to run around the neighborhood and deliver the goods.

A.J. was a speed demon like me, but he was a little accident-prone. He broke his ankle, he broke his finger, and then he broke his arm. One summer day, A.J. came running in the house with his arm hanging by his side looking like a broken tree branch. Sheri took one look at A.J.'s arm, and started screaming, "Oh my God, Greg - take him to the hospital right now. I can't look at that!" I took A.J. straight to Stevens Hospital, which was only 15 minutes away. When we got there, the emergency room was packed, so they couldn't take us in right away. The people around us were looking at A.J.'s arm and wincing, and I thought they were going to get sick. There was another guy there, a big black dude who had broken his finger playing football. When the guy saw A.J's deformed arm, he started yelling at the hospital staff, "What the h--- is wrong with you freaking people - this little boy has a broken arm! Get someone out here and take care of him - now!" The nurses immediately came out and got A.J., and took him in to set his arm.

Another time, we went to Hawai'i for our annual summer vacation, and the first day we were there, A.J. somehow broke his little finger surfing. Sheri took him to the clinic in Maui, and they put a hard plastic splint on his hand that looked like half of a cup. A.J. was back in the water the next day, saying, "This splint is great for paddling!" By the time we got home a month later, A.J was due for a follow-up exam on his finger. Sheri said, "A.J., I'm not taking you to the doctor. You've already been surfing on it for a month – you're fine." On another occasion, we went skiing up at Sun Peaks. Caleb was running around, teasing his brothers, and being a little pest. A.J. went to grab Caleb, but he slipped and fell hard on his arm. He said it hurt, so we put some ice on it, and gave him some Tylenol for it. Throughout our one-week trip, A.J. kept saying his arm was sore. Meanwhile, he kept right on skiing and snowboarding. We took him to the doctor when we got home a week later, and what do you know – A.J. had a hairline fracture in his arm. A.J. was always a tough kid, and he never complained. But he definitely had a knack for odd injuries.

When it was time for A.J. to go to college, he chose Western Washington University, in my old territory of Bellingham. A.J. had the same girlfriend from the time he was 16, and she lived right down the street from us, so he decided he didn't want to be too far away from her. He considered all the colleges that were closest to our home, before he settled on the University in Bellingham, which is about an hour and a half away. Even after A.J. went to college, it was like he never left home. He still came home every weekend to see his girlfriend and to visit our family. In a way, I wish A.J. would have cut himself loose from his familiar surroundings and really gone away, like his brothers and sisters have, so he could get a taste of life on his own. But A.J. has always been a great kid, and a smart kid, and a wonderful older brother for all of his younger brothers and sisters. More than anything, A.J. has always made Sheri and me proud of him in all he's done.

MANNY

My fourth child was my son, Immanuel, who was born in June, 1993. Manny was my second son, and he completed the scenario of two boys and two girls that I always wanted with my children. Immanuel is a Biblical name that means, "God is with us." By the time Manny was born, I was very conscious of the miracles that God had worked in my life, and I wanted to give my second son a name that would always remind Sheri and I how blessed we were. I remember when Manny was born, and we were at the hospital.

When the doctor came in to see us, I could tell right away that he'd been drinking a little. He was very smooth, and he hid it well, but that doctor was definitely under the influence. I was a veteran of countless AA meetings, and I could spot a drinker from a mile away. The doctor told us he wanted to use forceps to pull Manny out, but I refused to give him permission to do so. The doctor agreed to honor our wishes, and Manny was born shortly thereafter. Manny appeared to be a healthy baby, but for the first four months of his life, he cried a lot. Our pediatrician ran several tests to try to solve Manny's crying, and in the process, he discovered that Manny's collarbone had been broken during the delivery. The doctor had been very careless when he pulled Manny out, and my little boy cried because he was in so much pain. Sheri and I knew we had a legitimate legal case, but we never told anyone about how that doctor's poor judgment had hurt Manny. Fortunately, Manny's collarbone healed up fine.

Manny was always such a wonderful boy for us. He was probably the quietest of our kids to that point, and everyone loved his easy-going personality. To this day, Manny remains a straight-up gentleman, and because of that, his four sisters all love and appreciate him just as much as his brothers. Manny grew up in A.J.'s shadow, but Manny was a great athlete in his own right. When the boys played football, A.J. was the star running back, and Manny was the fullback. Manny was A.J.'s lead blocker, and Manny would knock defenders out of the way so his older brother could score all the touchdowns. A.J. was always more outgoing and cocky, but Manny never complained when A.J. got the spotlight. Manny just handled his business with a quiet grace. When A.J. and Manny were old enough to move up into the next bracket, Sheri suggested I let A.J. move on, while I stayed with Manny and coached his team. Sheri's motherly wisdom told her that Manny needed his time in the sun, without A.J. around. I thought that was a great idea, so I stayed and coached Manny's team for his last year. We moved Manny to running back, and then we turned him loose and let him run wild. To this day, Manny holds the Perry family record for most touchdowns in a game, with four.

Manny always had a strange ritual before he played football. Right before the game would start, Manny would start crying. There was no particular reason for Manny to cry. He wasn't upset or hurt or anything, but it was like he just needed to let go of some emotion before he took the field. Once the game started, Manny stopped crying and was back to his calm, cool self. But in his big record-setting game, Manny cried throughout the whole game. He ran for a 50-yard touchdown, and when he came off the field, he was bawling. I told Manny to keep right on crying, and keep right on scoring touchdowns. And he did! Later in the game, Manny ripped off a 70-yard score, and still he cried. I think Manny realized it was finally his time to shine, and all those emotions stayed with him on the field. A.J. was so upset when Manny broke his family touchdown record, because there had been a game the previous season in which A.J. scored 5 touchdowns, but two of them were called back because of penalties. After both plays, A.J. came back to the sideline all upset, saying, "I'm tired of scoring all these touchdowns and having them not count!" The boys had a little sibling rivalry going, but it was all in good fun.

Manny always worked hard and did well in school, so when he turned 16, I bought him a really nice used Mercedes sedan that one of my clients was selling. By his senior year in high school, Manny didn't want to play football anymore because the school's football team had lost a lot of games in recent years. I convinced Manny to play out his final year, and in the first game of the season, Manny was the KING-TV Player of the Week. It was so great to see Manny finally get that recognition after all his quiet leadership over the years. Manny also ran track for his school, and in his senior year, his team went to the State track championships and won big. Manny applied to several colleges around the Northwest, including Washington State University and the University of Oregon, and every school accepted him. Another local university recruited Manny to play football. The coaches came to visit Manny, and they wined and dined him a bit. They got Manny interested in their football program, but then he was turned down for the school. I talked to the administrators, and I let them know that we didn't appreciate them building Manny up and then letting him down like that. But we moved on, and Manny kept looking at nearby colleges. When Sheri took Manny to see Washington State University, he said he knew from the moment he walked on campus that was where he wanted to be.

One of the kids I coached in youth football, Alex, also went to WSU, and he belonged to Paul Allen's Phi Kappa Theta fraternity. Alex and Manny had played youth football together as kids, so Alex and his guys from the fraternity recruited Manny to join their chapter. At the same time, I was the Official Real Estate Partner of the Seahawks, which were owned by Paul Allen. Part of the fraternity's recruiting process included a pick-up football game at Qwest Field against alumni from WSU's in-state rivals, the University of Washington. Manny was invited to participate, and even though it was supposedly just a casual game, Manny dominated. Paul Allen set it up for the fraternity to get a personal tour of the Seahawks' stadium locker rooms. Manny decided to go to WSU simply because he liked the school and the fraternity so much. After Manny got to WSU, I thought he should try out for the football team. I tried to call the head coach to set up a tryout for Manny, but I couldn't get the coach to return my calls. Finally,

I called and told his secretary that I was the Official Real Estate Partner of the Seattle Seahawks. I explained that my relationship with the Seahawks went all the way to the top of the organization, and included Paul Allen and Pete Carroll. I let the secretary know that I wanted to talk to the head coach about my son, the star running back. Five minutes later, my phone rang and it was the head coach of WSU.

I told the coach who I was, and then I told him all about Manny's football career. I told the coach about all the championships Manny had won growing up with A.J. and me, and how Manny had exploded in his senior year at King's. I explained to the coach how Manny had never planned on attending WSU, but that he really connected with the guys in Paul Allen's fraternity. Most of all, I told him that he owed it to himself to at least give Manny a football tryout. The coach agreed to meet with Manny the following morning in his office, and told me Manny would need to fill out some paperwork for the NCAA. I told Manny about the appointment, and I forgot all about it. A few weeks later, we were having a big party at the house, and the whole family came in from out of town. Manny came home from WSU, and when the group was gathered together at dinner, I said, "Hey, Manny - I pulled some big strings to get you that meeting with the football coach. So what happened? You're all set up, right?" Manny looked at me, and said, "Uh, Dad – I didn't show up."

My blood started to boil. Did Manny just say what I think he said? I eyed Manny and said, "You what? What do you mean you didn't show up? Let me tell you something, my son, you little son of a b----. I called in a favor for you. No one gets a private meeting with the head coach, and a tryout with a Division I school, in the Pac-12, when you weren't even recruited by them, just by making a phone call. I did that for you. I talked to the coach, and he told me he would meet you the next day. All you had to do was go to his office, fill out the paperwork, and it's done. You're in. And you don't show up? That is unacceptable, Manny." The more I talked, the angrier I got. I grilled Manny good, in front of everyone. When I finished, Manny got up, walked out of the room, and out the front door of the house. I thought to myself, "Oh man, what did I just do? I can't believe I lost my cool with Manny like that." I went out to the front porch and Manny was standing there, crying. I felt God condemning my heart and saying, "This may be your dream, for Manny to play football. But this is not Manny's dream." I had humiliated my son in front of his own family, and I saw how wrong I was. I said, "Manny, I'm sorry. I didn't mean to do that to you." Manny said, "Dad, I'm sorry too. They told me in the frat that I really can't play football and be in the frat at the same time, because the academics are too important. I really want to do well in school, and I don't want to play football anymore." I said, "Manny, say no more. I'm sorry. I guess I wanted you to play football more than you wanted to play football. I got it, son. It's okay. Come on in the house." I brought Manny back inside, and I apologized to him again in front of the family. Then I humbled myself before everyone for making such a scene.

Manny went back to WSU after that incident, and became a true leader in his fraternity. His frat brothers love him for himself; for being the kind of person everyone always wants to be around.

The bottom line is that Manny has made us so proud of him with his dedication in the classroom. Manny will soon be graduating with a double major in Business, and after graduation, a career in International Business awaits him. Manny is the consummate gentleman of our family, and all of his brothers and sisters love and respect him so much. With his keen intelligence, his winning personality, and his even-keeled temperament, there is no limit to what Manny can accomplish in his life. I can't wait to watch Manny make his unique impact on the world.

DOMINIQUE

My fifth child was my daughter, Dominique, who was born in February, 1995. After A.J. and Manny followed Raquel and Royale, I finally had my ideal family arrangement, with two boys and two girls. We ran with that setup for about a year, then one day Sheri called me and said, "Daddy, I want a little girl." About a year or so later, God blessed us with a perfect little baby girl, in Dominique. I'll never forget, when she was born, Dominique had these big, beautiful silver dollar eyes. Dominique always had a gift for observing everything around her, and for understanding things that should have been way beyond her years. When Dominique started speaking at around 18 months, Sheri and I were amazed because Dominique was so articulate. She could speak better than her older brothers, even as a little girl. Dominique was always very clever too, probably from observing Raquel and Royale work on me. She used to drive Raquel crazy by claiming that she, and not Raquel, was her daddy's princess. Raquel and Dominique argued about that for years. Raquel would say, "I was the first girl, and that means I will always be Dad's only true princess." Then Dominique would say, "Well, you may have been the first, but I was the best, and the cutest – so deal with that." If I had a dollar for every time Sheri and I had to tell those two, "That's enough, girls – knock it off," I could buy Raquel another car!

Dominique was very clever and smart growing up. You could catch with her hand in the cookie jar, and say, "Dominique, your hand is in the cookie jar," and she'd just look back at you and say, "No it's not." No matter how many times or how many ways I tried to bust Dominique when she was little, she just acted like I was the crazy one and like she hadn't done anything wrong. It was pretty comical at times, because she was so bold, yet so convinced of her innocence. As she got older, Dominique followed her siblings into sports, where she eventually became a superstar athlete in her own right. Dominique was a great soccer player, and she also played volleyball, basketball, and ran track. Because Dominique was the youngest child in the family for a few years, and she grew up with two older brothers, she got picked on a lot. But Dominique grew tough because of that, and in time she gave her brothers all they could handle. The reason my office is still filled with awards and trophies from my kids is because the level of competition in our house was always greater than anything my kids faced in the outside world. All my kids had to be tough growing up in our house, or they would've been chewed up before they were even teenagers.

One time, when we were on vacation in Australia, me and the kids were walking on the beach in Surfer's Paradise. There was a set of monkey bars in one part of the beach, so I thought I'd mess with the kids a little. I pulled a $20 bill out of my wallet and said, "Let's have a little contest and see who can do the most pull-ups. The winner gets this $20 bill." A.J. stepped up and said, "I got this, Dad. That $20 is all mine." A.J. did about five pull-ups, and was feeling good about himself. Manny jumped up next, and he did about three pull-ups. Raquel and Royale were older, and they weren't all that interested in competing. Then Dominique said, "Let me try it, Dad." A.J. and Manny started laughing when Dominique grabbed the monkey bars, but those boys didn't laugh for long. Dominique got up there and started cranking, while I counted for her: "That's one, two, three, four, five, six, seven, eight, nine, and ten!" I'm pretty sure Dominique could've done a few more, but she had proven her point. A.J. and Manny didn't even know what hit them. I said, "Oh, so you boys are pretty quiet now, huh? Looks like your baby sister just kicked your butt!" I gave Dominique the $20 bill and a big kiss on the forehead. For the rest of the day, Dominique took every opportunity she could find to wave that $20 in her brothers' faces and remind them about that contest.

It was the same when I used to go watch Dominique play sports. She was a total sweetheart off the field, but once the game started, she was all business. Dominique was always so strong and physical when she was playing. In soccer, she would lay kids out and then turn around and play it off like she didn't even know what happened. Dominique was very protective of her brothers and sisters, and the whole family. If anyone ever said anything bad about anyone in our family, Dominique would be the first one to stand up and say something. Dominique has a certain confidence about herself, and a total lack of fear. She was surfing, snowboarding, skiing, and riding snowmobiles and jet skis since she was five years old. We used to jump off the cliffs in Hawai'i, and Dominique was always ready for the next adventure. After my bankruptcy, we had to pull the kids out of the private Christian school for a few years, so Dominique finished high school at the local public high school. She was a walk-on for several of the sports teams there, and the coaches were thrilled to have her. All my other kids had gotten their first cars when they were 15 or 16, but Dominique had to wait until she was out of high school. When she graduated, we had a big party for her, and I got her a brand new Volkswagen Jetta.

After she graduated, we talked about which college Dominique would like to attend. She said she was interested in the California schools like USC and UCLA, so we toured those campuses first. But the next thing I knew, Dominique had been accepted at WSU and had decided to go there. It seems that several of her girlfriends had been accepted there, and they had convinced Dominique to join them. By the time I uncovered the girls' conspiracy, it was too late. In the end, Dominique was happy to be with her friends again, so I didn't make a big deal out of it.

When the Seahawks made it to the Super Bowl in New York in 2014, I was very fortunate to be able to take my whole family plus a few friends to the game. I don't know how, but God worked everything out for us to be there, and of course, the Seahawks won the game in exciting fashion. We were sitting pretty close to the field, plus I had All-Access Passes, so we were able to go on the field for the Seahawks' victory celebration and the trophy presentation. I stood and watched as the confetti was falling on all of us, and it almost made me cry to see the pure joy on my kids' faces. I just quietly and humbly thanked God for that incredible moment, to be able to share that once-in-a-lifetime memory with my kids. A few months later, when the NFL Network produced their annual video tribute to the Super Bowl for a TV special called America's Game, I couldn't believe my eyes. During the Seahawks victory celebration, the NFL cameras followed Seahawks head coach Pete Carroll as he first saw his wife in the crowd, waved to her, then walked through the crowd on the field to share the magical moment with her. At the exact moment the coach and his wife embraced, there on the camera, I recognized some familiar faces. Standing right behind Pete was my youngest son, Caleb. He was pumping his fist and chanting, "Pete! Pete!" Standing right next to Pete and his wife was my princess, Dominique. As I watched the video on TV, I was struck again by the pure joy and amazement reflected in Dominique's eyes. I could tell she knew just how special that experience was, and she was cherishing every second of it.

Today, Dominique is still going strong at WSU, and working on an International Business and Marketing major. She's still that beautiful girl that the doctor first put in my arms, with her silver dollar eyes, and a million dollar smile to match. Dominique has grown into an incredible young lady. She's been around the world several times, and she has a maturity and sophistication about her that is simply contagious. I've always tried to teach my kids how to win at life, and not just sports. Dominique is definitely a winner, and she has made me so proud to be her dad.

JANAYE

My sixth child was my daughter, Janaye, who was born in August, 1996. Janaye's birthday is the day after Raquel's birthday, so every summer we get to have two big birthday parties. I always wanted two girls and two boys, but then Sheri said she wanted a little girl, so we had Dominique to make it five children. The problem was, I didn't like having an odd number of kids, so I told Sheri, "We need one more." I already knew Sheri would approve - all I have to do is look at her and she gets pregnant anyway. Pretty soon, God blessed us with Janaye, who we nicknamed Naye-Naye. Sheri always said the happiest times in her life are when she's pregnant. It's like all those hormones get balanced out and Sheri just glows with love and life.

Before Janaye was born, Sheri and I had agreed that this baby would be our last, and that Sheri would get her tubes tied right after the baby was born. Sheri told me she wanted to stop at six so that we could enjoy a fair amount of quality adult time after the children were grown, and we'd still be young enough to enjoy being grandparents. Then Janaye was born and the doctor put that beautiful baby girl in my arms. By the way, I was there for the births of all my kids; the doctors put every single one of my babies in my arms when they were born. I went out into the hall with Janaye, while Sheri was wheeled into surgery. I was walking down the hall to the nursery when I looked down at Janaye's face and said, "Thank you, God, for this beautiful little healthy girl, this perfect bundle of love." That's when something changed my heart. I turned and ran back into the room where the nurses were prepping Sheri for surgery, and I yelled, "Stop!" Sheri took one look at me and I could see in her eyes that she knew exactly what I was thinking. Sheri turned to the doctors and told them, "Stop right now. Don't do it. We're not having the surgery." The doctors looked at Sheri and I like we were crazy, but we didn't care. Something touched our hearts, and we knew what to do.

A short time later, Sheri was lying in her hospital bed, holding Janaye. Sheri's mom walked into the room with Dominique, who was about 18 months old at that point. Dominique took one look at that baby, her new little sister, then turned to Sheri and shot her a stare-down dirty look that I'll never forget. Then Dominique turned and walked out of the room without saying a single word. Those two girls have been going at it ever since. Dominique and Janaye are great sisters, and they'll do anything for each other. They love and support each other through everything. But those two girls can go at one another like nobody's business.

Growing up, Janaye was always a runner. All my kids have been great athletes, but Janaye is fast even by our family's standards. When Janaye was two years old, she used to ask us to let her out of the car a block from our house so she could race the car home. Then we'd drive real slow and watch Janaye run like the wind ahead of us. When she got a little older, she used to come to my football practices with the boys, and Janaye could outrun all of them, despite being several years younger. I'd make the boys run wind sprints with Janaye out in front, and none of the boys ever caught her. Finally, the boys gave up and said, "No, Coach – we're not chasing Janaye no more." Later on, Janaye got into sports herself and she became a superstar soccer player. I remember a game when Janaye was still little, when her team had a corner kick. Usually, youth soccer teams

used corner kicks to try to pass the ball to the front of the net.
Janaye lined up for the corner kick, kicked the ball, and I watched
as it sailed toward the front of the net, then hooked in perfectly for
a goal. The parents on the sidelines stood there for a moment with
their mouths open, like they'd just seen a ghost or something, and
then we all erupted in cheers. None of us had ever seen a kid do
anything like that before, and that's when I realized Janaye was a
special talent.

Another time, Janaye got the ball around midfield and started
dribbling toward the goal. A girl from the other team was right
on her tail, trying to catch her and steal the ball. Janaye glanced
over her shoulder and saw the girl coming up behind her. Then
Janaye popped the ball up in the air in front of her, and did a flying
sidekick and blasted the ball past the goalie right into the net. Once
again, the crowd went crazy cheering for my little superstar. I didn't
even understand the game of soccer, but I knew talent when I saw
it. I said to myself, "Dang, my little girl is baaad!"

I'll never forget when Janaye was in the 4th grade, and we had
her parent-teacher conference. Her teacher told us Janaye could
be President of the United States someday, because she was such
a natural-born leader and she was so organized. The teacher said,
"Janaye could run my class right now without me being there." I
used to notice those same traits at home, too. I could come home
late from work, and ask the other kids what was going on, or where
everybody was, and nobody knew anything. But when I asked
Janaye, she knew exactly what everyone was doing, and where they
were, and what time they would be home. Janaye has a way about
her that is like an adult trapped in a kid's body. She was the only
one of my kids that I never had to hassle about doing homework. If
Janaye got tired at night, she'd go up to her room and go to bed, even
if it was still early. Janaye always took care of her personal business

in a very mature and confident way. She is a natural leader, and the kind of person everyone wants to be around. Janaye has always been very adventurous and outgoing, even as a kid. One summer when we were all in Maui, she said, "I think it would be fun to get a big group of kids together and just travel around the world and go surfing at all the best beaches." Now, my wife probably wouldn't approve of that idea, but I wouldn't be the least bit surprised if Janaye actually did that someday.

When she was only 16, Janaye blew out her ACL in a Select game. By then, Janaye was so good, and in such high demand, that she was playing soccer almost year-round. I had told Sheri to give Janaye a break, and let her have an offseason to heal up. But every time Janaye tried to shut it down for a while, some other team would come calling and she'd be right back playing again. I think her knees just got tired from all the wear and tear. Janaye also played volleyball, and ran track for her school. But it didn't matter what sport she was playing, or what was at stake. Janaye had a fiery, competitive spirit that drove her to succeed. She always had to be faster, or stronger, or last longer than the other kids. I wasn't surprised by that, considering Janaye grew up in a house with five older siblings, all of whom excelled at sports.

Janaye was always such a trooper. She had an inner strength that allowed her to roll with stuff that would've derailed other kids. When she blew out her knee playing soccer, we tried to get her the best doctors. We had a female doctor who was supposed to be one of the best. Right before Janaye was to go in for surgery, the doctor bent Janaye's leg back to test it, and Janaye screamed out in pain. We all looked at the doctor as if to say, "What the heck are you doing? You just injured her even more!" Janaye had the surgery and the doctors rebuilt her knee. But as she was going through the rehab process, Janaye kept saying, "Dad, my knee doesn't feel right." I told Janaye to keep working on her rehab, and that she'd be fine with time. One day Janaye came to me in tears, saying, "Dad, all the other kids who had their ACLs done are running around and feeling great. My knee still isn't right. I can tell something is wrong." We took Janaye back to the hospital and had her knee thoroughly checked by a specialist, who confirmed Janaye's suspicions. The doctor told us Janaye's knee was too loose in the back, and too tight in the front. He recommended another surgery to fix everything, and we set it up so Janaye could finish volleyball season and have surgery over Christmas break. Her knee healed up perfectly the second time, and Janaye is still as active and in shape as ever.

Janaye has talked about going on missions after college, and helping kids in communities around the world. She's such a loving person, and so smart, that if she put her mind to helping others in that way, Janaye would have an amazing impact. She already had two jobs when she was just 16, because she had the time and wanted to stay busy. After Janaye graduated from high school, she became the only one of my seven kids to go out of state for college. She enrolled at the University of San Diego, which is a small, private Catholic school with only 5,700 students. Sheri cried when her baby girl crossed the state line, but Janaye is a very independent young lady, and she knows exactly what she's doing with her life. Janaye may be only a freshman at USD, but she's already worked her way into some leadership positions at the school. That's just Janaye's nature, and I will never be surprised by her success. Janaye is a girl who is really going places in this world.

CALEB

My seventh child was my son, Caleb, who was born in September, 1998. Caleb bust on the scene like a tiger cub, and he was roughhousing with all his older siblings before he could even walk. Caleb's older brothers tossed that little boy like a salad, but he bounced right back up and kept going. I had Caleb in the pool learning to swim when he was just an infant. Just like his brothers and sisters before him, Caleb learned how to play the game by watching all the older kids. By the time he was a year old, Caleb was already a master at getting his way. He was a man-child, and a little king, and he knew it. Being the youngest and cutest, Caleb got a lot of attention, which he soaked up like a sponge. We were traveling around the world, enjoying great family adventures together, and Caleb loved every minute of it. One summer, instead of our usual trip to Maui, we decided to go to Bermuda. It started when all the kids came to Sheri and me and said, "We love Maui, and we want to go there too - but can we go to L.A. to see Dad's family, and then we can go to Disneyland and Magic Mountain, and then we can go to Bermuda?"

Sheri and I thought it over for about two seconds, then I said, "Okay, good thinking guys – let's do it." The kids screamed in celebration, and we were on our way. We flew to L.A. for a week, then on to Maui for two weeks, then back home for about eight hours to do laundry and change our luggage, then on to Bermuda for a final week. It was crazy, but that's just the way the kids wanted it, and they had a blast the whole time. Everywhere we went, Caleb was right in the middle of everything with the bigger kids. Caleb was only 11 months old, but he could already swim. In Bermuda, we played a fun game in the hotel pool. I threw him up in the air as high as I could, right into the deep end of the pool. Caleb would hit the water, go under for a second or two, then he'd pop out of the water with his arm extended like he was holding a torch. I'd snatch Caleb's arm and pull him up out of the water, while the mothers around the pool glared at me like I was a child abuser. Every time I threw Caleb, the women started clucking and pointing at him, and pretty soon Caleb figured out that he was the star of the show. I'd pull him out of the water, and Caleb would just say, "Again, Dad! Again!" Caleb always liked being the center of attention, and he provided non-stop entertainment.

One year when we were in Maui, Caleb was almost three years old. He was still running around with his older brothers and sisters, and doing everything they did, only in a miniaturized version. We were at a hotel near Black Rock in Kaanapali, and I was entertaining the kids while Sheri went to get her hair done. I was trying to get the kids to jump off the cliff at Black Rock. I started with A.J., but he kept chickening out at the last minute. Then I started working on Manny, but he wasn't going for it either. Manny said, "I don't care what you say, or what you call me – I'm not jumping off that cliff. Period." Meanwhile, Caleb just sat and watched us from his beach blanket. Raquel and Royale were off running around town, so it was down to Dominique and Janaye. But the girls just shook their heads and said, "No way, Dad. You do it, and we'll watch." Then Caleb jumped up and said, "Hey Dad, I'll jump." I said, "What do you mean, you'll jump?" Caleb said, "Off the cliff. I'll jump off the cliff with you, Dad." I pointed to the cliff and said, "You'll jump off the cliff with me? That big black cliff over there?" Caleb just smiled and said, "Yeah, Dad – I'll jump. Take me out there with you." I put some water wings on Caleb, and we headed toward the cliff at Black Rock.

I had the older kids paddle out into the ocean with their boogie boards so they could watch Caleb jump from below the cliff. Then Caleb and I slowly climbed up the rocks and made our way over to the jump spot. The local Hawaiian boys saw me coming up there with my little man-child and said, "What's up, man?" I said, "My little homeboy here is gonna jump off the cliff. They looked down at Caleb, then back at me, then down at Caleb, then back at me.

Then one of the guys said, "No way. The little dude is jumping off the cliff? That's 25 feet down, Bro." I just said, "I know. Don't worry, he's got it." Caleb got up onto the edge of the cliff and looked down at the water. I said, "You ready?" He said, "Yep, I'm ready, Dad." I said, "Hit it!" Caleb jumped off that cliff, hit the water, and popped right back up like a fishing bobber. I yelled down to him, "Awesome! How was it?" Caleb said, "Scary, scary." I asked him if he wanted to do it again, and Caleb said, "No Dad, that's scary." I took him ashore, and then I started roasting A.J., Manny, Dominique, and Janaye like they were marshmallows. I said, "How is it that the four of you couldn't jump, because you were too chicken, and yet your little brother who isn't even three years old did it?! You guys are a bunch of wimps!" Caleb and I were high-fiving each other, and celebrating like we'd just won a gold medal. Of course, the older boys beat Caleb's butt that night back in the room, but he didn't care.

Speaking of kicking Caleb's butt - man, my boys used to love to roughhouse and beat the crap out of each other. I would come home from work, and we'd have big pillow fights. The boys would be jumping around on the beds, and I'd be swinging those pillows trying to knock them off the bed. Sometimes when I came home, Caleb would say, "Dad, A.J. and Manny have been picking on me. Will you help me get 'em?" I said, "Heck yeah, I'll help you get 'em!" I'd pick up Caleb, hold his body and let him swing his legs around and pound on his brothers for a few minutes. Of course, as soon as I left the room, A.J. and Manny would go right back to whaling on Caleb. They showed that boy no mercy, which is probably why he grew up to be so tough and persistent. I'll never forget one time when Caleb made me laugh so hard I cried. Manny had been picking on Caleb again, but this time Caleb had a plan. He waited until Manny was done playing and was no longer paying attention. Then Caleb struck like a cobra. Manny was walking through the family room when Caleb came flying down the hall, jumped, flew through the air like Bruce Lee, bounced off the top of the couch, and landed a perfect flying roundhouse punch to the side of Manny's head. Manny started screaming and crying, and I thought I would die laughing.

Another time in Maui, we took the long and winding road to Hana to see the waterfalls and trails. We stopped along the way to go swimming, and when we spotted some people jumping off some high cliffs, we decided to give it a try. This time, A.J. and Manny didn't bother waiting for me to mock them for not jumping. The boys got out there and jumped off those cliffs before I could get Caleb out there. Sheri came out to take some pictures of all of us, but when she saw Caleb on top of a huge cliff, she went berserk. "Greg Perry, you get my baby off that cliff right now! Are you crazy? Don't you dare make him jump from up there! Bring him to me right now!" Caleb started crying, because he wanted to jump off a big cliff again, but Sheri wasn't having it. I brought him down, while Sheri read me the riot act and threatened to divorce me if I kept using her baby as a stunt kid.

One thing about Caleb is, he has a certain mentality and a toughness that developed from doing everything his big brothers have done, ever since he was little. When we were at Big Beach, on the other side of Maui, the waves were really big and strong. That water could wash swimmers and bodysurfers all the way up on shore in just a few seconds. Caleb was only three or four years old, but he loved bodysurfing on that beach. He'd run and dive at the waves, right when they crested near the shore. Caleb would disappear under the crashing waves for about five seconds, then he'd emerge on the beach, about 50 yards up onto the sand. He couldn't get enough of it. Meanwhile, all the tourists were freaking out, watching this little boy bodysurfing just like the big boys. The women, especially, kept hollering at me to get Caleb out of the water, but I told them, "It's okay – he's fine. He loves it." Eventually, the tourists got out their cameras and started taking pictures of Caleb doing his thing. The more attention he got, the more Caleb hammed it up.

Caleb was equally enthusiastic when we took our winter vacations. He loved to ski just like the rest of the kids. One year, when Caleb was five, we went up to Sun Peaks for a week or so. We all climbed up to a black diamond, and lined up to ski down the hill. As soon as we got on top, Caleb was itching to go down. When I asked him if he was ready, Caleb said, "Yeah, Dad – let's hit it!" Keep in mind, it was Caleb's first time on a black diamond because he'd just graduated from the lower courses. Caleb took off and flew down the hillside so fast even Manny started freaking out. Manny said, "Dad, you better watch Caleb – he's out of control!" I said, "You're just mad because he's faster than you." Manny screamed, "I'm telling you, he's crazy, Dad!" I said, "He's not crazy, he's just not scared like you." We got down to the bottom, and it struck me what I was seeing. Caleb's daredevil act was fun, but more importantly, I realized that with Caleb able to do the big runs, all seven of my kids could ski together with me for the first time ever. There was Raquel, Royale, A.J., Manny, Dominique, Janaye, and now Caleb. It was a perfect moment, and I thanked God once again for blessing me with my amazing family.

The following year, we returned to Sun Peaks and rented out a condo on the slopes, just like we always did. After a long session in the morning, I came down the hill for the last time and skied right up to the front door. All the kids came in behind me, except for Caleb. I turned around and asked A.J. and Manny, "Where's Caleb?" The boys said, "We thought he was with you." I said, "No, he's not with me. I thought he was with you guys." Sheri panicked, thinking her baby was out there on the slopes all by himself. I put my gear back on and was just about to go back out and find him when Caleb came skiing up to the door. I said, "Where were you just now?" Caleb said, "Oh, I found a shortcut down the mountain." I said, "A shortcut? How did you find that?" He said, "Well, you guys all took off, and I knew I had to go around a certain way to get here, so then I cut through and here I am." I guess that shouldn't have surprised me, because even as a little kid, Caleb was always very independent and mature for his age.

I'll never forget another time when we were in Maui, and I was driving through Lahaina to take some of the older kids surfing just down the road at Puamana. I hadn't seen Caleb since earlier that morning, when he was out in the yard playing with his friend, Aiden. Caleb was only seven, but we had been to Maui so many times over the years that all the locals knew my family and me, so I never worried about the kids. I was driving along, and I saw Caleb and Aiden walking through town. I pulled up and said, "Hey, what's going on? You guys need a ride?" Caleb said, "No Dad, we're good. We're just heading down to the harbor." I said, "Okay, well let me know if you need anything." Caleb replied, "Okay, Dad - see ya." That was about the time I realized that my little main man was growing up faster than I could keep up.

When Caleb turned six, he told me he wanted to start playing football. He was always at practice with me anyway, but kids had to be six to play in the Pee Wee leagues. I told Caleb I would coach his team, but when A.J. and Manny found out, they threw a fit. A.J. said, "Dad, you can't coach Caleb's team – you're coaching our team." I told the boys there wouldn't be a problem, because I could coach both teams at the same time. I made a commitment to all three of my boys, and then I followed through. By season's end, both of my teams had made it all the way to their championship games. As I mentioned before, we couldn't find football fields to practice on, so I called in a favor with Tod, the CEO of the Seahawks, and he let me hold two practices simultaneously at Qwest Field. In the meantime, Caleb had already become a little superstar football player. He had watched and learned from his older brothers, who were both great players, and he learned well. Caleb hit the ground running, literally, and was a dynamic running back, just like his brothers before him.

A.J. was my offensive coordinator for Caleb's team. Over the last four years of coaching Caleb, we made it to four straight championship games and we won three of them. The only game we lost was in double overtime. Fast forward to Caleb's freshman year in high school. I had retired from coaching youth football after the previous season. Caleb was already playing for his school team, but he wasn't very happy because the school didn't have a freshman team; they only had a JV team. Caleb begged me to coach his same group of kids on the side, but I told him I couldn't do it because I had already retired, and there was no going back. Besides, the group of kids Caleb had played with in youth football had split up and they'd all gone on to play at various high schools in the area. I told Caleb all the reasons why it wouldn't work, but he didn't want to hear it. Finally, I gave in and told the kids I would coach them on the side, but only as long as our schedule together didn't conflict with their regular high school teams. I checked the schedules for every kid, and then we figured out a way to practice without any scheduling conflicts. We only practiced twice a week, but we made up for the lack of time with our intensity. I had coached this whole group of kids in youth football, so they knew my drill.

We went undefeated in the senior division, and we beat Eastside Catholic in the championship. Eastside was a local powerhouse team that rarely lost to anybody. They were used to winning year after year, but we took it to those Eastside boys. Caleb wasn't used to playing high school football. He was playing on the JV team, but those boys were a lot bigger than him, and usually older. But Caleb was so tough, even for a smaller player. One time, when Caleb didn't go down on first contact, a player came and hit Caleb hard and broke a couple of his ribs. I told him he was going to miss some time, and that he needed to go to the doctor, but Caleb wouldn't go. He told Sheri, "I'm fine, Mom – really." I said, "Caleb, you're not fine. You've got broken ribs." Caleb said he didn't want to go to the doctor, because then he wouldn't be able to play the rest of the season. I called Caleb's coach and explained the situation to him. He agreed to let Caleb take it easy for a few games, but in the meantime, Caleb still wanted to play for my team. I made him wear a protective vest, and Caleb got through it without a problem.

The same week we had our senior division championship game, Caleb's coach told me he needed Caleb to play for him that week too, because some other kids were out of the game. I told the coach, "No problem, Caleb will be ready." We were on the ferry, heading to Whidbey Island for the game, when I asked Caleb where his uniform and gear was. He said, "Oh, I'm not playing this week." I said, "Yes, you are – I left you a message earlier, telling you to bring your uniform because the coach needs you to play." Caleb said, "Well, I don't want to play for the JV team – I just want to play in the championship for our team." I said, "Listen to me, little man. If you don't play for your school team, you can't play for me. You're not going to cherry-pick which games you want to play in, or which teammates you don't care about. You're either all in, or you're all out – which is it?" Caleb sighed, and said, "Okay Dad, I guess I'll play." After the ferry arrived on Whidbey, I turned around, called Sheri, and told her to bring Caleb's gear to the ferry dock. I grabbed Caleb's jersey, and made it back to the game in the nick of time. Caleb not only played that day, but he busted out big with the first two-touchdown game of his high school career. A few days later, our Mukilteo team won the senior division championship over Eastside. That was only the beginning of Caleb's high school football career, which quickly turned spectacular.

Caleb also ran track as a freshman, once again following in the footsteps of his older siblings. In his first year of running track, Caleb broke the State record for 1A in the 100-meter run. Then he broke the State record for 1A in the 200-meter run. Caleb was the only freshman on the 4x100 relay team. That summer, Caleb participated in an open track camp, where about 15 schools from 1A, 2A, 3A, and 4A divisions came for an exhibition. Caleb excelled even against the older kids from larger schools. That's when I knew we were on to something special. After track season was over, Caleb took his football game to a whole new level. I went to see the football coach, and he told me, "Caleb is my Ferrari. All I do is take him out of the garage, give him the ball, and he scores touchdowns. Nobody can catch him." Caleb went into his sophomore football season, and it was clear that the school's football team wasn't as good as it could have been. But it didn't matter, because Caleb became a non-stop highlight reel all by himself. The team could hardly block for Caleb, but it hardly mattered because nobody could catch Caleb. He only needed an inch of daylight, and then he was gone. Caleb literally ran wild all over the JV league as a sophomore, like a man among boys.

As I sit here today, Caleb has just recently broken a couple of his personal best records in track. He is now #1 in the State for his age group in 1A in both the 100-meters and the 200-meters. If we take his age and class out of the equation, Caleb is now in the top seven for all age groups in both the 100-meters and 200-meters. He still has two more years of eligibility after this season, and the sky is the limit for Caleb. Caleb recently returned from Houston, where he had a few private training sessions with a former Gold medal Olympic champion. The best part is, for all of Caleb's growth and success as a young athlete, he has remained a very humble spirit. He's not flashy like A.J., or smooth like Manny. Caleb is his own man; quiet and calm. Even when Caleb scores a touchdown in football, he just hands the ball to the referee and walks away. When A.J. scored touchdowns, he had all these elaborate celebrations, but that's not Caleb's style. Caleb lets his actions do the talking for him.

I think being the baby all these years, and watching the rest of the kids grow up, Caleb figured out early on who he was and how he wanted to be. I remember when my good friend, TD, who is an actor and comedian, came over to my house for an event. TD saw a highlight reel of Caleb and he just shook his head. He said, "Greg, I've known Caleb since he was little. It's just a mentality he has that makes him special." Caleb is 5-9, and 155 pounds. He's still growing and filling out, and the way he's going, he will be breaking records for a few years to come. But Caleb doesn't seem to really care about it all that much. He doesn't talk about himself, or what he's done, or even what he wants to do in the future. Caleb just handles his business in the best way possible. It's clear to me that Caleb's motivation and drive is all internal; he just has a motor that runs a little faster than the rest. I can't help but think back to that time in Maui when Caleb was only two years old, and he jumped off that cliff at Black Rock. It didn't matter to Caleb that he was only two, or that his older brothers and sisters were afraid to jump. Caleb was determined to beat everyone else in the family, and prove himself, and he has. Caleb has carried that same spirit of quiet humility and powerful action into his teenaged years, and I can't wait to see how far it takes him in his life.

CHAPTER 54

A PH.D. IN LIFE

THE KEY TO everything in my life is my faith in G-O-D. That's what has made me the man I am, the father I am, and the husband I am. I always tell people, Bill Gates is not the richest man in the world - I am. I live in a constant state of gratitude, because God has blessed me with a beautiful, loving wife, seven happy and healthy children, and all the personal blessings I could ever ask for. I have my God, my sobriety, my wife, and my kids. Everything else beyond that is extra. My life has taught me this: money does not equal success. I've made lots of money in my life, and it's not because I'm so smart and clever. I don't take the credit for any of my success; all the credit goes to God. If I had gotten what I truly deserved, I would've been fertilizer 30 years ago. It's been God's grace, working in my life, forgiving me, blessing me, and watching over me.

You won't find any diplomas hanging on my office wall. But I've got a Ph.D. in Life, a Master's Degree from the School of Hard Knocks, and I graduated with Honors from None University. So what do you want to know? I'm a living, breathing miracle, and there's no denying it. Whenever people question my life story, or try to downplay the role of God in their lives, I tell them, "It's okay if you have a problem with God, because He doesn't have a problem with you. It's okay if you don't understand God, because He understands you. It's okay if you hate God, because He loves you. So get over it. There is a God, and you're not it. Give God the credit He deserves." If I had to go back and live my life 10 times over again the same way I've lived this time, I'd be dead all 10 times because I never would've made it out of South Central alive. There are a couple of cold, hard truths I've learned in this life: 1) nobody gets out of here alive; and 2) if money could buy more life, rich people would never die. But they always run out of life before they run out of money.

God is the ultimate scorekeeper, and He always evens the score. When I was growing up and running the streets, we talked about hitting The Big Payoff – and getting hit by The Big Payback. In the streets, I was going to get you before you could get me. Now, I just bless all my enemies, because God is the scorekeeper, and He takes care of everything. God always wins in the end, so I've learned to go with God, because I want to be on the winning team. If people don't agree with me, or don't believe me, or don't understand me, that's okay. I've been blessed beyond my wildest imagination. I've traveled all over the world. I've taken my family everywhere we could ever want to go, as my wife says, "Crafting eternal memories." I've mentored everyone from billionaires, to world leaders, to the guys in the penitentiary. Everyone else is easy after that.

I've crashed and burned so many times, and yet God always pulls me out of the fire in the nick of time. I'm not perfect, I'm not a saint, and I don't always do the right thing in every moment. I'm not here to tell you what you should or shouldn't do with your life. But I'll tell you this for sure: you pay the cost to be the boss, and there's a price to pay for everything you do. There are no free lunches in this life, so how much do you want to pay? The Laws of the Universe are very simple. The key to living is giving. If you want love to come back to you, if you want more love in your life, then give more love. Whatever you dish out is what you get back. It's all about your actions. God is not interested in what I'm thinking or how I'm feeling. He's interested in what I do. What I do is who I really am, because talk is cheap and actions speak louder than words. An old football coach once said, "What you do speaks so loudly, I can't hear a word you say." I can say anything, or justify just about anything, but when I take action, that's when my true direction and intention is revealed. Actions create reactions, and actions have consequences.

When I do something, I do it out of love, with no expectancy of return, and I don't tell anybody what I'm doing. When I live that way, all the blessings come back to me. Somehow, some way, God always keeps score, and I always keep winning. I used to cheat to win, but now I don't need to cheat. I just go with God, and do the right thing, and He takes care of the rest. That's why I'm happy, joyous and free. I have peace on the inside, regardless of what happens on the outside. Life is like a rollercoaster; you're going to have some ups and downs. The problem is, when you identify with the outside world, and try to live that way, you suffer for it. When the rollercoaster goes up, you're up and everything is great. But when the rollercoaster goes down, you hit bottom and get depressed. You have to stay in the middle. When life goes up, you stay in the middle. When life goes down, you stay in the middle. When my life is going great on the outside, I'm grateful and I give all the credit to God. That's what keeps me humble and keeps my feet planted firmly on the ground.

I remember one time in my real estate career when my company told me I'd won 172 monthly sales awards in a row. I told them I didn't want any more awards because they didn't matter to me. So the company created a few new categories of sales awards so the other agents wouldn't feel like they could never make it to the top in sales. My assistant used to say, "Those are your awards, and you deserve them." But I didn't care, because I had my sights set on something bigger. In the real estate business, being in the Top 1% of agents is like winning the Super Bowl in the NFL. I've achieved the Top 1% designation a total of 13 times in my 22-year career, and have just barely missed several other times. It would be easy to pat myself on the back and take the credit for being successful. The truth is, if it weren't for my faith in God, and Him always working the highest good in my life, I never would've made it past my first year in the real estate business. But real estate is just one part of my life, and just one aspect of how God has blessed me. The truth is, there are many other aspects and layers to me that I want to share with the world. This book is merely the launching pad for the second half of my incredible life.

My entire beloved family, at Alki Beach in Seattle, summer 2015.

CHAPTER 55

THE HERE AND NOW

IT'S ALWAYS BEEN my goal and my dream to change the world and make a difference. Everything I've been through in my life has prepared me for this moment. All the ups and downs, joys and pains, rights and wrongs, good and bad, and the successes and failures. All the learning lessons, all the roads I've ever been down, around the world. Through it all, I've learned how to play the game of Life and win. So what do you want to know? I've already lived everything in my nearly 55 years of life. Through it all, I've realized that the greatest gifts I have are the ability and the desire to help others. I can't take any credit for any of it, because it's not me. I didn't do anything to deserve this gift; in fact the opposite is true. It's only because God has blessed me despite myself. I've messed up my life so many times and so many ways that God needed a whole crew of guardian angels to keep me on track.

Through every avenue I've gone down, and through all the experiences I've had, God has bailed me out over and over again. From being a self-made millionaire to being flat broke. From being in gangs to working in organized crime; from living the

GREG PERRY

rich life with a Jewish family to living with a drug addiction and a gambling addiction; from being a superstar real estate agent to filing bankruptcy a few times; from traveling all over the world to being a worldwide success trainer for a Chinese billionaire. From mentoring world leaders in foreign countries to being an athlete trying to make it in the NFL. From being a businessman running a marketing machine to being locked out of my own business. I could go on and on about the different experiences I've had and the roads I've traveled. Now, I can see it was all for a higher purpose. It was all preparation for an even greater destiny to be fulfilled. It was all part of God's plan, and all for the purpose of making me the person I am today.

Right now, I'm in the process of truly fulfilling my most important goals and dreams. I want to teach everyone that they too can live the lifestyles of success, and that they can use the success principles I've shared in this book to achieve complete balance in every aspect of their life. The ideas and life lessons I've shared through my life story have the power to positively transform the spiritual, emotional, mental, physical, family, financial, health, and business aspects of your life, just like they did in my life.

I've recently set up 12 different new companies, as part of my vision of creating a new Lifestyles of Success empire that will be second to none in terms of helping people change their lives and fulfill their goals and dreams. My intention is to be a powerful force for good in this world. My personal goal is to be the number one success trainer in the world. My dream is to coach, mentor, and train the most influential people in the world, including millionaires, billionaires, world leaders, and the rich and powerful. I will mentor and train superstar athletes from every major sport, and professional sports franchises. I will help actors and actresses, movie stars, Fortune 500 CEOs, and corporate leaders. I'm starting with the most influential people in the world because my life experience has taught me that they need it the most, and because they have the power and sphere of influence to help millions of people. I've always believed that Bill Gates is one of the few wealthy individuals who have figured out how life really works, because he understands the key to living is giving. Bill is considered the richest person in the world - but in truth, he is the wealthiest person in the world. Bill never sold out to the world; he just keeps on giving back and spreading his blessings all over the world, helping countless people in countless ways. He gives out of love, with no expectancy of return, and he doesn't promote or publicize everything he does. That's why he will remain the wealthiest person in the world, because the Laws of the Universe will continue to reward him and bless his life beyond his wildest imagination.

Here is a brief summary of all 12 of the Lifestyles of Success companies I've created to make my personal dreams come to life:

1. Lifestyles of Success Management, which oversees all of the Lifestyles of Success companies. The goal is to manage and direct the entire Lifestyles empire to sustained success by promoting the values of wealth, balance and peace in all aspects of business.

2. Lifestyles of Success American Way Youth Foundation, which benefits children across the USA. The goal is to go into the inner cities and teach under-privileged kids how to win at the game of Life by utilizing the principles of success.

3. Lifestyles of Success International Charities, which is a global outreach program for missionary work. The goal is to identify and support Godly organizations that embody the core values of the Lifestyles brand, and to facilitate their success around the world.

4. Lifestyles of Success Real Estate, which is the next stage of my successful residential and commercial real estate business. The goal is to continue to expand on my 22-year history of record-breaking sales and outstanding customer satisfaction in real estate.

5. Lifestyles of Success Development, which promotes commercial development and building infrastructure. The goal is to use my real estate expertise to positively impact commercial, residential, and retail development locally, nationally, and internationally.

6. Lifestyles of Success Global Technology, which facilitates emerging technologies and new inventions. The goal is to create and promote positive, life-enhancing technologies for the local, national, and international technology marketplace.

7. Lifestyles of Success Sports Agency, which helps athletes be successful during and after their careers. The goal is to be the number one sports agency in America, by teaching pro athletes how to win at the game of Life on and off the field, by giving back to society.

8. Lifestyles of Success Fashion, which designs, manufactures, and sells a full line of Lifestyles branded clothing and apparel. The goal is to create a global brand that stands for quality, success, and excellence in the world of fashion and design.

9. Lifestyles of Success Dream Life, which creates and produces books, films, TV, and multimedia projects. The goal is to create a media company that embodies and promotes the core values and principles of the entire Lifestyles of Success program.

10. Lifestyles of Success Life Academy, which teaches all the concepts within a successful, balanced life. The goal is to

teach people from all walks of life how to win at the game of Life, by using the Laws of the Universe to create wealth, balance, and peace in their lives.

11. Lifestyles of Success Wealth Academy, which promotes financial investment, growth, and management. The goal of the Lifestyles Companies is to be a billion-dollar company, which will attract influential, like-minded investors who wish to support our programs.

12. Lifestyles of Success Consulting, which advises companies, organizations, national and global entities. The goal is to consult world leaders, Fortune 500 companies and CEO's, professional sports teams, and influential organizations to help them change the world.

I created my original Lifestyles of Success Institute several years ago to accomplish these kinds of goals. Now, the time is right to crank it up, roll it out, and make a lasting impact on the world. In my life, I've learned that in order to succeed, people need a road map for success. That is what all my companies are designed to provide. Regardless of the particular field of endeavor with any of the Lifestyles of Success companies, their mission is always the same: to teach people how to live the life of their dreams. I want to teach people that they have the power within them to create the life they want. The entire series of Lifestyles of Success companies will teach people how to win at the game of Life and how to achieve true wealth, not just financial riches. I recently saw a sign that said, "Some people are so poor, all they have is money." That statement captures an essential aspect of my overall message to the world: the best things in life are free. There's a huge difference between being wealthy and being rich. Being wealthy means having an abundance of the best things in life. Being rich means having an abundance of money, without regard for the true quality of your life. When I had the opportunity to choose between those two states several years ago, I chose being wealthy over being rich, and it has made all the difference in my life.

One of my favorite sayings is, "If it's meant to be, it's up to me." That saying means you can be anything, do anything, and achieve anything, if you set your mind to it and follow through with action. Nothing is impossible; all things are possible for those who believe. You have to believe, you have to have faith, you have to make a plan of action, you have to take action, and you have to follow through to the end. If you do that, there is absolutely, positively, nothing you can't achieve. But remember, it's impossible to please God without faith, so you must have faith in God, who strengthens you and sustains you. Your faith will be tested along the way; that's just a fact of life. But you must keep your faith strong. I never ever gave up for one second of my life, even when the scorecard read double zeroes and I had nothing left to lose. God always has the last word, and I teach people how to not only succeed, but how to succeed the right way. That means perfect balance on the outside, and perfect peace on the inside. It means understanding the meaning of the phrase, "The key to living is giving." That's why I'm doing all of this - to give back. I've been so blessed over my lifetime, and now I want to give it all back to God and to all His people.

I am going to teach people how to leave their old unsatisfying life behind, and how to be the best they can be. That means being the best dad, the best mom, the best husband, the best wife, the best son, the best daughter, the best boss, the best employee, the best teacher, the best student, the best athlete, the best whatever. There is a secret, and a method, that works every single time, and I'm going to share it with the world, starting right now. As I've said before, nobody gets out of here alive, and all the money in the world can't buy you another hour, minute, moment or second of life. If money could buy more life, rich people would never die. They always run out of life before they run out of money. So, the time is always now. There is no tomorrow, there is only today. God has never promised you tomorrow, He's only blessed you with today. That's why they call it the present, that's why they call it the gift of life. The time to do what you most want to do in your life is not in some far distant future. The time to act is now. Don't forget who you are, or where you came from. Stay humble, stay true to your highest vision of yourself, and you will live an incredibly rich and rewarding life.

Thank you for reading my life story in this book. I hope you laughed and I hope you cried. I hope you learned and I hope you loved reading it. I hope my story has inspired you to transform your life and go for the life of your dreams. I hope reading my book was just the first step toward a new beginning for you. Always remember to dream big. The sky is the limit. The only limits you have are the ones you place on yourself. Don't put any limits on your dreams. If you do your best, God will do the rest. God already knows your innermost desires anyway, but being willing to dream big lets God know you have faith in His power to work miracles in your life. Don't be afraid to hit your knees and pray, because my life is living proof of the power of prayer. I've always said if people only knew the true power of prayer, they'd be praying all the time. Finally, remember to give back to others. None of us can ever be truly successful without the help of others. The best way to show your gratitude is to constantly give back to others and help them be successful, too.

God bless you, in all that you do.

GREG PERRY'S
TOP 30 SUCCESS TIPS

1. Discover the power within yourself.
2. If you are willing, great things are possible.
3. Never hesitate to tackle the most difficult problems.
4. Generate power: pray.
5. For success, first look to yourself.
6. Nothing can keep you from reaching your goals.
7. People often need your love the most when it appears they deserve it the least.
8. You're the master of every situation.
9. If it's meant to be, it's up to me.
10. Life is what you make it. Always has been, always will be.
11. Clear your mind of "can't." You can do anything you truly believe you can do.
12. Doubt is the biggest dream destroyer.
13. Your principles mean more to you than any money or success.

14. No journey is too great if you find what you seek.
15. There are many things in life that will catch your eye, but only a few will catch your heart. Pursue these.
16. There's a big difference between seeing an opportunity and seizing an opportunity.
17. Never let the urgent crowd out the important.
18. God helps those who help themselves.
19. Make use of your finest talents.
20. Life is a boomerang – whatever you dish out you get back.
21. You must take a chance.
22. Until you try, you don't know what you can do.
23. Be so good they can't ignore you.
24. Give everybody love.
25. Your determination will make you succeed in everything you do.
26. Enjoy the pleasures of life to the highest degree, and share them.
27. The key to living is giving.
28. Realize how good you really are. God made you perfect.
29. You may occasionally give out, but never give up.
30. Silence is golden.

You Must Not Quit

When things go wrong, as they sometimes will,
When the road you're trudging seems all uphill,
When funds are low and debt is high,
When you want to smile, but you have to sigh,
When caring is pressing you down a bit,
Rest if you must, but don't you quit.
Life is strange with its twists and turns,
As every one of us sometimes learns,
Many a failure turns about,
When you might have won had you stuck it out,
Don't give up though the pace seems slow,
You may succeed with another blow.
Success is failure turned inside out,
The silver tent of the clouds of doubt,
You never can tell how close you are,
It may be near when it seems so far.
So stay in the fight when you are hardest hit,
It's when things seem worst,
That you must not quit!

DEDICATIONS

I dedicate this book to my Heavenly Father, for blessing me beyond my wildest imagination. This book is not about me – it's about God, and all the miracles He has worked in and through my life.

Thanks to my mom, Lois, for showing me the true meaning of unconditional love, and for being my spiritual teacher. You have always been the greatest mom in the world.

Thanks to my dad, John, for bringing me into the world, and for teaching me the importance of love, honesty, and respect during the eight years we had together.

Thanks to my Jewish family, for changing my life in the best possible way, and for branding me forever with your example of the perfect family. To David, for being my second father, for loving me like one of your own kids, and for showing me the true meaning of love. To Margy, for being my second mom, and for also being one of the greatest moms in the world in your own gentle, loving, and caring way. To Steve, for being my brother to this day. To Pam and Scott, who I will always love as my family.

Thanks to my first wife, Rae, for blessing me with two beautiful daughters, Raquel and Royale.

Thanks to my wonderful and beautiful wife, Sheri, for being true blue and always believing in me through thick and thin. Thanks for blessing me with all of our beautiful, healthy children. You have always been my rock, and you will always be my girl.

Thanks to my wonderful children: Raquel, Royale, Abraham, Immanuel, Dominique, Janaye, and Caleb. You have been my drive and my motivation. You have all enriched my life in more ways than you could possibly imagine, and you have inspired me to be the best father I can be.

Thanks to my son-in-law, Ryan, and my three grandchildren; Cameron, Carter, and London, for making me a grandfather and for making my family life even more blessed and complete.

Thanks to my brother, Michael, and my sisters; Gail, Brenda, Adrienne, and Angela. Thanks for always loving and protecting your little brother. Special thanks to my sister, Brenda, who passed at 20, and left us a little bundle of love, London, who later joined her mom in heaven.

Thanks to all my uncles, aunts, nieces, nephews, cousins, friends, and everyone who ever played a role in my life, or helped me in life, for making me the person I am today. Blessings to you all.

Thanks to all my anonymous brothers and sisters in the 12-Step program – you know who you are – for all your love and support. May God bless all that you do.

Thanks to my spiritual advisor, Joel, for mentoring me and teaching me the word of God, and for always keeping me humble and grounded in the Lord.

Thanks to my ghostwriter, Gordon Majack, for being divinely inspired and helping me write my life story. I've watched how God has transformed your life during this process, and I hope my story has the same effect on everyone who reads it.

Special thanks to Phyllis, my personal administrative assistant and dear, loving friend, who is worth her weight in gold. Thanks for over 20 years of dedicated, trusted service and a friendship like no other. You have been a priceless asset in my life, and a key to all of my success. You will always have a special place in my heart.